A HISTORY AND CRITIQUE
OF SCHOLARSHIP CONCERNING
THE MARKAN ENDINGS

Steven Lynn Cox

MELLEN BIBLICAL PRESS
Lewiston/Queenston/Lampeter

Library of Congress Cataloging-in-Publication Data

Cox, Steven Lynn, 1956-
    A history and critique of scholarship concerning the Markan
endings / by Steven Lynn Cox.
       p.   cm.
    Includes bibliographical references and index.
    ISBN 0-7734-2380-X
    1. Bible. N.T Mark XVI--Criticism, interpretation, etc.-
-History. 2. Gar (The Greek word)   I. Title.
BS2585.2.C67 1993
226.3'066--dc20   93-33176
                                                  CIP

A CIP catalog record for this book
is available from the British Library.

The Edwin Mellen Press   The Edwin Mellen Press
Box 450   Box 67
Lewiston, New York   Queenston, Ontario
USA 14092   CANADA L0S 1L0

The Edwin Mellen Press, Ltd.
Lampeter, Dyfed, Wales
UNITED KINGDOM SA48 7DY

Printed in the United States of America

To my parents
and parents in-law

Table of Contents

ACKNOWLEDGEMENT

A project of this magnitude is impossible for a single person to complete alone. The library of the Southern Baptist Theological Seminary offered a scholarly atmosphere that was conducive to research. The library staff of Dr. Ronald Deering was gracious and expedient in supplying the resources that I requested in connection with this and all projects undertaken while a student at the Southern Baptist Theological Seminary. I would like to express gratitude to each professor at Southern who taught and challenged me to be a critical thinker.

My graduate committee deserves special mention, for they encouraged me to pursue the publication of this project while it was still in the dissertation form. Dr. David Garland taught me to question the obvious. His critical insights into the scriptures and the literature preceding the New Testament allowed me to develop a deeper appreciation for the Greco-Roman world. Dr. Wayne Ward exhibited how a scholar shares the Gospel of Christ in the pulpit as well as in the classroom. His theological presence is an inspiration to each generation that comes under his tutelage. Dr. James Blevins has been a friend and at times, a father to me. Dr. Blevins has vastly contributed to this project and my personal academic career. His scholarship is unique and its presentation is vivid. The greatest lesson that I learned from him is that in order to become a good teacher, one must be studious but also compassionate.

I would also like to thank Dr. Michael Palmer, of Bluefield College, for his support, advice, and criticism of ideas proposed in this research. Mike is a scholar who would not turn away a friend, even though he was busy with academics and writing for publication. Mike is a friend who would not let my dream die.

The grandest appreciation goes to my wife for her patience during the writing of the dissertation and the editing for publication. She selflessly labored several hours typing and collating materials for the completion of this work.

TABLE OF ABBREVIATIONS

ABR	*Austrian Biblical Review*
AJT	*American Journal of Theology*
ANF	The Ante-Nicene Fathers
Bib	*Biblebhashyam*
BR	*Biblical Research*
BS	*Bibliotheca Sacra*
BZ	*Biblische Zeitschrift*
CBQ	*Catholic Biblical Quarterly*
CT	*Christianity Today*
CTM	*Concordia Theological Monthly*
EJ	*Encyclopedia Judaica*
ET	*Expository Times*
ETh	*Evangelische Theologie*
ETL	*Ephemerides Theologicae Lovanienses*
HTR	*Harvard Theological Review*
Int	*Interpretation*
ISC	Ibycus Scholarly Computer
JBL	*Journal of Biblical Literature*
JE	*The Jewish Encyclopedia*
JETS	*Journal of Evangelical Theological Society*

JTS	*Journal of Theological Studies*
JTSA	*Journal of Theology For Southern Africa*
KJV	King James Version of the Bible
LCL	The Loeb Classical Library
MAR	*Michigan Alumnus Review*
NPNF1	A Select Library of the Nicene and Post-Nicene Fathers of the Christian Church, series 1
NPNF2	A Select Library of the Nicene and Post-Nicene Fathers of the Christian Church, series 2
NTeS	*NeoTestamentica et Semitica*
NTS	*New Testament Studies*
PG	Patrologiae cursus completus . . . series Graeca (ed. Migne)
PL	Patrologiae cursus completus . . . series Latina (ed. Migne)
R&E	*Review and Expositor*
RSV	Revised Standard Version of the Bible
RUO	*Revue de l'Universite d'Ottawa*
RV	Revised Version of the Bible
Std	*Studien*
TDNT	*Theological Dictionary of the New Testament*
TL	*Theologische Literaturzeitung*
TZ	*Theologische Zeitschrift*
UBS	United Bible Societies
YA	*The Yearbook Annales*
ZNW	*Zeitschrift für die neutestamentliche Wissenschaft*
ZTK	*Zeitschrift für Theologie und Kirche*

CHAPTER 1

Introduction

This book will attempt to survey and evaluate the scholarly views on the problems associated with the ending of Mark's gospel.[1] Such a holistic approach may give insight to the modern interpreter in the consideration of the text. Attention will be given to the possibility of a gospel ending in γάρ, a view that has been debated from the second century to the present day.

The ending of Mark has been variously interpreted in New Testament research, and therefore warrants a *Forschungsgeschichte*. James L. Blevins confirmed the legitimacy of such an enterprise: "There is a real need periodically

---

[1]For the sake of brevity, Mark refers to the evangelist, without making any assertions about the writer's actual identity. For discussion about the identity of the evangelist see: Hugh Anderson, *The Gospel of Mark*, The New Century Bible Commentary (Grand Rapids: Wm. B. Eerdmans, 1976), pp. 29-32; Werner Kelber, *Mark's Story of Jesus* (Philadelphia: Fortress Press 1979), p. 13; Werner Georg Kümmel, *Introduction to the New Testament* (Nashville: Abingdon Press, 1984 rpt.), pp. 95-97; William Lane, *Commentary on the Gospel of Mark*, The New International Commentary on the New Testament (Grand Rapids: Wm. B. Eerdmans, 1974), pp 21-23; Dennis E. Nineham, *The Gospel of St. Mark*, The Pelican Gospel Commentaries (London: Adam and Charles Black, 1963), pp. 38-41; and Vincent Taylor, *The Gospel According to St. Mark: The Greek Text With Introduction, Notes, and Indexes*, 2nd ed., Thornapple Commentaries (Grand Rapids, Michigan: Baker Book House, 1966), pp. 26-31.

to pause and evaluate the course of study in a particular field,''[2] with the hope of laying the foundation for new research.

The value of a *Forschungsgeschichte* of a biblical text is twofold. Initially, an inquiry into how a pericope is interpreted by the church through the period of its history ought to help the scholar arrive at an exegesis as enlightened and responsible as possible. History bears witness to exegetical results examined and discarded by a consensus of responsible scholars in a former time, which are sometimes returned to currency by interpreters uninitiated of the hard fought conclusions of the past. Furnished with a survey of the interpretation of a text in history, the interpreter has at his command a valuable tool for attaining a correct understanding of its meaning.[3]

A second rationale is that such a study mirrors the thought of the various historical periods considered.[4] Dogmatic assumptions and interpretive principles adopted by a particular movement or 'school' in a given time are examined for their ''true'' value.[5] By this process the reader may grasp the causal relationship between dogmatic and hermeneutical presuppositions and the resultant exegesis.

---

[2]James L. Blevins, ''The Messianic Secret in Markan Research, 1901-1964'' (Ph. D. dissertation, The Southern Baptist Theological Seminary, 1964), p. 1.

[3]Bruce Demarest, *A History of Interpretation of Hebrews 7:1-10 from the Reformation to the Present* (Tübingen: J. C. B. Mohr [Paul Siebeck], 1976), p. 1.

[4]See Kurt Aland, ''Luther as an Exegete,'' *Expository Times*, 69 (1957), 45, who cited this as a principle reason for scholarly interest in the history of exegesis of biblical texts.

[5]See Demarest, *A History of Interpretation*, p. 1, n. 2. Demarest stated: ''An objective assessment of a movement or 'school' of interpretation can be made only in retrospect. Karl Bornhäuser commented on the difficulty of correctly evaluating one's immediate situation: 'No theologian can write concerning the present without considering himself as part of that present, and without permitting his own participation in the movements to influence him.''' See also Karl Bornhäuser, ''The Present Status of Liberal Theology in Germany,'' *American Journal of Theology*, 18 (1914), 191.

A useful dividend of a historical survey of this sort is often a refining of principles of hermeneutics.[6]

Statement of Problem

Robert Stein has stated:

> The way an author concludes his work is certainly an indication of what that individual is seeking to say. One need only think of how often people try to ascertain what a book is about by turning to the concluding chapter or summary! Of all the sections of a work, the conclusion is usually the most significant for our understanding.[7]

The Gospel of Mark presents the reader with the serious problem that the ending is highly debated. The ending of Mark has attracted careful and systematic investigation and has been characterized as "the greatest of all literary mysteries."[8]

Over the past nineteen hundred years, several scholars have grappled with the problem of the Markan ending in articles within New Testament introductions, translations, commentaries, theologies, and journals. It is unfortunate that the ending of Mark has been glossed over without a comprehensive study of its own. These scholars appear eager to write on one perspective without adequately dealing with perspectives differing from their own. When writers do deal with opposing views of the ending of Mark, they often fail to deal with the interpretation through the perspective of the whole Christian Era.

---

[6]Ibid.

[7]Robert Stein, *The Synoptic Problem: An Introduction* (Grand Rapids, Michigan: Baker Book House, 1987), p. 256.

[8]Nineham, *Saint Mark*, p. 439.

James Keith Elliott, assisted by the Institute für neutestamentliche Textforschung in Münster, has listed the textual evidence for the ending of Mark:

(1) Manuscripts which include the longer ending (Mark 16:9-20):

> A C D E H K M S U W X Y Γ Δ Θ Π A Φ Ω 47 055 0211 f13
> 28 33
> 274 (text) 565 700 892 1009 1010 1071 1079 1195 1230 1242 1253
> 1344 1365 1546 1646 2148 2174 etc.
> Lect. 60 69 70 185 547 883
> Lat. (vt. aur c d^{supp} ff^2 l n o q) (vg). Syr. (c p h pal)
> Cop. (sah boh fay) Gothic (Ms. lacks 12-20) Arm.^{mss} Geo.^{B}
> Diat. (Arabic, Italian, and Old Dutch).

(2) Manuscripts which add the longer ending marked with an asterisks or qbelli, or with a critical note added:

> f 137 138 1110 1215 1217 1221 1241 (vid) 1582.

(3) Manuscripts which add the shorter ending before the longer ending:

> L Ψ 099 (incomplete up to συντόμως) 0112(omits
> πάντα. . .μετὰ δέ) 579 274 (mg) Lect. 1602 Syr. (h^{mg})
> Copt. (sah^{mss} boh^{mss}) Eth.^{mss}

(4) Lat. (vt. k) reads only the shorter ending after Mark 16:8. Lat. (vt. a) also may have originally contained only the shorter ending.

(5) Manuscripts which end at Mark 16:8:

> ℵ, B (a large space follows 16:8)
> 304, (2386 and 1420 have a page missing at this point). Syr.(s), Arm.^{8mss},
> Eth.^{3mss},   Geo.^{1}a.[9]

---

[9]James Keith Elliott, "The Text and Language of the Endings to Mark's Gospel," *Theologische Zeitschrift* 27 (1971), 255-256. See chapter five, pages 163-163 for Elliott's results on the variant endings appended to Mark 16:8. The textual apparatus of the third edition of the United Bible Societies' *Greek New Testament* confirmed the textual evidence for the ending of Mark as offered by Elliott. See Kurt Aland, Matthew Black, Bruce Metzger, and A. Wikgren, eds. *The Greek New Testament*. 3rd. ed. (London: United Bible Societies, 1975), p. 196. This book will investigate the endings of Mark in connection with the textual evidence listed above, with the exception of the addition of

The question, "Could a document/book end in γάρ" has been a popular point of scholarly debate, in connection to the ending of Mark. Several scholars argued from a literary perspective that Mark could not have ended his Gospel with γάρ,[10] because such an abrupt ending was not common at the time in which the Second Gospel was written.[11] Such a position would lead the scholar to defend one of the possible endings of Mark (options one through four above). The likelihood of Mark 16:8 being the authentic ending of Mark has recently been defended.[12] Most scholars in recent years, however, have attested to the authenticity of the 16:8 ending of Mark, with γάρ concluding the Gospel (see above the texts of option 5).[13]

---

the section on reconstructed endings in chapter four.

[10]See H. B. Swete, *The Gospel According to St. Mark* (London: Macmillan and Company, Ltd., 1898), p. 399; B. H. Streeter, *The Four Gospels* (London: Macmillan and Company, Ltd., 11924), pp. 335-364; R. R. Ottley, "ἐφοβοῦντο γάρ, Mark XVI 8." *Journal of Theological Studies*, 27 (1926), 407-409; C. H. Kraeling, "A Philological Note on Mark 16:8," *Journal of Biblical Literature*, 44 (1925), 357; H. J. Cadbury, "Mark 16:8," *JBL*, 46 (1927), 344f.; W. L. Knox, "The Ending of St. Mark's Gospel," *Harvard Theological Review*, 35 (1942), 13-23; Vincent Taylor, *The Gospels* (London: The Epworth Press, 1938), p. 49f.; *Mark*, p. 610; and Frederick W. Danker, "Postscript to the Markan Secrecy Motif," *Concordia Theological Monthly*, 38 (1967), 26.

[11]According to Taylor, Knox argued that there is no parallel in the beginning of Mark, in the conclusion of any other Markan pericope, or in Jewish and Hellenistic literature in general. Vincent Taylor, *Mark*, p. 609, stated that the hypothesis implies by pure accident Mark lighted on a conclusion which 'suits the technique of a highly sophisticated type of modern literature'. See Knox, "The Ending of St. Mark's Gospel," 13-23.

[12]Robert P. Meye, "Mark 16:8--The Ending of Marks Gospel," *Biblical Research*, 14 (1969), 33.

[13]Thomas Boomershine and G. L. Bartholomew "The Narrative Technique of Mark 16:8," *JBL*, 100 (2, 1981), 214, argued that Mark 16:8 was probably the intended and original ending based on three major narrative techniques identified in 16:8: (1) the use of extensive narrative commentary; (2) the use of intensive inside views; and

Besides the endings of Mark based on textual variants, two other theories on the ending of Mark have emerged. The first proposal is a suggested theory of D. Bernhard Weiss by George Salmon. Salmon comments, "Weiss considers the mention of the names of the women (Mary Magdalene and Mary the mother of James) so soon again (Mark 15:47 and Mark 16:1 consecutively) suggests that chapter xv. closes St. Mark's Gospel, as originally planned, and that chapter xvi. begins a new little work,"[14] composed by Mark the evangelist. It is ironic that Weiss ended the Second Gospel at 16:8 without marking the end of chapter 15 with an asterisk, in his *das Neue Testament* and *Lehrbuch der Einleitung in das Neue Testament*.[15]

Etienne Trocmé proposed a second theory in which the original edition of the Gospel of Mark consisted of chapters 1-13.[16] To this original "an anonymous ecclesiastic of the Roman community" attached chapters 14-16, which may have been based on a small document from Jerusalem and lent to the whole (chapters 1-16) the authority of Peter and the name of Mark.[17] Trocmé speculated that the group represented by Mark is represented with the seven who were chosen for servile roles in the church (Acts 6), and that the author of the authentic Mark is

---

(3) the use of short sentences.

[14]George Salmon, *The Human Element in the Gospels: A Commentary on the Synoptic Narrative* (New York: E. P. Dutton and Company, 1907), p. 528.

[15]See D. Bernhard Weiss, *A Commentary On the New Testament*, vol. 1, George H. Schodde and Epiphanius Wilson (New York and London: Funk & Wagnalls, 1906), pp. 374-377; idem., *das Neue Testament* vol. 1 (Leipzig: J. C. Hinrichs'sche Buchhandlung, 1905), pp. 278-279; and idem., *Lehrbuch der Einleitung in das Neue Testament* (Berlin: Verlag von Wilhelm Hertz, 1897), pp. 491-497.

[16]Etienne Trocmé, *The Formation of the Gospel According to Mark*, trans. Pamela Gaughan (London: SPCK, 1975), pp. 248f. See also page 100 below.

[17]Ibid.

Philip the evangelist (see Acts 6:5 and 8:26ff.). The motif of such conjecture is that of discipleship.[18] These two theories are ingenious, yet both lack plausibility and textual support, and are of no value in accounting for the form that Mark has come to us. Generally, scholarship has not accepted these two propositions, therefore, they will not constitute consideration.

Throughout the critical era (the era following the Reformation to the present day) the study of the ending of Mark has attracted several approaches. A popular approach that has been used was the discipline of philology, for discussing the syntactical issue as well as the vocabulary of the ending of Mark.[19] The theological issues of the ending of Mark has raised interest in the Christology of Mark as well as the call of discipleship.[20] Within the last twenty years numerous articles have been written regarding the literary aspect of the Second Gospel's ending.[21]

These works provide New Testament study with valuable information concerning the research on the ending of Mark, however, it is obvious the debate over the ending of Mark is far from completion. Each of these works are limited according to their purpose and provide only a limited perspective on the question, therefore, a broader approach is necessary.

---

[18]Ibid., pp. 179-183.

[19]Elliott, "The Text and Language," 255-262; Farmer, *The Last Twelve Verses of Mark*, pp. 79-103; and Kraeling, "A Philological Note on Mark 16:8," 357-364.

[20]Jack Dean Kingsbury, *The Christology of Mark's Gospel* (Philadelphia: Fortress Press, 1983); Nineham, *The Gospel of St. Mark*; Augustine Stock, *Call to Discipleship: A Literary Study of Mark's Gospel* (Wilmington: Michael Glazier, Inc., 1982).

[21]See Meye, "Mark 16:8," 33 and Norman R. Petersen, "When is the End Not the End? Literary Reflections on the Ending of Mark's Narrative," *Interpretation*, 34 (April, 1980), 151-166.

Limitations

The task of researching scholarly material on the ending of Mark entails certain limitations that may guide the researcher to produce a helpful source in New Testament studies. The first limitation mandates that I be selective with the sources that I use. This selectivity does not seek to be biased or persuasive for one view, but to prevent repetition, so that I may have a manageable number of sources to work with, on the works representing various perspectives on the subject. I will, therefore, select scholars who add distinctive and pertinent information concerning the ending of Mark. It should be observed that though I may not cite scholars (i.e., Church Fathers and authors dating from the pre-Reformation era) I will consider the value of their contributions to the subject at hand.

The second limitation is that of space and time. At the initial stage of this research I am amazed at the vast amount of material available that pertains to this subject. It is obvious that research of this nature can only serve to clarify and evaluate the various perspectives on this topic. A final and conclusive answer about the ending of Mark is not possible at this stage and may never be!

The greatest limitation of this research is to remain as neutral as possible until I make conclusions in chapter six. Scholars representing each perspective have valid reasons for supporting their view, some of which may not be easily dismissed. The limitations of fairness and honesty will be guides this research.

Methodology

This book will attempt to survey and evaluate select scholarship on the ending of Mark. One can perceive several delimitations within this proposal. This study will critically analyze the debate surrounding the ending of Mark from the ante-Nicene Fathers to the present day. The ending of Mark is a problem within New Testament scholarship that calls for a clarification of the state of this research. It will be an imperative to consider the intentional and the unintentional reasons Mark may have concluded his Gospel at 16:8. Realizing the various peripheral issues associated with the ending of Mark, care must be taken not to overextend the boundaries of the study. This study, therefore, will recount the problems of whether the Markan ending of 16:8 was intentional or whether the original ending was lost, and the theories of the legitimacy of the inclusion of 16:9-20. The question that will guide this research is whether ἐφοβοῦντο γάρ is a legitimate ending of a work.

The design for this research will be determined by the development of interpretation of the ending of Mark from the Ante-Nicene Fathers to the present. This research will exhibit the developing major divisions and sub-divisions to ensure valid points of distinction.

The format of this book will function in a two-fold fashion of survey and evaluation. The goal of this methodology will be an assessment of pertinent issues of the debate concluded by an appraisal of the direction for the resolution of the problem.

Organization

The succeeding chapters will have their unique adgenda. The second chapter will survey the pre-critical period and three major sections will follow the chapter introduction. The first section will contain three sub-sections on the Ante-Nicene through the Post-Nicene Fathers' perspectives of the Markan endings. This section will contain three subsections: (1) The Fathers who favor the longer ending; (2) The Fathers who favor the short ending; and (3) A third tradition as evidenced by Jerome. The second section will include the prominent Medieval theologians' (i.e., Bede, Euthymius, and Thomas Aquinas), perspective on the Markan ending and the third section will include the perspectives of prominent Reformation theologians such as Erasmus, Luther, Calvin and Zwingli. A summary will conclude the chapter.

The third chapter will survey the prominent scholars who accepted the authenticity of 16:9-20. The first section of this chapter will be a summary and critique of John Burgon's perspective on the ending of Mark. This section will review Burgon's treatment of the Byzantine text, his defense of the authenticity of Mark 16:9-20, and a critique of his work. The second section of this chapter will be a summary and critique of George Salmon's works.[22] The third section of this chapter will be a summary and critique of Farmer's work *The Last Twelve Verses of Mark*[23] and will trace how the perspective of the Markan authenticity of 16:9-20 has evolved up to the now. A summary will conclude this chapter.

The fourth chapter will survey and critique select scholars who held that the longer ending was not authentic to Mark the evangelist, but were not willing to accept the 16:8 ending as the intended ending of Mark. The first section of this chapter will discuss the scholars who maintained 16:8 is an unintentional ending of Mark, based on the proposal of one of three theories: (1) the original ending of Mark was lost; (2) the evangelist never completed his Gospel; and (3) 16:8 is a suppressed ending. The second section of this chapter will consider the various theories of reconstruction, most notable Eta Linnemann[24] and Gerald Trompf[25]

---

[22]George Salmon, *A Historical Introduction to the Study of the Books of the New Testament* (London: John Murray, 1885); idem., *The Human Element in the Gospels: A Commentary on thess Synoptic Narrative* (New York: E. P. Dutton and Company, 1907); idem., *Some Thoughts on the Textual Criticism of the New Testament* (London: John Murray, 1897).

[23]William R. Farmer, *The Last Twelve Verses of Mark* (Cambridge: Cambridge University Press, 1974).

[24]Eta Linnemann, "Der Wiedergefundene Markusschluss," *Zeitschrift für Theologie und Kirche*, 66 (3, 1969), 255-287. The reader should be aware that Linnemann has renounced the entire historical-critical tradition and her former writings in response to her "born again" experience. See idem., *Historical Criticism of the Bible: Methodology or Ideology? Reflections of a Bultmannian turned Evangelical*, trans. by Robert W. Yarbrough from *German Wissenschaff oder Meinung* (Grand Rapids, Mich.: Baker Book House, 1990).

who assumed Mark did conclude his Gospel, but the ending was lost or suppressed. The third section will consist of a sub-section that discusses the text of the Freer Logion and the second subsection will discuss the shorter ending. Each of these sub-sections will be followed by a critique. The major sections of this chapter will be concluded by a critique, but the sub-section on Linnemann will be immediately followed with a critique by Kurt Aland. A summary will conclude the chapter.

The fifth chapter will discuss the scholars who reject the authenticity of 16:9-20 and argue that Mark intended to conclude his Gospel with γάρ. This chapter will include select scholars who surveyed the question of the ending of Mark based on textual criticism, form criticism, redaction criticism, and literary criticism respectively. A summary will conclude the chapter.

The final chapter will offer a summary of pertinent issues divulged from this research. A second and final section of this chapter will offer subjects for future studies in connection with the ending of Mark.

---

[25]Garry W. Trompf, "The First Resurrection and the Ending of Mark's Gospel," *New Testament Studies*, 18 (1972), 308-330 and idem., "The Markusschluss in Recent Research," *Australian Biblical Review*, 21 (October, 1971), 15-26.

CHAPTER 2

Pre-Critical Positions on the Ending of Mark

This chapter proposes to establish the foundations of the critical evaluations offered by scholarship since the Reformation, by surveying the pre-critical period. This chapter will contain two major sections. The first section will contain three sub-sections with the Ante-Nicene, the Nicene, and Post-Nicene Fathers' perspectives on the Markan ending. Within this section, the early church Fathers will be consulted, in order to secure an understanding of the churches' perspective on the ending of the Second Gospel. From this investigation, pertinent questions such as "Why did Mark end his Gospel the way he did" or "Why did the church append the 'longer ending' to the Second Gospel," may be answered.

The next two sections will include the prominent Medieval and Reformation theologians' perspective on the Markan ending, respectively. At this point, I do not know how important of an issue the ending of the Second Gospel was to the church in that era. It is important to delineate an understanding of what the theologians of that time thought of the Markan ending, for such questions on similar textual problems in the New Testament surely initiated modern critical methods for interpretation.

A summary will conclude the chapter.

An Appeal to Antiquity

Text critics were dependent on three primary sources of information for determining the text of the New Testament: (1) manuscripts, (2) versions, and (3) Church Fathers. Most text critics assumed that the earliest manuscripts, versions, and Fathers were the most trustworthy witness. With these three sources, early manuscripts were considered the most valuable help in establishing the precise text of scripture than can be rendered by any translation, and the translations are rendered with greater authority than the Fathers. John Burgon listed three reasons why the Fathers are listed as a less decisive authority:

> (a.) Fathers often quote Scripture loosely . . . and sometimes allude only when they seem to quote. (b.) They appear to have too often depended on their memory, and sometimes are demonstrably loose and inaccurate in their citations . . . (c.) Copyists and Editors may not be altogether depended upon for the exact form of such supposed quotations.[1]

In the task at hand, the Fathers become the most important evidence in the determination whether Mark 16:9-20 was original to the Second Gospel. As seen above, the earliest extant text available is from the first half of the fourth century, yet several Fathers predate the primitive manuscript witnesses B, ℵ, A, C, and D (which date from A.D. 300 to A.D. 600) and about two hundred Fathers exist contemporary with these manuscripts. It is evident that any objection to quotations from scripture in the writings of ancient Fathers can apply only to the form of these quotations, not to their substance. This gives the text-critic the assurance whether the passage in question was found in the text which he was accustomed to, which belonged to him, or to the church which he served. Burgon affirmed,

---

[1]John W. Burgon, *The Last Twelve Verses of the Gospel According to St. Mark* (Oxford: James Parker and Co., 1871), pp. 19-20.

"The earliest of the Fathers are observed to . . . allude rather than to quote,"[2] therefore, it is not their memory at fault, but their judgment.

The Fathers' Opinion on the Ending of Mark

After investigating the question of the Fathers' opinion on the original ending of Mark, this research turns to the task of assessing the value of the Fathers' opinion in the task of textual criticism. It is obvious that this conclusion will be based primarily on the Father's use of the last twelve verses of Mark compared with a lack of use of these verses. Attention will be given to the location, date of the Fathers, and the references to the verses of the longer ending that the Fathers may have used.[3]

Fathers Who Support the the Longer Ending

Several of the Fathers from Papias to Euthymius alluded to and quoted the longer ending, however, some of the testimonies of these Fathers were considered to be greater, because of the frequency of use and the way in which these verses were used.

Of the Anti-Nicene Fathers, Tatian was the first to quote from every verse of the longer ending. Tatian, a student of Justin Martyr, was recognized as one of the early great apologists, based on his *Address to the Greeks*, where he "attempts to show the superiority of what he calls 'barbarian religion' (Christianity) over the culture and religion of the Greeks."[4] Tatian's method in his *Diatessaron*, was to "combine distinctive phrases preserved by only one Evangelist with those

---

[2]Ibid., p. 100.

[3]See Appendix A for a listing of the Fathers' use of Mark 16:9-20.

[4]Justo L. González, *A History of Christian Thought*, vol. 1 (Nashville: Abingdon Press, 1983 rpt.), p. 112.

preserved by another, (by this) he arranged the several sections of the Gospel into a single narrative."[5] An example of his use of scripture is a segment from Mark 16:10 sandwiched between Luke 24:9 and Luke 24:10:

> . . . and returning from the tomb they reported all these things to the eleven and to all the rest. She went and reported to those who had been with him, as they mourned and cried; Now they were Mary the Magdalene and Joanna and Mary the mother of James; and the rest (of the women) with them told these things to the apostles.[6]

According to Metzger, "Tatian's Harmony of the Gospels contained several textual alterations which lent support to ascetic or encratite views;"[7] and H. von Sodon blamed the alteration of the Four Gospels as leading to the corruption of subsequent transmissions of the New Testament text.[8] Kurt and Barbara Aland supported this to a degree, particularly in the notion of the transmission of the New Testament into the Syriac Versions:

> Peculiarly among the versions, the first stage of the tradition was not a translation of the four canonical Gospels, but Tatian's Diatessaron. . . . The many historical and critical textual problems of the Syriac version

---

[5]Bruce M. Metzger, *The Text of the New Testament: Its Transmission, Corruption, and Restoration* (New York and Oxford: Oxford University Press, 1968), p. 89.

[6]Tatian, *Harmoniae Evangeliorum* (Rome: 1888), p. 95. The Latin reads: "Et regressae mulieres illae, nuntiaverunt haec omnia undecim, et ceteris discipulis, et his, qui cum eo fuerant, quia erant tristes et flentes. Et ipsae erant Maria Magdalene, et Ioanna, et Maria mater Iacobi, et ceterae, quae cum eis eramt, et hae fuerunt, quae dixerunt ad Apostolos."

[7]Metzger, *The Text of the New Testament*, p. 201.

[8]For a discussion of von Sodon's theory, see ibid., pp. 141-142; Hermann Freiherr von Sodon, *Die schriften des Neuen Testaments in ihrer älteseten erreichbaren Textgestalt* (Berlin: 1902), pp. 405 ff.; and Kurt Aland and Barbara Aland, *The Text of the New Testament: An Introduction to the Theory and Practice of Modern Textual Criticism*, trans. Erroll F. Rhodes (Grand Rapids, Mich.: William B. Eerdmans, 1987), pp. 22-23.

may be traced to it. For not only does the Syriac tradition present translation problems which are formidable, but the ubiquitous heritage of the Diatessaron must also be dealt with properly. In the course of history a constant process of revision produced a whole series of Syriac New Testament versions with the result that they cannot always be distinguished from each other with precision: besides the Diatessaron there is the Old Syriac (Vetus Syra), the Peshitta, the Philoxeniana and the Harklensis, as well as Palestinian Syriac version.[9]

Metzger may not go as far as von Sodon or the Alands in blaming Tatian for a widespread corruption of New Testament texts, however, he conceded, "not a few instances of harmonization of the text of the Gospels in certain witnesses (notably the Western witnesses) are to be ascribed to Tatian's influence."[10]

The value of Tatian's citation of the longer ending is that it placed an undeniable reference to each verse as early as the second century and in the world capital of Rome. The use of the verses of the longer ending along with the verses of the other Gospels (which have long been considered authentic) would appear to validate the authenticity of the verses of the longer ending.

Irenaeus (who also dates from the second century) went one step farther than Tatian by citing Mark as the author of verse 16:19, in his *Against Heresies*, *Book Three*: "Towards the conclusion of his Gospel, Mark says: 'Therefore, after the Lord Jesus had spoken to them, he was received up into heaven, and sits on the right hand of God. . . .'"[11] Harry A. Sturz confirmed that Irenaeus "used Greek texts other than the Byzantine" and later added that his text was different

---

[9]Aland and Aland, *The Text of the New Testament*, pp. 188-189.

[10]Metzger, *The Text of the New Testament*, p. 92.

[11]Irenaeus, *Contra haereses*, *libre 3*, Patrologiae Cursus Completus, Series Graeca, ed. Jacques Paul Migne, vol. 7 (Paris: Seu Petit-Montrouge, 1857), p. 879. The Latin reads as "In fine autem Evangelii ait Marcus: 'Et quidem Dominus Jesus, postquam locutus este eis, receptus est in coelus, et sedet ad dexterum Dei. . . .''

from the Alexandrian text-type that Origen used.[12] (This is not to say that the Alexandrian type did not exist at the time prior to Origen).[13]

Metzger noted the seriousness of Irenaeus' interest of ensuring accuracy in transcription by quoting Irenaeus' conclusion of *On the Ogdoad*:

> I adjure you who shall copy out this book, by our Lord Jesus Christ and by his glorious advent when he comes to judge the living and the dead, that you compare what you transcribe, and correct it carefully against this manuscript from which you copy; and also that you transcribe this abjuration and insert it in the copy.[14]

The text in which Irenaeus used contained the longer ending, or he would not have cited 16:19 as authentic to Mark. Irenaeus further attacked the Valentinians for changing the tense of a verb. In essence, Irenaeus "derides this impiety by pointing out that through such tampering they exalt themselves above the Apostles."[15]

This is also significant, because it affirmed the early (second century) reference of the longer ending having spread to Gaul, therefore, validating the view that the longer ending was in an early widespread usage. Another point of consideration is the early reference of Mark as the author of the Gospel, including the longer ending. The testimony of Tatian and Irenaeus, by reason of location and date, added support not only to the authenticity of the verses of the longer ending of Mark, but also to the theory that considered Rome to be the place of origin.

---

[12]Harry A. Sturz, *The Byzantine Text-Type and New Testament Textual Criticism* (Nashville: Thomas Nelson Publishers, 1984), pp. 42-43 and 80.

[13]Ibid., p. 80.

[14]Metzger, *The Text of the New Testament*, p. 21. Metzger obtained this quote from a statement made by Eusebius, as found in Eusebius, *Historia ecclesiastica, libri 5* PG, vol. 20, p. 494.

[15]Sturz, *The Byzantine Text-Type*, p. 116.

G. D. Kilpatrick questioned "whether there are any readings which can be demonstrated to be later than A.D. 200."[16] He concluded:

> From the third century onward the freedom to alter the text which had obtained earlier can no longer be practiced. Tatian is the last author to make deliberate changes in the text of whom we have explicit information. Between Tatian and Origen Christian opinion had so changed that it was no longer possible to make changes in the text whether they were harmless or not.[17]

Metzger added:

> In the earlier ages of the Church, Biblical manuscripts were produced by individual Christians who wished to provide for themselves or for local congregations copies of one or more books of the New Testament. Because the number of Christians increased rapidly during the first centuries, many additional copies of the Scriptures were sought by new converts and new churches. As a result speed of production sometimes outran accuracy of execution.[18]

In a footnote in Augustine's *Harmony of the Gospels*, Philip Schaff confirmed that the verses of Mark 16:9-20 appear in nearly all Latin codices.[19] According to the Alands, "the earliest Latin texts are found in Tertullian's numerous quotations of the New Testament."[20] They continued:

---

[16]Ibid., p. 96.

[17]Ibid., p. 97. Sturz's quote of G. D. Kilpatrick is from G. D. Kilpatrick, "Atticism and the Text of the Greek New Testament," *Neutestamentliche Aufsätze*, Festschrift für Prof. Josef Schmid. ed. by J. Blinzler, O. Kuss, E. Mussner (Regensburg: Puster, 1963), pp. 129-130.

[18]Metzger, *The Text of the New Testament*, p. 14.

[19]See Philip Schaff, ed., "*Saint Augustine, Harmony of the Gospels*," A Select Library of the Nicene and Post-Nicene Fathers, Series 1, vol. 6 (Grand Rapids, Mich.: Wm. B. Eerdmans Publishing Company, 1956), p. 214, n. 11.

[20]Aland and Aland, *The Text of the New Testament*, p. 182.

> These quotations are of little use in the tracing the history of the Latin
> versions because Tertullian evidently translated his scripture quotations
> . . . directly from Greek, in which he was quite competent, making no use
> of any manuscripts of the Latin New Testament. Not until Cyprian . . .
> is there any evidence of the use of such manuscripts.[21]

In his *On Christian Doctrine*, Augustine complained that anyone obtaining a
Greek manuscript of the New Testament would translate it into Latin, regardless
of their knowledge of either language.[22] Jerome agreed with Augustine's analysis
of the translations by confirming, "There are almost as many different translations
as there are manuscripts."[23]

It is not surprising that Augustine quoted from these verses, however, he
did more than quote these verses. In his work *The Harmony of the Gospels*,
Augustine cited Mark as the author of the verses of the longer ending in which
he quoted:

> . . . Mark also attests to these facts: for after telling us how the women
> went out from the sepulcher, trembling and amazed, and said nothing to
> any man, he subjoins the statement, that the Lord rose early the first day
> of the week, and appeared first to Mary Magdalene, out of whom he had
> cast seven devils, and that she went and told them who had been with
> him, as they mourned and cried, and that they, when they heard that he
> was alive, and had been seen of her, believed not.[24]

---

[21]Ibid.

[22]Ibid.

[23]Ibid., p. 183.

[24]Augustinus, *De Consensu Evangelistarum, libri 3*, Patrologiae Cursus Completus, Series Latina, vol. 34, ed. Jacques Paul Migne (Paris: Seu Petit-Montrouge, 1865), p. 1203. The Latin reads as " . . . Et visa sunt ante illos sicut deliramentum verba ista, et non credebant illis. 'His et Marcus attestatur. Nam posteaquam commentoravit eas trementes et paventes exiisso a monumento, et nemini quidquam dixisse, adjunxit quod resurgens Dominus apparuerit mane prima sabbati, primo Mariae Magdalene, de qua ejecerat septem daemonia; et quia illa vadens nuntiavit iis qui cum eo fuerant lugentibus

Augustine (fourth century) repeatedly brought these verses forward, at times discussing them as the work of Mark and then at other times not mentioning their origin.[25] According to David Otis Fuller, Augustine "remark(ed) that 'in dielus Paschalilus,' St. Mark's narrative of the resurrection was publicly read in the church.'"[26] This is significant because Augustine flourished from 390-440.

There is no question of Augustine's belief in the inspiration of scriptures.[27] This is very important because Augustine is the first Father who cited each verse of the longer ending (individually, not collectively) as authentic to Mark, predating the earliest manuscript evidence that we have (either supporting or rejecting the longer ending). Augustine's use of the longer ending suggested that at the beginning of the fourth century, the longer ending was widely held as authentic by the Eastern church. From Augustine on it appears that the longer ending was incorporated in the manuscripts used by the Fathers, therefore, these verses were considered to be both authoritative and authentic.

---

et flentibus; et quia illi audientes quod viveret, et visus esset ab ea, non crediderunt.''

[25]Schaff, ed., *"Saint Augustine, Harmony of the Gospels,"* pp. 217-220, 223, and 224; idem., *"Saint Augustine, Sermons on New Testament Lessons, Lesson XXI.,"* NPNF1, vol. 6, p. 323; idem., *"Saint Augustine, On Forgiveness of Sins, and Baptism,"* NPNF1, vol. 5, pp. 30, 70, and 71; idem., *"Saint Augustine, Against Two Letters of the Palagians, Book I.,"* NPNF1, vol. 5, p. 390; idem., *"Saint Augustine, On Baptism, Against the Donatists,* NPNF1, vol. 4, p. 497; idem., *"Saint Augustine, Expositions on the Book of Psalms,"* NPNF1, vol. 8, pp. 293, 307, 329, and 330; idem., *"Saint Augustine, On the Soul and its Origin,"* NPNF1, vol. 5, pp. 339 and 342; and idem., ed. *"Letters of St. Augustine,"* NPNF1, vol. 1, p. 404.

[26]David Otis Fuller, ed., *Counterfeit or Genuine: Mark 16? John 8?* (Grand Rapids, Mich.: Grand Rapids International Publications, 1984 rpt.), p. 45.

[27]Sturz, *The Byzantine Text-Type*, p. 40.

The Fathers Who Support the Short Ending

The textual tradition which ends the Second Gospel at 16:8 is traced back to the fourth century manuscripts ℵ and B and "presumably back to their third-century prototype."[28] If the intimate agreement between B and $\mathfrak{P}^{75}$ in Luke and John extended to Mark, this could lead to a second century prototype.[29]

The arguments of the supporters of the short ending are based on the silence of several of the Fathers commenting on the verses of the longer ending (note Theodoret, Clement of Alexandria, and Origen). An argument based on silence is generally non-conclusive, yet Origen has attracted much attention.[30] On several occasions Origen had the opportunity to refer to the longer ending in response to Celsus, but declined from doing so. In one incidence, while dealing with Celsus' criticism of the Christian belief of the post-resurrection appearances of Jesus, Origen referred to the post-resurrection accounts of Matthew, Luke, and John while making no reference to Mark 16:9-20. At another point, Origen answered Celsus' charge that Jesus revealed himself secretly to only one woman (this point is one in which Celsus could have supported if he had appealed to Mark and John). Origen responded: "Now it is not that he showed himself to one woman only; for it is stated in Matthew. . . ."[31] It is obvious that at this point,

---

[28]William R. Farmer, *The Last Twelve Verses of Mark* (Cambridge: Cambridge University Press, 1974), p. 30.

[29]Ibid.

[30]See for example Kurt Aland, Matthew Black, Bruce Metzger, and A. Wikgren, eds., *The Greek New Testament*. 3rd. ed. (London: United Bible Societies, 1975). p. 196; Farmer, *The Last Twelve Verses of Mark*, pp. 26-31; and Bruce Metzger, et al., eds. *A Textual Commentary on the Greek New Testament* (London and New York: United Bible Societies, 1976 corrected edition), p. 123.

[31]Origenes, *Contra Celsum*, *libri 2*, PG, vol. 11, p. 905. The Greek reads: "Ἀλλ᾽ οὐδ᾽ ὅτι ἑνὶ μόνῳ γυναίῳ ἐφάνη, ἀληθές ἐστιν· γέγραπται γὰρ ἐν τῷ κατὰ Ματθαῖον Εὐαγγελίῳ. . . ."

Origen had at least the negative opportunity to refer to the longer ending of Mark. In other places, Origen referred to the post-resurrection appearances of Jesus in Matthew, Luke, and John, but never in Mark 16:9-20.

Unlike Augustine, Origen in *Against Celsus* never dealt with discrepancies between the Gospel accounts. Celsus' failure of commenting on the discrepancies of the Four Gospels is remarkable in that one would not expect Celsus, the critic of Christianity who is best known for drawing attention to the inconsistent texts and illogical aspects of Christian doctrine, to have missed the discrepancy of Matthew 28:1 and Mark 16:9.[32]

Origen sought to be a "peacemaker," as he understood the term:

(A peacemaker) demonstrates that which appears to others to be a conflict in the scripture is no conflict, and exhibits their concord and peace. . . . For he knows that all scripture is the one perfect and harmonized instrument of God which from different sounds gives forth one saving voice to those willing to learn. . . .[33]

Guided by this principle, Origen commented on the text of scripture, not by emphasizing discrepancies, but by demonstrating the work of a "peacemaker" or harmonizer. To Origen, "all that appears as discord is in reality a special case of harmony."[34] The different statements of the four evangelists about the same topics compliments each other without conflict.

---

[32]See Burgon, *The Last Twelve Verses*, pp. 44-46 for a discussion and attempted harmonization of these two texts.

[33]Origenes, *In Matthaeum, tomo 2*, PG, vol. 13, p. 832. The Greek reads: ". . . ὁ τὴν ἄλλοις φαινομένην μάχην τῶν Γραφῶν ἀποδεικνὺς εἶναι οὐ μάχην, καὶ παριστὰς τὴν συμφωνίαν καὶ τὴν εἰρήνην τούτων. . . . Ἐν γὰρ τὸ τέλειον οἶδε καὶ ἡρμοσμένον ὄργανον τοῦ θεοῦ εἶναι πᾶσαν τὴν Γραφὴν μίαν ἀποτελοῦν ἐκ διαφόρων φθόγγων θωτήριον τοῖς μανθάνειν ἐθέλουσι θωνήν. . . ."

[34]Farmer, *The Last Twelve Verses of Mark*, p. 29.

Within the church, the practice of harmonizing or conflating the text of the Gospels began at a very early date. Frank Pack confirmed that Origen used examples of the Gospels in which the text of one Gospel had been altered by harmonizing it with the text of another Gospel, and that Origen also engaged in such harmonistic conflation.[35] Origen bitterly complained about those who made additions to and deletions from the text of New Testament manuscripts, yet this did not prevent him from making changes which he thought were justified. Based on his ideal of "peacemaker," many of the changes that Origen made in his New Testament texts were influenced by his principle of the unity and harmony of scriptures.[36]

In reference to the Eusebian response to the questions posed by Marinus,[37] the first solution may have appealed to Origin as an Alexandrian-trained scholar, since the harmonizing changes made in his New Testament citations included examples of omission, however, the second would have appealed to him as an ecumenically oriented Christian.[38] Farmer was correct in his assertion, "There seems to be no way to proceed beyond these generalizations to any positive statement about what Origen actually thought about the questions of the authenticity of Mk 16:9-20."[39]

---

[35]Frank Pack, "The Methodology of Origen As A Textual Critic in Arriving at the Text of the New Testament" (Ph. D. Dissertation, University of Southern California, 1948), pp. 182-207.

[36]Ibid.

[37]See below pages 25-28.

[38]Farmer, *The Last Twelve Verses of Mark*, p. 30.

[39]Ibid.

According to Farmer, there have been some who maintained that the twofold solution to the question of Marinus may have originated with Origen, but this is only conjecture.[40] It is interesting that this theory has been held by proponents both for and against the authenticity of the longer ending. As shown above, this twofold solution is Origenic in nature. If this solution "is from Origen, it provides evidence for the existence of manuscripts ending with ἐφοβοῦντο γάρ in the third century in such quantities as conservatively to argue for a late second-century origin of this reading."[41]

Eusebius is the Father who is most associated with the argument in favor of the short ending. As noted in the above paragraph, he is often quoted as saying that the Second Gospel ends with ἐφοβοῦντο γάρ in the more accurate manuscripts.

According to D. S. Wallace-Hadrill, the *Gospel Questions and Solutions* of Eusebius exist in two versions:

> . . . the first and longer being known in Greek and Syriac fragments, the shorter, known as the *Epitome*, existing in the form of sixteen answers to questions posed by Stephanus concerning the infancy narratives of the Gospels, and four chapters to Marinus on the Resurrection narratives.[42]

In the first question Marinus asked Eusebius, "How according to Matthew, the savior appears to have risen 'at the end of the Sabbath,' but according to Mark

---

[40]Ibid.

[41]Ibid.

[42]D. S. Wallace-Hadrill, *Eusebius of Caesarea* (London: A. R. Mowbray & Co. Limited, 1960), p. 60.

'early the first day of the week?'''[43] Eusebius then proceeded with the solution of the problem:

> This problem calls for a twofold solution. The one who is in favor of getting rid of the whole passage, will say that it is not in all the copies of the Gospel of Mark. The accurate copies, at all events, makes the end of Mark's narrative come after the words of the young man who appeared to the woman and said, 'Do not be afraid, you seek Jesus of Nazareth;' and to which in the next place the evangelist adds, 'and when they heard it, and no one said anything, for they were afraid.' For in these words in almost all the copies of the Gospel according to Mark, comes the end: But what follows might be done away with, especially if it contradicts the testimony of the other evangelists. This then is what a person will say who is for evading and entirely getting rid of a problem.[44]

The second question Marinus asked Eusebius is: "How is it that according to Matthew (Mary) the Magdalene saw the risen Lord at the end of the Sabbath, while according to John the same woman on the first day of the week stood

---

[43]Eusebius, *Questiones evangelica ad Marinum, libri 1*, PG, vol. 22, p. 937. The Greek reads as: "Πῶς παρὰ μὲν Ματθαίῳ 'ὀψὲ σαββάτων' φαίνεται ἐγηγερμένος ὁ Σωτήρ, παρὰ δὲ τῷ Μάρκῳ 'πρωὶ τῇ μιᾷ τῶν Σαββάτων.'"

[44]Ibid. The Greek reads as: "Τούτου διατὴ ἂν εἴη ἡ λύσις· ὁ μὲν γὰρ τὸ κεφάλαιον αὐτὸ τὴν τοῦτο σάσκουσαν περικοπὴν ἀθετῶν, εἴποι ἂν μὴ ἐν ἅπασιν αὐτὴν φέρεσθαι τοῖς ἀντιγράφοις τοῦ κατὰ Μάρκον Εὐαγγελίου. τὰ γοῦν ἀκριβῆ τῶν ἀντιγράφων τό τέλος περιγράφει τῆς κατὰ τὸν Μάρκον ἱστορίας ἐν τοῖς λόγοις τοῦ ὀφθέντος νεανίσκου ταῖς γυναιξὶ καὶ εἰρηκότος αὐταῖς, "μὴ φοβεῖσυε, Ἰησοῦν ζητεῖτε τὸν Ναζαρηνόν·" καὶ τοῖς ἔξης, οἷς ἐπιλέγει, "καὶ ἀκούσασαι ἔφυγον, καὶ οὐδενὶ οὐδεν εἶπον, ἐφοβοῦντο γάρ." ἐν τούτῳ γάρ σχεδὸν ἐν ἅπασι τοῖς ἀντιγράφοις τοῦ κατὰ Μάρκον Εὐαγγέλιον περιγέγραπται τὸ τέλος· τὰ δὲ ἑξῆς σπαμίως ἔν τισιν ἀλλ' οὐκ ἐν πᾶσι φερόμενα περιττὰ ἂν εἴη, καὶ μάλιστα εἴπερ ἔχοιεν ἀντιλογίαν τῇ τῶν λοιπῶν εὐαγγελιστῶν μαρτυρίᾳ· ταῦτα μὲν οὖν εἴποι ἂν τις παραιτούμενος καὶ πίντη ἀναιρῶν περιττὸν ἐρώτημα.

crying by the tomb?''[45] As in the first question, the first part of question two appeared to conflict with the second part. Farmer obviously pointed out that both of these questions are related, therefore, it can be debated whether Eusebius is responsible for the views expressed in the second answer, based on how one interprets Matthew's ὀψὲ δὲ σαββάτων (at the end of the Sabbath).[46] Eusebius pointed out that ὀψὲ δὲ σαββάτων can be interpreted in a general way as 'early the first day of the week.'[47] This broad interpretation of the text of Matthew tends to place the resurrection during the night between the Sabbath and the morning of the first day of the week. The resurrection as recorded in Mark, therefore, could have taken place as recorded in Matthew (as asked in question one).

The first question is answered by the interpretation of ὀψὲ δὲ σαββάτων. If one interprets this phrase in a literal manner, a serious time discrepancy cannot be avoided. If one interprets this phrase in a broad sense, there is no time discrepancy, however, if one interprets ὀψὲ δὲ σαββάτων as 'early the first day of the week,' the first solution to Marinus' first question is unnecessary and the second solution to the second question is invalid, for it appears to presuppose a view of Matthew's use of ὀψὲ δὲ σαββάτων as being repudiated.[48] Farmer concluded:

---

[45]Ibid., p. 940. The Greek reads as: "Πῶς κατὰ τὸν Ματθαῖον ὀψὲ Σαββάτων ἡ Μαγδαληνὴ τεθεαμένη τὴν ἀνάστασιν, κατὰ τὸν Ἰωάννην ἡ αὐτὴ ἑστῶσα κλαίει παρὰ τῷ μνημείῳ τῇ μιᾷ τοῦ Σαββάτου.''

[46]See Farmer, *The Last Twelve Verses of Mark*, p. 5.

[47]Ibid.

[48]Ibid., p. 6.

This clearly shows the text . . . is more like a developed compilation in
which earlier more or less effective answers to variously closely related
questions have been edited and reissued by someone (possibly Eusebius)
without reworking the whole according to any single and consistent set
of critical presuppositions.[49]

From the above discussion one may conclude: (1) Both Burgon and Farmer
have shown that Mark 16:9 does not contradict Matthew 28:1, for the broad
interpretation of ὀψὲ δὲ σαββάτων appears to be the correct one. (2) It is obvious
Eusebius was well aware of several good texts of the New Testament which did
not include Mark 16:9-20. Knowledge of texts that did include the longer ending
is not a claim of authenticity for that ending. (3) The proposal that Eusebius may
not have been the original author of the answers to the questions of Marinus,
points to the probability of an older tradition.[50] If that be the case, the questions
of Marinus have been worked over as well as the answers to his questions,
therefore, based on the traditions of these questions and answers, the knowledge
of texts with and without the longer ending go back to the third and possibly the
second century. This testimony affirmed that a large part of the Greek copies did
not include the longer ending. Eusebius did not discuss the authorship of these
verses, however, it is obvious Eusebius did not believe that these verses were
written by Mark: "According to Mark, after the resurrection it is not said that he
was seen by the disciples."[51]

---

[49]Ibid.

[50]Ibid.

[51]See Samuel Prideaux Tregelles, *An Account of the Printed Text of the Greek
New Testament with Remarks on Its Revision Upon Critical Principles* (London: Samuel
Bagster and Sons, 1854), p. 247. The Greek reads as κατὰ Μάρκον μετὰ τὴν
ἀνάστασιν οὐ λέγεται ὤφθαι τοῖς μαθηταῖς.

According to Tregelles, the arrangement of the Eusebian Canons are also an argument that Eusebius did not have the verses of the longer ending, for "in genuine copies of the notation of these numbers do not go beyond verse 8, which is marked σλή."[52] Some manuscripts include this notation as far as the end of verse fourteen and some to the end of the chapter, however, these are unauthorized additions. This is contradicted by both good copies which contain these sections (such as A and Codex Amiatinus) and also by a scholion which is found in several manuscripts at verse 16:8. According to Tregelles, "It has been objected that these sections show nothing as to the MSS. extant in Eusebius' time, but only the conditions of the Harmony of Ammonius, from which the divisions were taken."[53] This objection is self destructive for it carries back the evidence from the fourth to the third century, therefore, "just as Eusebius found these verses absent in his day from the best and most numerous copies, so was also the case with Ammonius when he found his Harmony in the preceding century."[54]

Another fact text critics fail to observe is the evidence Eusebius gave in agreement with the ministry of Mark. Eusebius, in his *Ecclesiastical History, Book II.*, informed the reader that "with every kind of exhortation they encouraged Mark, whose Gospel is extant. . . ."[55] Since this Gospel was in existence, it is obvious that Eusebius was familiar with the contents of the Second Gospel and how it ended. A few lines down, Eusebius not only discussed the written Gospel of Mark, but also his preaching:

---

[52]Ibid., pp. 247-248.

[53]Ibid., p. 248.

[54]Ibid.

[55]Eusebius, *Historica ecclesiastica, libra 2*, PG, vol. 20, p. 172. The Greek reads as: ". . . παρακλήσεσι δὲ παντοίαις Μαρκον, οὗ τὸ Εὐαγγέλιον φέρεται. . . ."

But it is said this same Mark was the first to be sent to preach in Egypt the Gospel which he had also written, and was the first to establish churches in Alexandria itself. The number of men and women who believed at the first attempt was so great, and their asceticism was so extraordinarily philosophic, that Philo thought it appropriate to to describe their activities and assemblies and meals and all the rest of their conduct.[56]

From this we are able to uncover elements of internal and external evidence pertaining to the ending of Mark.

The external evidence is obvious. Since Mark preached "his Gospel" and settled several churches in Alexandria, we should expect the Alexandrian texts to be very accurate. Burgon maintained that the short ending dominated the Alexandrian texts, which he considered inferior to the Byzantine texts.[57] Since the text of Mark was extant up until Eusebius' day (according to Eusebius' testimony above) one would have to argue the superiority of the Alexandrian texts rather than their inferiority, therefore, the reliability of the short ending appears to be correct.

The internal evidence is based on the contradictory testimonies of the longer ending of Mark and Eusebius concerning the personality of the Markan converts and the text of the longer ending: "The number of men and women who believed at the first attempt was so great, and their asceticism was so

---

[56]Ibid., p. 173. The Greek reads as: "Τοῦτον δὲ Μάρκον πρῶτόν φασιν ἐπὶ τῆς Αἰγύπτου στειλάμενον, τὸ Εὐαγγέλιον ὃ δὴ καὶ συνεγράψατο, κηρύξαι, ἐκκλησίας τε πρῶ ἐπ᾽ αὐτῆς Ἀλεξανδρείας συστήσασθαι. Τοσαύτη δ᾽ ἄρα τῶν αὐτόθι πεπιστευκότων πληθὺς ἀνδρῶν τε καὶ γυναικῶν ἐκ πρώτης ἐπιβολῆς, συνέστη, δι᾽ ἀσκήσεως φιλοσοφωτάτης τε καὶ σφοδροτάτης, ὡς καὶ γραφῶν αὐτῶν ἀξιῶσαι τάς διατριβὰς καὶ τὰς συνηλύσεις, τά τε συμπόσια, καὶ πᾶσαν ἄλλην τοῦ βίου ἀγωγὴν τὸν φίλωνα."

[57]Edward F. Hills, "Introduction," John W. Burgon, *The Last Twelve Verses of the Gospel According to St. Mark* (Erlanger, Ky.: Faith and Facts Press, rpt.), pp. 21-30.

extraordinarily philosophic. . . . .''[58] It would seem logical if the converts were "extraordinarily philosophic," surely Mark the evangelist would be.[59] This is contradictory to the testimony of Mark 16:17-18:

> And these signs will follow the ones (who) believe: in my name they will cast out demons, they will speak with new tongues; they will take up serpents and if they drink anything deadly by no means will it harm them, they will lay hands on them and they will recover.[60]

The above information as supplied by Eusebius is valuable in supporting the argument of the authenticity of Mark ending at 16:8 with ἐφοβοῦντο γάρ. Many critics based their view of authenticity or lack of authenticity of the longer ending solely on the question of Marinus, however, Eusebius' testimony of Mark's ministry in Alexandria appears to be the most conclusive in support of the short ending, when considered in connection with present day manuscript evidence of the Alexandrian texts.

---

[58]Eusebius, *Historica ecclesiastica, libri 2*, PG, vol. 20, p. 173. The Greek reads: "Τασαύτη δ' ἄρα τῶν αὐτόθι πεπιστευκότων πληθὺς ἀνδρῶν τε καὶ γυναικῶν ἐκ πρώτης ἐπιβολῆς συνέστη, δι ασκήσεως φιλοσοφωτάτης τε καὶ σφοδοροτάτης.''

[59]See B. H. Throckmorton, "Philosophy, *"The Interpreter's Dictionary of the Bible*, vol. 3, eds. et al. (Nashville: Abingdon Press, 1962) p. 799. In an article on "philosophy," B. H. Throckmorton stated: "A number of philosophies were influential in the speech and thinking of man in the street in the Hellenistic Age, especially Cynicism and Stoicism. But Epicureanism, Platonism, and Neo-Pythagoreanism were other options." It is important to note that the following verses in no way resembles the thought of any of these philosophies.

[60]Kurt Aland et al., eds. *Novum Testamentum Graece [Nestle-Aland text]*, 26th ed. (Stuttgart: Deutsche Bibelstiftung, 1979), pp. 148-149. The Greek reads as: "σημεῖα δὲ τοῖς πιστεύσασιν ταῦτα παρακολουθήσει· ἐν τῷ ὀνόματι μου διαμόνια ἐκβαλοῦσιν, γλώσσαις λαλήσουσιν καιναῖς, [καὶ ἐν ταῖς χερσὶν] ὄφεις ἀροῦσιν κἂν θανάσιμον τι πίωσιν οὐ μὴ αὐτοὺς βλάψῃ, ἐπὶ ἀρρώστους χεῖρας ἐπιθήσουσιν καὶ καλῶς ἕξουσιν.''

There are several other Fathers who are cited as accepting the short ending, including Victor of Antioch, Gregory of Nyssa, Hesychius of Jerusalem, and Severus of Antioch, however, evidence shows the possibility that these Fathers borrowed from Eusebius or each other.[61]

Gregory of Nyssa in his second *Homily on the Resurrection*, followed Eusebius' argument:

> In the more accurate copies, the Gospel according to Mark has its end at 'for they were afraid.' But in some copies this is also added: 'Now he was arisen early the first day of the week, he appeared first to Mary the Magdalene, out of whom he had cast seven demons.'[62]

The second *Homily on the Resurrection*, which was printed in the third volume of the works of Gregory of Nyssa, is "word for word the same Homily which Combifis in his 'Novum Auctarium,' and Gallandius in his 'Bibliotheca Patrum' printed as the work of Hesychius, and vindicated to that Father, respectively in 1648 and 1776."[63]

Besides the question of authorship of this passage, Gregory was actually a hostile witness to the argument for the short ending, for he quoted Mark 16:19 in the above work.[64]

---

[61]Burgon, *The Last Twelve Verses*, pp. 39-41, 57-67.

[62]Gregorii Nysseni, *In Christi resurrectionem, libri 2*, PG, vol. 46, pp. 644-645. The Greek reads: "Ἐν μὲν τοῖς ἀκριβεστέροις ἀντιγράφοις τὸ μετὰ Μάρκον Εὐαγγέλιον μέχρι τοῦ, Ἐφοβοῦντο γὰρ, ἔχει τὸ τέλος. Ἐν δὲ πρόσκειται καὶ ταῦτα· Ἀναστὰς δὲ πρωΐ πρώτη Σαββάτου ἐφάνη πρῶτον Μαρίᾳ τῇ Μαγδαληνῇ, παρ' ἧς ἐκβεβλήκει ἑπτὰ δαιμόνια."

[63]Burgon, *The Last Twelve Verses*, p. 40.

[64]Gregorii Nysseni, *In Christi resurrectionem, libri 2*, PG, vol. 46, p. 652.

Several pages of this same *Homily* re-appeared verbatim as attributed to Severus of Antioch and were printed as his by Montfaucom in his *Bibliotheca Coisliniana* (1715) and by Cramer in his *Catena* (1844),[65] including the above statement as cited from Gregory of Nyssa. Burgon confirmed, "Competent judges have declared that there are sufficient reasons for giving it (a claim of authorship) to Hesychius rather than to Severus, while no one is found to suppose that Gregory of Nyssa was its author."[66] Burgon affirmed Hesychius was only reproducing what he had received from Eusebius: "The words indeed are by no means the same; but the sense is altogether identical. He seems to have also known Victor of Antioch."[67]

Victor of Antioch quoted the same questions that Marinus asked Eusebius (see footnotes 43 and 45). Victor's commentary on Mark, as was almost every ancient commentary in existence, is to a great extent a compilation, in which he transcribed from several Fathers before him.[68] In the first twelve lines of his commentary on Mark at verse 16:9, Victor did not give any hint that the material is not original, however, the latter half of the entry "professes to give substance of what Eusebius had written on the same subject."[69] Each of these above named Fathers appeared as reiterating in some form or fashion the statements of Eusebius on these verses, (see above pages 26-27).

---

[65]Burgon, *The Last Twelve Verses*, p. 40.

[66]Ibid., p. 119.

[67]Ibid., p. 136.

[68]See for instance: Origen, Apollinarius, Theodore of Mopsuestia, Eusebius, and Chrysostom.

[69]See Fuller, *Counterfeit or Genuine?*, p. 56.

Farmer followed Burgon by arguing that these above named Fathers are only quoting Eusebius and were not advocating for the authenticity of the short ending. We should question whether Eusebius was referring to the verses of the longer ending based on a rhetorical argument against the notion that there are discrepancies in the Gospel. This by no means is an endorsement for the longer ending! We should, however, accept the testimony of these Fathers that the short ending dominated the better texts.

A Third Tradition as Evidenced by Jerome

Jerome is often cited as a defender of the short ending based on a letter written in A.D. 406 or 407, in response to a question pertaining to the question of the seeming inconsistencies between Matthew 28:1 and Mark 16:1-2, from a lady of Gaul named Hedibia: "How are the discrepancies in the Gospel narrative to be accounted for? How can Matthew 28:1 be reconciled with Mark 16:1-2?"[70] Burgon and Farmer insisted that this question originated with Eusebius: "Whether Jerome is utilizing another Latin or Greek form of the same text published by Mai, or whether he is modifying this text, it is clear that his letter to Hedibia is secondary to the text attributed to Eusebius."[71] Burgon and Farmer dealt with this question as if they were dealing with Matthew 28:1 and Mark 16:9 (a view connecting this question to the longer ending), however, Jerome clearly stated Matthew 28:1 and Mark 16:1-2. To a critic of the longer ending, this discrepancy of the verses cited would appear as a ploy to prove the authenticity or at least Jerome's reference to a verse of the longer ending.

---

[70]Hieronymi, *Epistolae, epistolae CXIX*, PL, vol. 22, p. 980. The Latin reads as: "Quae causa sit, ut de resurrectione et apparitione Dominini Evangelistae diversa narrauerini. Et cur dicente Matthaeo, quad vespere sabbati illucescente in una sabbati Dominus surrexit, Marcus mane cum alterius diei asserat surrexisse."

[71]Farmer, *The Last Twelve Verses of Mark*, p. 22. Farmer appeared to reiterate Burgon's position on these questions. See Burgon, *The Last Twelve Verses*, p. 133.

Jerome explained his method in handling such discrepancies:

> I have presented you with the opinions of all the commentators; for the
> most part, translating their very words, to put you into possession of
> ancient authorities on the subject . . . This has been hastily dictated in
> order that I might lay before you what have been the opinions of learned
> men on this subject, as well as the arguments by which they have
> recommended their opinions. . . .[72]

Jerome added:

> My plan is to read the ancients; to prove all things, to retain that which
> is good; to remain constant in the faith of the Catholic Church.
>   I must now dictate replies, either original or second hand, to other
> questions which lie before me. . . .[73]

In his response to Hedibia, concerning the question of a conflict between
Matthew and Mark, Jerome wrote:

> This difficulty admits of a twofold solution. Either we reject the
> testimony of Mark, which is met with in scarcely any copies of the
> Gospel-almost all the Greek codices being without this passage . . . or
> else, we shall reply that both evangelists state what is true.[74]

---

[72]Hieronymi, *Epistolae, epistolae CXIX, CXIX*, pp. 967 and 978. The Latin
reads as: "Itaque et ego tempore coarctatus, singulorum vobis, qui in sacram Scripturam
commentariolos reliquerunt, sententias protuli, et ad verbum pleraque interpretatus sum;
ut et me liberum quaestione, et vobis veterum tractatorum mittatur auctoritas . . . Haec
celeri sermone dictavi, quid cruditi vivi de utroque sentirent loco, et quibus argumentis
suas vellent probare sententias. . . ."

[73]Ibid., p. 980. The Latin reads as: ". . . Meum propositum est antiquos
legere, probare singula, retinere quae bona sunt, et a fide Ecclesiae Catholicae non
recedere.
     Volens ad alias quaestiunculas respondere, et vel mea, vel aliena dictare extemplo,
a fratre Sisinnio admonitus sum, ut et ad vos et ad caeteros sanctos fratres qui nos amare
dignantur litteras scriberem. . . ."

[74]Ibid., p. 987. The Latin reads as: "Hujus quaestionis duplex solutio est; aut
enim non recipimus Marci testimonium, quod in raris fertur Evangeliis, omnibus Graeciae
libris pene hoc capitulum in fine non habentibus, praesertim cum diversa atque contraria
Evangelistis caeteris narrare videatur; aut hoc respondendum, quod uterque verum

It is obvious that Jerome knew of Greek and Latin manuscripts which did not include Mark 16:9-20. By the reason he included these verses in his Latin translation of the New Testament and also treated them in his *Commentary on Mark*. This suggests that Jerome not only testified to the existence of a twofold textual tradition, but infers that Jerome preferred to include these verses rather than omit them from the ending of the Second Gospel.

In his *Against the Pelagians*, Jerome confirmed that in some copies, and especially in Greek codices, an extensive addition is found at the end of the Gospel of Mark (at the end of verse 16:14): "At length Jesus appeared to the Eleven as they were at the table; he upbraided them for their lack of faith and hardness of heart, in that they did not believe those who had seen him after he had risen"[75] Following verse 16:14, the text proceeds immediately with the following addition:

> And they excused themselves saying, 'This age of lawlessness and unbelief is from Satan, who by means of unclean spirits does not allow the true power of God to prevail over unclean things of the spirits. Therefore reveal thy righteousness now'. They spoke to Christ, and Christ replied to them that 'the term of years for Satan's power has been fulfilled, but other terrible things draw near. And for those who have sinned I was delivered over to death, in order that they might turn to the truth and sin no more; that they might inherit the spiritual and incorruptible glory of righteousness which is in heaven.[76]

---

dixerit.''

[75]Mark 16:14.

[76]This quote of the longer ending is from Aland, eds. et al., *The Greek New Testament*, p. 197. The Greek reads as: ''ἐπίστευσαν κἀκεῖνοι ἀπελογοῦντο λέγοντες ὅτι ὁ αἰὼν οὗτος τῆς ἀνομίας καὶ τῆς ἀπιστίας ὑπὸ τὸν Σατανᾶν ἐστιν, ὁ μὴ ἐῶν τὰ ὑπὸ τῶν πνευμάτων ἀκάθαρτα τὴν ἀλήθειαν τοῦ θεοῦ καταλαβέσθαι δύναμιν· διὰ τοῦτο ἀποκάλυψον σοῦ τὴν δικαιοσύνην ἤδη. ἐκεῖνοι ἔλεγον τῷ Χριστῷ, καὶ ὁ Χριστὸς ἐκείνοις προσέλεγεν ὅτι πεπλήρωται ὁ ὅρος τῶν ἐτῶν τῆς ἐξουσίας τοῦ Σατανᾶ, ἀλλὰ ἐγγίζει ἄλλα δεινὰ καὶ ὑπὲρ ὧν ἐγὼ ἁμαρτησάντων παρεδόθην εἰς

Jerome did not reveal where he found this passage. No manuscript with this ending was known until the twentieth century, when the passage turned up in a Greek manuscript (W) which Charles L. Freer had bought from an Arab dealer in Gizeh near Cairo.[77]

Jerome's reference to "the addition at the end of the Gospel of Mark" proved that by the time of Jerome, at least three traditional endings to the Second Gospel existed. This did not prove or disprove the authenticity of either the short or longer ending, but it is obvious that both of these endings predate the ending offered by W.

The Medieval Theologians

By the seventh century, the widespread acceptance and use of the longer ending was common to commentaries, such as the ones produced by Bede, Euthymius, and Thomas Aquinas. This widespread acceptance and use of the longer ending marked an age of reluctance to question the Church, scripture, or God.

The tradition that Bede (672-735) represented was the connecting link between antiquity and the theological and philosophical awakening that took place in the medieval period.[78] Bede, known affectionately as "the Venerable," was

---

θάνατον ἵνα ὑποστρέψωσιν εἰς τὴν ἀλήθειαν καὶ μηκέτι ἁμαρτήσωσιν· ἵνα τὴν ἐν τῷ οὐρανῷ πνευματικὴν καὶ ἄφθαρτον τῆς δικαιοσύνης δόξαν κληρονομήσωσιν ἀλλά.''

[77]Metzger, *The Text of the New Testament*, p. 153.

[78]González, *A History of Christian Thought*, vol. 3, p. 105.

one of the great leaders of the scholarship of the monasteries of the eighth century.[79]

According to Peter Hunter Blair,

(Bede) was devoted to studying the meaning of Holy Writ and its interpretation in the light of the writings of the Fathers. If the church was the spiritual heart of the monastery, the Bible was the ultimate source of spiritual knowledge.[80]

Blair continued, "Copies of the Gospels comprise far the greater part of the manuscripts which had English associations during the age of Bede."[81] G. F. Browne added, "There is very little indeed of criticism of the text in Bede's sermons. He takes it (the text) as he finds it, and he expounds it."[82] Browne continued: "The Bible which was in the hands of his (Bede's) readers and hearers was of course the Latin Bible."[83] Coupled with this is the continuous use by many of Tatian's *Diatessaron*, which came to enjoy a wide circulation in the Syrian-speaking churches, and later translated into Latin.[84]

Based on the influence of works that contained the longer ending of Mark, which dated back as far as the second century, it is not surprising that Bede

---

[79]Williston Walker, *A History of the Christian Church*, 3rd edition (New York: Charles Schribner's Sons, 1970), p. 183.

[80]Peter Hunter Blair, *The World of Bede* (New York: St. Martin's Press, 1970), p. 212.

[81]Ibid., p. 219.

[82]G. F. Browne, *The Venerable Bede: His Life and Writings* (London: Society for Promoting Christian Knowledge and New York: The Macmillan Company, 1930), p. 233.

[83]Ibid. See also pages 19-20 above.

[84]Ibid., p. 218.

included the longer ending in his *Commentary on Mark*.[85] Bede "was always careful to point out omissions, and to warn his readers against mis-translations into which the Latin might lead them if they were not warned."[86] With the longer ending being in tact in the Latin versions, it is obvious Bede had no question concerning their authority or authenticity.

Euthymius Zigabenus wrote a compilation on the Gospels in the early part of the twelfth century, from which he is often cited as a supporter of the short ending. He affirmed, "It is said by the interpreters the Gospel according to Mark ends here: but (these verses of the longer ending) were subsequently added."[87] According to Burgon, "This clearly is his (Euthymius') version of the statement of one or more of the Fathers."[88] This statement by Euthymius, alone, appears as solid evidence in favor of the authenticity of the short ending, however, he went on to say, "This (discrepancy between Matthew 28:1 and Mark 16:9) should also be explained, since there is nothing destructive to the truth."[89] Euthymius did include the longer ending in his commentary (compilation) on the Gospel of Mark and it is not conclusive as to his position on the ending of Mark.

---

[85]Bede, *Expositio in Marci*, PL, vol. 92, pp. 300-302.

[86]Browne, *The Venerable Bede*, p. 234.

[87]Euthymii Zigabeni, *In quatuon evangelia: In Marcum*, PG, vol. 129, p. 845. The Greek reads as: "Φασὶ δὲ τῶν ἐξηγητῶν ἐνταῦθα συμπληροῦσθαι τὸ κατὰ Μάρκον Εὐαγγέλιον· τὰ δὲ ἐφεξῆς προθήκην εἶναι μεταγενεστέραν."

[88]See Burgon, *The Last Twelve Verses*, p. 69. Burgon made this statement in a chapter discussing the Fathers who accepted the short ending of Mark. The context of this sentence is of the four Fathers (Eusebius, Victor of Antioch, Gregory of Nyssa, and Jerome) who dominated the discussion in this chapter. See pages 39-68.

[89]Euthymius, *In quatuon evangelia: In Marcum*, PG, vol. 129, p. 845. The Greek reads as: "Χρὴ δὲ καὶ ταύτην ἑρμηνεῦσαι, μηδὲν τῇ ἀληθείᾳ λυμαινομένην."

Euthymius did not prove or disprove the authenticity of either the short or longer endings of the Gospel of Mark. This testimony is a direct reference to the knowledge of the debate concerning the two endings in various manuscripts,[90] and that the question about the ending of Mark was a topic of concern as late as the twelfth century.

Thomas Aquinas (1225-1274), often considered as one of the greatest theologians of all time, was a Dominican theologian who maintained the philosophy of Aristotle[91] was very valuable and should not be rejected for the sole reason that it was opposed to the philosophical outlook that had served as the background for earlier theological formulations.[92] Aquinas' motive was not to leave aside Christian orthodoxy, but rather to adopt Aristotle and his philosophy as the philosophical tool for a theological understanding of Christianity.[93] He made a distinction between philosophy and theology: "Philosophy deals only with those truths which reason can attain; but theology, whose proper field is that of revealed truth, is concerned not only with these, but with truth in all its forms."[94]

Aquinas produced several works in the areas of philosophy as well as theology. In the field of theology, Aquinas' three most significant works are his

---

[90]Burgon alluded to Euthymius continuing the questions of the discrepancies between Matthew 28:1 and Mark 16:9 and these Fathers commented on the longer ending being absent from some of the earlier manuscripts. See ibid.

[91]Walker, *A History of the Christian Church*, pp. 246-251 for a discussion of Aristotle's influence on Aquinas and his theology.

[92]González, *A History of Christian Thought*, vol. 2, p. 255.

[93]Ibid.

[94]Ibid., p. 259.

Commentary on the Sentences, the *Summa contra gentiles,* and the *Summa theologiae.* On several occasions Aquinas referred to Mark 16:12, 15-20 as authentic by citing the reference to the Gospel of Mark (e.g., Mark 16:16). In his *Catena Aurea: Commentary on St. Mark,* Aquinas included the testimony of several of the above named Fathers who supported the longer ending of Mark, including Augustine, Bede, and Theophylacti. Aquinas occasionally cited Mark the evangelist as the author of the verses of the longer ending of Mark: "Mark, when about to finish his Gospel, relates the last appearance of our Lord to His disciples after His resurrection, saying, 'For the last time He appeared unto the eleven as they sat at meat.'"[95]

Even though the Medieval theologians considered the issue of the manuscript evidence of the longer and short endings of Mark, these theologians continued to include the longer ending in their translations and commentaries. The fact remains, however, that the evidence of the Medieval theologians perspective on the authenticity of verses 16:9-20 is inconclusive. No matter how these theologians viewed the longer ending's authenticity, it is obvious that they viewed these verses as canonical and authoritative. Euthymius affirmed, "This should (Mark 16:9-20) also be interpreted, since there is nothing destructive to the truth."[96]

The Reformation Theologians

The dominance of the longer ending continued from the Medieval period, as shown above, through the age of the reformation, based on the widespread use of the Latin texts which continued the Byzantine tradition. This was confirmed in

---

[95]Thomas Aquinas, *Catena Aurea: Commentary on the Four Gospels Collected Out of the Works of the Fathers, St. Mark* (Oxford and London: James Parker and Co., 1874), p. 343.

[96]See footnote 89.

the various works of Erasmus, Zwingli, Luther, and Calvin. With the reformation came an age of questioning the method of the interpretation of scripture, however, there remained a reluctance to questioning God or scripture.

Desiderius Erasmus (1469-1536) is included in this period because of his influence on the text which Martin Luther later translated into German.[97] Erasmus produced five (constantly revised) editions of the New Testament[98] based on four or five manuscripts of the twelfth/thirteenth century which represented the Byzantine text,[99] that included the verses of the longer ending of Mark. In this process, he took manuscripts which were available to him for each part of the New Testament and entered corrections in the places where he deemed it necessary. Erasmus made these corrections by comparing the text to the text of the common Latin version.[100]

---

[97]Compare with page 44 at footnote 110.

[98]See Metzger, *The Text of the New Testament*, pp. 99-103 for a discussion of these five editions. The first edition (1516) consisted of a compilation of the Greek manuscripts (each of these manuscripts did not contain a whole copy of the New Testament) to form a Greek New Testament which included his Latin translation. The final six verses of Revelation were missing in the Greek manuscripts, therefore, Erasmus depended on the Latin Vulgate to translate these verses into Greek. The Second edition (1518) consisted of an elegant Latin translation which often differed from Jerome, that included brief annotations used to justify his translation. The major criticism of this Greek and Latin New Testament was that the text lacked a part of the last chapter of 1 John. Erasmus inserted this passage in the third edition (1522), but he also included a footnote to remark on his doubt of the authenticity of these verses. The fourth edition (1527) included the text of the New Testament in three parallel columns, the Greek, the Latin Vulgate, and his own Latin translation. The major change of the fifth edition (1535) was Erasmus' deletion of the Latin Vulgate.

[99]See Aland, *The Text of the New Testament*, p. 4, 72. Metzger, *The Text of the New Testament*, p. 102, stated: "The text of Erasmus' Greek New Testament rests upon a half-dozen minuscule manuscripts.

[100]See Aland, *The Text of the New Testament*, p. 4, and Metzger, *The Text of the New Testament*, pp. 99-100. Compare this to footnote 19 above in this chapter where Schaff confirmed the Latin translations usually included the verses of the longer ending.

From Erasmus to Martin Luther, the dominance of the Byzantine text and the longer ending of Mark continued as a result of the Latin text's inclusion of the verses in question. Metzger confirmed, "The second edition (of Erasmus' New Testament) became the basis of Luther's German translation,"[101] in which he included the verses of the longer ending.[102] In a footnote Metzger continued:

> It has often been debated how far Luther's translation reads on the Greek text. In recent times H. Dibbelt (Archiv für Reformationgeschichte, xxxviii [1941], pp. 300-39) has maintained that the translation reflects only an occasional consultation of the Greek; on the other hand, H. Bornkamm (Theologische Literturzeitung, lxxii [1947], pp. 23-28) holds that Luther translated from the combination of Greek and Latin texts in Erasmus' edition and from the Vulgate, which he had in his head.[103]

To Luther, the Word of God is the starting point for theology.

His concept of "Word of God" was a complex idea. González described this concept:

> The Word is the eternal second person of the Trinity, which existed in God from all eternity; the Word is God's power as manifested in the creation of all things; the Word is the incarnate Lord; the Word is the Scriptures, which witnesses to it; the Word is the proclamation through which the Word in Scripture is actually heard by believers.[104]

---

[101]Metzger, *The Text of the New Testament*, p. 100.

[102]*Die Bibel oder die ganze heilige Schrift des Alten und Neuen Teftaments nach der deutfchen uberfehung D. Martin Luther* (New York: American Bible Society, 1816).

[103]Ibid.

[104]González, *A History of Christian Thought*, vol. 3, p. 41.

With such a high view of Scripture, it is not surprising that Luther accepted the verses of the longer ending as authentic, for the longer ending was the dominant ending of Mark that circulated in the Latin versions of Luther's day which were subsequently translated into German.[105] From a theological perspective, the verses of the longer ending do not provide any information that contradicts any portion of Scripture.[106]

The usefulness of some of these verses to Luther is debatable. Luther freely quoted the verses of Mark 16:15-20 and cited them as "recorded in the last chapter of Mark, however, in no place did he cite Mark 16:9-14."[107] Luther cited Mark the evangelist as the author of the longer ending in an allusion to Mark 16:16: "Without faith no one can be saved, as Mark says in his last chapter."[108] He appeared particularly fond of Mark 16:16, therefore, he maintained, "This is a strict command if a person wants to be saved, let him (or her) be baptized; otherwise he (she) is in God's disfavor."[109] In his *Church Postil, Gospels: Epiphany, Lent, and Easter Sermons*,[110] Luther offered three Easter Sermons from Mark 16:1-8, however, he used Luke 24:13-35 when he continued with the

---

[105]See above footnotes 101 and 102.

[106]See González, *A History of Christian Thought*, vol. 3, p. 42 where González said, "His (Luther's) own practice was to reject only those traditional views and practices which contradicted 'the clear sense of Scripture.'" Such logic would also apply to Scripture as well.

[107]Helmut T. Lehmann, eds et al., *Sermons, II.*, Luther's Works, vol. 51 (Philadelphia: Fortress Press, 1974), p. 182. This is only one example of this occurrence.

[108]Ibid., p. 254.

[109]Ibid., vol. 52, p. 183.

[110]Martin Luther, *Church Postil, Gospels: Epiphany, Lent, and Easter Sermons* (Minneapolis, Minn.: Lutherans in all Lands Co., 1906).

post-resurrection sermons. One would wonder why Luther did not present Mark 16:9-20 in the continuation of the resurrection story.

The reform movement that began with Luther quickly accumulated support from various parts of Europe. This reformation movement, which was greater than one person, soon produced "various views that agreed with Luther on some points, but strongly disagreed on others."[111] González continued, "It is possible to classify Protestant theology in the sixteenth century into four basic groups or traditions: the Lutheran, the Reformed, the Anabaptist, and the Anglican."[112]

Huldreich Zwingli (1484-1531) was the person in whom the Reformed tradition had its earliest theologian. Even though Zwingli agreed with Luther in many respects, they also had many differences. Luther followed an anguished spiritual pilgrimage which dealt with the basic issue of his relationship with God, whereas, Zwingli was led by patriotic and intellectual considerations.[113] According to González, "Zwingli's intellectual interests ran along the lines of Erasmian humanism."[114]

The primary influence of Erasmus on Zwingli took place through Scripture. Zwingli maintained that the Bible apart from its inspiration, had historical priority, therefore, it is a better witness than latter tradition.[115] Scripture is infallible and is the believer's "sole authority."[116]

---

[111]González, *A History of Christian Thought*, vol. 3, p. 63.

[112]Ibid.

[113]Ibid., p. 64.

[114]Ibid., p. 64. See also Walker, *A History of the Christian Church*, p. 321.

[115]Ibid., p. 65.

[116]Ibid., pp. 66-67.

The church (the unseen body of believers) "cannot err, for it is predestined to be obedient to Christ."[117] With such a high view on Scripture and the authority of the "unseen church," it is not surprising that Zwingli made frequent use of the verses of the longer ending of Mark. On several occasions Zwingli quoted or alluded to each verse of the longer ending of Mark, with the exception of verse 20. (Note that Mark 16:20 is the only reference in the four Gospels of the disciples fulfilling the "Great Commission.") Zwingli did, however, cite the verses of the longer ending of Mark as being authentic to Mark the evangelist, except for Mark 16:18 and 20. In his work *On True and False Religion*, Zwingli unequivocally attributed Mark the evangelist as the author of Mark 16:9-14:

> . . . and these women could not have been other than the Magdalene and her companions, whose tale Mark [16:9-14] describes vividly, at the same time mentioning those who were going to Emmaus, and telling how, when they returned and said that Christ had appeared to them, some did not believe them. "Postea" (afterward) Mark says, where our version has "novissime" (finally), as if that was the last appearance of Christ, though the Greek is ὕστερον, which cannot possibly mean "Novissime," but "postea"-- he says, then, "afterward," when the men returning from Emmaus had told what had happened to them, as the Eleven had sat at meat on the very day of the Resurrection.[118]

Zwingli made more use of the Markan "Great Commission" (Mark 16:15-16) than he did of the Matthean "Great Commission" (Matthew 28:18-20), usually by citing the passage as from Mark the Gospel and on a few occasions he cited Mark the evangelist as the author: "Mark puts it this way [Mark 16:15-16]: "Go ye into all the world, and preach the Gospel to the whole creation. He that

---

[117]Ibid., p. 72.

[118]Huldreich Zwingli, *Commentary on True and False Religion*, eds. Sammuel Macauley Jackson and Clarence Nevin Heller (Durham: The Labyrinth Press, 1981 rpt.), p. 170.

believeth and is baptized shall be saved; but he that believeth not shall be condemned.[119]

Zwingli undoubtedly had no reservation as far as the canonicity and the authenticity of the verses of the longer ending of Mark. As seen above, this may in part be a result of Erasmian influence.

The best way to understand John Calvin's (1509-1564) position as to the authenticity of the longer ending to Mark, is to understand his view of Scripture and to observe his use of Scripture. Calvin maintained that scripture is self authenticating and receives its authority from God, therefore, it is not right to subject it to proof and reasoning.[120] He vowed, "Scripture has its authority from God, not from the church,"[121] furthermore, "while the church receives and gives its seal of approval to the Scriptures, it does not thereby render authentic what is otherwise doubtful or controversial."[122] Calvin concluded:

> When that which is set forth is acknowledged to be the Word of God, there is no one so deplorably insolent--unless devoid also both of common sense and of humanity itself--as to dare impugn the credibility of Him who speaks."[123]

---

[119]Ibid., p. 379.

[120]John T, McNeil, ed., *Calvin: Institutes of the Christian Religion*, The Library of Christian Classics, vol. 1, trans. Ford Lewis Battles (Philadelphia: The Westminster Press, 1960 ed.), p. 80.

[121]Ibid., p. 74.

[122]Ibid., p. 76. This quote is a strong indication that since Mark 16:9-20 is included in text of his copy of Mark, he did not consider these verses as conflicting with any of the New Testament.

[123]Ibid., p. 74.

With such a view on scripture, it is not surprising that Calvin, along with the influence of tradition and scholastic investigation, accepted the verses of the longer ending as being authentic to Mark. At no time did Calvin stop at the end of Mark 16:8 and discuss the issue of their authenticity or the possibility of these verses being a spurious addition. On several occasions Calvin alluded to or quoted from verses of the longer ending in his *Institutes of the Christian Religion*.[124] Calvin used these verses in conjunction with the verses of the other Gospels in the presentation of doctrines in his systematic theology.

In his *Harmony of the Gospels*, Calvin sought to solve the discrepancy between Mark and Matthew, as far as Christ's initial appearance and to whom: a plural group as attested by Matthew 28:8-10 or a singular person (Mary Magdalene) as attested by Mark 16:9-11 of the longer ending of Mark.[125] Calvin offered a solution to this problem by saying, "It is more likely that she (Mary Magdalene) alone was named by Mark because she had a first sight of Christ, in a special way before the others, apart from Christ's appearance to her companions in due course."[126] On the next page Calvin continued this discussion in connection to 16:11:

> Mark records the testimony of Mary alone, yet I am sure that Christ's orders were jointly related by them all. This passage confirms better what I have just said, that there is no discord between the Evangelists in one

---

[124]See John T. McNeill, ed., Calvin: *Institutes of the Christian Religion*, vol 2. See the index on, p. 1571.

[125]David W. Torrance and Thomas F. Torrance, eds., *A Harmony of the Gospels Matthew, Mark and Luke Volume III. and the Epistles of James and Jude*, trans. A. W. Morrison (Grand Rapids, Mich.: Wm. B. Eerdmans Publishing Company, 1972), p. 227.

[126]Ibid.

attributing to Mary Magdalene in particular what, according to the rest, was shared by them all.[127]

Calvin was the first theologian to discuss possible contradictions between Mark and the other Gospels since Jerome did in the fourth century. These two theologians did not discuss the same point of conflict, however, they did apply the same method by explaining these "conflicts" in a manner where the idea of conflict is dismissed. It is obvious Calvin not only presented these verses as authentic, but unlike previous theologians, he presented Mark the evangelist as a creative thinker, writing from his own agenda (i.e., focusing in on the particular personality of Mary Magdalene rather than the general personality of the crowd as offered in Matthew).

The theologians of the Reformation era followed the theologians of the Medieval period in accepting the verses of the longer ending as authentic to Mark the evangelist without any debate. It is obvious that the Latin texts' inclusion of these verses led the theologians of the Reformation to view these verses as authentic, canonical, and authoritative, since they are not "doubtful or controversial."[128]

Chapter Summary

The Fathers provide much information on the traditions of the ending of Mark: (1) Several Fathers who advocated for the longer ending, affirmed that there were some manuscripts which ended abruptly at 16:8 with ἐφοβοῦντο γάρ. Some of these manuscripts traced the tradition which א and B follows back to the third

---

[127]Ibid., p. 228.

[128]See footnote 122 above. Compare also with footnotes 89 and 96.

and even late second century.[129] (2) A majority of the Fathers affirmed the existence of the longer ending, however, only three of these Fathers cited the longer ending as authentic to Mark. It is important to remember that Tatian cited Mark as the author of the verses of the longer ending as early as the late second century. (We must remember that a most of the Latin texts included the longer ending). (3) Jerome offered evidence that as early as the late second century, there existed a third ending appended at the end of 16:14. As noted above, this ending was not known until the twentieth century when Charles Freer discovered a manuscript (W) which included this ending.[130]

The Byzantine texts included the longer ending and were considered to be more reliable than the Alexandrian texts which commonly ended with ἐφοβοῦντο γάρ.[131] Eusebius countered that Mark preached in Alexandria and settled churches there[132] and Bede confirmed this point![133] From this, one may assume the priority of the Alexandrian texts rather than their inferiority.

Besides the testimony of Tatian, Irenaeus, and Augustine (who supported the longer ending) and Eusebius (who supported the short ending), the testimony of the Fathers from the second through the sixth centuries was inconclusive. It is obvious that the longer ending was in widespread use by the early part of the third

---

[129]Farmer, *The Last Twelve Verses of Mark*, p. 26.

[130]This is the only manuscript that is known to have this appendage at the end of 16:14. Common sense would tell us that originally this was not the only manuscript to have ended in this manner.

[131]See footnote 57 above.

[132]Eusebius, *Historia ecclesiastica, libri 2*, PG, vol. 20, p. 173.

[133]Bede, *Opera Historica*, vol. 2, The Loeb Classical Library Series, trans. J. E. King (London: William Heinemann and New York: G. P. Putnam's Sons, 1930), p. 337.

century, however, use does not prove authenticity. The early testimony of Tatian and Eusebius is the most conclusive arguments representing each side of the debate. We must remember that even though Eusebius did say that the longer ending was absent from most of the texts in use at his time, nowhere does he say that the authentic ending of Mark was ἐφοβοῦντο γάρ. It does appear that after the third century the longer ending began to dominate the texts used by the Church.

From the sixth century to the end of the Reformation the Latin texts were dominant, which in turn signaled the dominance of the longer ending of Mark. The value of the theologians of this time span is not helpful in a critical evaluation of the longer ending of Mark, because of this widespread acceptance of the Latin traditions. Bede, Theophylacti,[134] and Euthymius all included the longer ending of Mark in their commentaries, without any discussion of the textual tradition(s) behind the longer ending or the textual tradition behind the short ending. The theologians of the Reformation era, likewise, did the same.

This chapter confirmed that the early theologians were aware of and concerned about the question of the authenticity of the longer ending of Mark. Based on the result of the research of the works of the Fathers and theologians on this question, the results are inconclusive, therefore, the subject calls for further consideration by the critical methods of scholars from the seventeenth century to the present day. The three subsequent chapters will investigate the critical scholarship concerning the ending of Mark: (1) Chapter 3 will survey select scholars who accepted the longer ending of the Second Gospel as being authentic to Mark the evangelist; (2) Chapter 4 will survey select scholars who maintained that the original ending of the Second Gospel is missing; and (3) Chapter 5 will investigate select scholars who accepted Mark 16:8 as the authentic ending of the Second Gospel.

---

[134]Theophylacti, *Enarratio In Marci Evangelium*, PG, vol. 56, pp. 678-682.

CHAPTER 3

Scholars Who Support
the Longer Ending of Mark

This chapter will summarize and evaluate the critical studies of John Burgon, George Salmon, and William Farmer, who support or are at least receptive of the idea of the authenticity of the longer ending of Mark. The first section will be a brief summary of the major scholarship prior to John Burgon. The next section will discuss John Burgon's contribution to textual criticism and his defense of the longer ending, based on the dominance of the Byzantine text. The discussion of Burgon will dominate this chapter, because his text critical analysis laid the foundation for modern scholarship which accepts the longer ending as authentic. George Salmon continued the defense of the authenticity of the longer ending based on both external and internal evidence. Salmon was the first critic (as far as I found) who argued that a literary work could not end with γάρ. William Farmer, the most acclaimed twentieth century defender of the authenticity of the longer ending, called for a "re-investigation" of the possibility that Mark did originally end with the longer ending. Farmer's approach was primarily a reconsideration of Burgon's external and internal evidence, however, he was not as dogmatic as Burgon. The last section will be a brief discussion of the scholarship after Farmer, (this scholarship is very limited) which also defended the authenticity of the longer ending. A summary will conclude the chapter.

Scholars Who Accept the Longer Ending
of Mark Prior to John Burgon

Critical editions of the New Testament prior to Johann Jakob Griesbach,[1] did not question the authenticity of the longer ending of the Gospel of Mark. John Mill in his *Novum Testamentum* Graecum[2] (a text that is similar to the text of Stephanus) "presents a wealth of textual material with an able introduction."[3] After a review of the evidence he was acquainted with, Mill concluded that there was no reason for doubting the authenticity of Mark 16:9-20.

Twenty-seven years after the printing of Mill's text, J. J. Bengel's edition of the New Testament appeared.[4] In essence, Bengel re-published Textus Receptus, because as Robertson stated it, "he could not then publish a text of his own. Neither the publisher nor the public would have stood for it.'"[5] Bengel's

---

[1]Johann Jakob Griesbach, *Commentarius Criticus in Textum Novi Testamentl* (Ienae: Apud J. C. G. Goepferdt, 1774/1775).

[2]John Mill, *Novum Testamentum Graecum* (1907). In the production of this text Mill consulted 78 manuscripts, including the Peshitta Syriac, the Old Latin Versions, the Vulgate, and several patristic quotations.

[3]A. T. Robertson, *An Introduction to the Textual Criticism of the New Testament* (Nashville, Tenn.: Sunday School Board of the Southern Baptist Convention, 1925), p. 24.

[4]Johann Jakob Bengel, *Gnomon Novi Testamenti*, vol. 1 (Tübigin: Sumtibus Ludov Frid. Fues., 1850).

[5]Ibid., p. 25. See also Caspar René Gregory, *Canon and Text of the New Testament* (New York: Charles Schribner's Sons, 1907), p. 447. Gregory gave an example of the people's disdain over the alteration of a text: "In the book of Revelation he (Bengel) altered nineteen passages to suit the manuscripts. So many people railed at his

method was to "put the good readings into the text when they had already appeared in some previous printed edition."[6] He initiated the foundation for modern textual criticism by providing marginal notes for five classes of readings: (1) the genuine readings, (2) those better than the text, (3) those just as good as the text, (4) those that were not as good as the text, and (5) the rejected readings.

J. J. Wettstein published a Greek New Testament in two volumes[7] based primarily on the Elzevir text.[8] According to Robertson, "He was the first to distinguish the uncial manuscripts by capital letters and the cursives by Arabic numbers."[9] Wettstein placed the readings which he considered genuine below the Elzevir text.

The importance of the latter two editors is they left Mark 16:9-20 in an undisputed position of its place.[10] This is primarily based on their adherence to the Textus Receptus.

---

edition that he published a "Defence of the Greek Testament. . . ."

[6]Ibid.

[7]J. J. Wettstein, *Novum Testamentum Graecum*, 2 vols. (Amsterdam: 1751).

[8]Robertson, *An Introduction to the Textual Criticism*, p. 20. The Elzevir text was published at Leyden and Amsterdam between 1624 and 1678. These editions of the New Testament were based on the work of Beza and of Stephanus and have little critical value because of their similarities. The 1633 edition contained, in the preface, the words '*Textus ergo habes nunc ab omnibus receptum*, from which the phrase *Textus Receptus* comes. This 1633 edition became the standard for the continent, as did the 1550 Stephanus edition for Great Britain.

[9]Ibid., p. 26.

[10]See Bengel, *Gnomon Novi Testamenti*, pp. 236-239 and Wettstein, *Novum Testamentum Graecum*, pp. 639-642.

John W. Burgon

John W. Burgon (1813-1888) spent a large part of his adult life at Oxford, as a Fellow of Oriel College and later as Vicar of the University church (St. Mary's) and Gresham Professor of Divinity. From 1876 to his death, Burgon was the Dean of Chichester.[11] Burgon's major works were: *The Last Twelve Verses of the Gospel According to St. Mark*; *The Revision Revised*;[12] and two works pieced together by E. Miller after Burgon's death, *The Traditional Texts of the Holy Gospels*;[13] and *The Causes of the Corruption of the Traditional Text of the Holy Gospels*.[14]

Burgon on Textual Criticism and the Byzantine Text

John Burgon maintained a steadfast defense of the Scriptures as the infallible word of God and labored in textual criticism to substantiate this claim. Such a bold claim was made because of his favor of the Byzantine text, which dominated the Greek New Testament manuscripts and was the norm by which

---

[11]Edward F. Hills, "Introduction," John W. Burgon, *The Last Twelve Verses of the Gospel According to St. Mark* (Erlanger, Ky.: Faith and Facts Press, rpt.), p. 18. This work contained an extensive introduction to the question of the validity of the longer ending of Mark and textual criticism and also contained a reprint of Burgon's work, *The Last Twelve Verses of the Gospel According to St. Mark*. The Burgon/Hills edition was complimented by an extensive introduction.

[12]John W. Burgon, *The Revision Revised* (London: John Murray, 1883).

[13]Idem., *The Traditional Texts of the Holy Gospels*, ed. E. Miller (London: George Bell & Sons, 1896).

[14]Idem., *The Causes of the Corruption of the Traditional Text of the Holy Gospels*, ed. E. Miller (London: George Bell & Sons, 1896).

texts are judged.[15] He renamed the Byzantine text the "Traditional Text," thus suggesting his conviction that the Byzantine text was the true text by which a perpetual tradition passed down from the second century, generation after generation, without fail by the Church.

Burgon condemned the non-Byzantine texts in the strongest of terms, deeming them depraved and inferior to the Byzantine text found in the vast majority of Greek New Testament texts. He considered Codex D as the most corrupt text.[16] Burgon maintained a similar view of ℵ and B:

> As for the origin of these two curiosities, it can perforce only be divined from their contents. That they exhibit fabricated texts is demonstrable. No amount of honest copying--preserved in for any number of centuries,--could by possibility have resulted in two such documents. Separated from one another in actual date by 50, perhaps by 100 years, they must needs have branched off from a common corrupt ancestor, and straightway become exposed to fresh depraved influences.[17]

Burgon attributed the false readings which are present in ℵ, B, D, and other non-Byzantine manuscripts to two main causes:

> The first one was the deliberate falsification of the New Testament texts by heretics during the second and third centuries . . . and (2) the efforts of certain learned Christians during this same period to improve the New Testament text through the use of conjectural emendation.[18]

---

[15]Harry A. Sturz, *The Byzantine Text-Type & New Testament Textual Criticism* (Nashville: Thomas Nelson Publishers, 1984), p. 32.

[16]Burgon, *Revision Revised*, p. 12.

[17]Ibid., p. 318.

[18]Hills, "Introduction," p. 24.

A third contributor to the "false readings" was the "self constituted critics (who) were the corrupting influences which were at work throughout the first hundred years after the death of S. John the Divine."[19]

Burgon maintained that the arguments of Tischendorf, Tregelles, Westcott, and Hort (who claimed, as a result of their work, the true New Testament had been discovered after having been for nearly fifteen centuries) were weak for "it would appear that the Truth of Scripture has run a very narrow risk of being lost for ever to mankind."[20] Hort contended that more than half the New Testament text lay *perdu* on a forgotten shelf in the Vatican Library, whereas, Tischendorf maintained that it had been deposited in a waste-basket in the convent of Saint Catherine at the foot of Mount Sinai, from which he rescued it in 1859.[21] Burgon believed that the "Author of Scripture" was careful to secure its preservation:

> I am utterly disinclined to believe--so grossly improbable does it seem--that at the end of 1800 years 995 copies out of every thousand, suppose, will prove untrustworthy; and that the one, two, three, four or five, which remain, whose contents were till yesterday as good as unknown, will be found to have retained the secret of what the Holy Spirit originally inspired. I am utterly unable to believe, in short, that God's promise has so entirely failed, that at the end of 1800 years much of the text of the Gospel had in point of fact to be picked by a German critic out of a waste-paper basket in the convent of St. Catherine; and that the entire text had to be remodeled after the pattern set by a couple of copies which had remained in neglect during fifteen centuries, and had probably owed their survival to that neglect; whilst hundreds of others

---

[19]Ibid., p. 27.

[20]Burgon, *Revision Revised*, p. 343.

[21]Ibid.

had been thumbed to pieces, and had bequeathed their witness to copies made from them.[22]

John Burgon believed that the history of the New Testament text was similar to the history of the New Testament canon. During the early Christian centuries Satan attacked not only the New Testament canon, but also the New Testament text. Shortly after the New Testament books had been given to the Church through the inspiration of the Holy Spirit, Satan began his attempt to corrupt their texts and render them useless.[23] These efforts were nullified. Just as God directed the Church to reject all non-canonical books and to receive only the "true" canonical books, (after a period of doubt), He lead the Church to reject false readings and to receive into common usage the "true" New Testament text.[24]

Burgon continued that the primary mistake of his contemporary New Testament textual critics (Tischendorf, Tregelles, Westcott, and Hort) was they ignored the unique fact, that the New Testament is a "Divinely inspired and providentially preserved Book."[25] Burgon regarded the Divine inspiration and providential preservation of the New Testament as two fundamental verities which make New Testament textual criticism different from the textual criticism of any other book. He concluded that the Byzantine text was the means of this providential preservation.

---

[22]Idem., *The Traditional Text of the Holy Gospels*, p. 12.

[23]Ibid., p. 20.

[24]Ibid.

[25]Ibid., p. 21.

Burgon and the Last Twelve Verses of Mark

In his work *The Last Twelve Verses of the Gospel According to St. Mark*, Burgon offered a defense of the last twelve verses of Mark being genuine, based on the authority of the Byzantine text. According to Burgon,

> The manuscript evidence is so overwhelmingly in their favor that no room is left for doubt or suspicion:--That there is not as much as one of the Fathers, early or late, who gives it as his opinion that these verses are spurious:--and, That the argument derived from internal considerations proves on inquiry to be baseless and unsubstantial as a dream.[26]

Burgon investigated both the external and internal evidence which favored and attacked the authenticity of the longer ending of Mark. He quickly dismissed the external evidence against the authenticity of the longer ending of Mark. Seven Fathers constantly emerged as having detrimental testimony against the authenticity of the longer ending of Mark,[27] however, Burgon was emphatic that six of these Fathers were quoting Eusebius (who Burgon questioned as opposing these verses, based on his observation that Eusebius nowhere said that the genuineness of the verses of the longer ending was suspected). Eusebius' elaborate discussion of the contents of these verses convinced Burgon that individually, Eusebius regarded them with favor.[28] Burgon concluded that these Fathers who

---

[26]Burgon, *The Last Twelve Verses*, p. 1.

[27]These Fathers are: Eusebius, Jerome, Gregory of Nyssa, Hesychius of Jerusalem, Severus of Antioch, Victor of Antioch, and Euthymius.

[28]Burgon, *The Last Twelve Verses*, p. 212. According to Burgon, "The last Twelve Verses of S. Mark's Gospel were anciently often observed to be missing from the copies. Eusebius expressly says so. I (Burgon) observe that he nowhere says that their genuineness was anciently suspected. As far as himself, his elaborate discussion of their contents convinces me that individually, he regarded them with favor. The mere fact,--(it is best to keep to his actual statement,)--that 'the entire passage' was 'not met with in all the copies,' is the sum of his evidence."

quoted Eusebius did not accept what many assumed as Eusebius' argument, that the manuscript that end at 16:8 dominate.

Burgon noted that only two manuscripts (א and B) have Mark ending at 16:8.[29] א and B are manuscripts of the fourth century, whereas, the testimony for the longer ending of Mark was confirmed at an earlier time (the late second century) by Tatian and Justin. Burgon concluded:

> The omission of 'The Last Twelve Verses' of S. Mark's Gospel (appeared) to have originated in a sheer error and misconception on the part of some ancient Copyist. He saw το τελος written after ver. 8: he assumed that it was the Subscription, or at least that it denoted 'the End,' of the Gospel.[30]

Because of the enormous amount of manuscripts that include the longer ending, Burgon insisted that the verses of the longer ending of Mark

> constitute an integral Ecclesiastical Lection; which lection,--inasmuch as it is found to have established itself in every part of Christendom at the earliest period to which liturgical evidence reaches back, and to have been assigned from the very first to two of the chiefest Church Festivals,--must needs be a lection of almost apostolic antiquity.[31]

Burgon listed some twenty Fathers, dating from the second century to the eighth century, who testified to the authenticity of the longer ending of Mark, based on their frequent citations of these verses. He noted that six of these Fathers predate א and B. He further added to his argument of external evidence by referring to the deluge of manuscripts which included this ending (a large number

---

[29]Note that this statement predated the discovery of many manuscripts that also end at 16:8, and W which appends the Freer Logion after Mark 16:14.

[30]Burgon, *The Last Twelve Verses*, p. 241.

[31]Ibid., pp. 212-213.

of these manuscripts are connected to the Byzantine tradition). Of the above manuscripts mentioned that support the longer ending, Burgon stated: "Manuscripts, Fathers, and Versions alike, are only not unanimous in bearing consistent testimony. But the consentient witness of the MSS. is even extraordinary."[32]

The witness of the Lectionaries (even though consistently overlooked) on the genuineness of the longer ending are important, because of the dominance of the longer ending in both the Eastern and Western Lectionaries. According to Burgon, "From the very first, S. Mark xvi. 9-20 has been everywhere, and by all branches of the Church Catholic, claimed for two of the greatest Festivals,--Easter and Ascension."[33] He further stated:

> . . . there is found to have been at least at that time (the third century)
> fully established throughout the Churches of Christendom a Lectionary,
> which seems to have been essentially one and the same in the West and
> in the East. That it must have been of even Apostolic antiquity may be
> inferred from several considerations.[34]

Burgon concluded that the testimony of the lectionaries represents the united testimony of all the churches.

A final matter of external evidence which Burgon considered was the possible reasons that $\aleph$ and B ended abruptly at Mark 16:8. The two more likely possibilities were a torn leaf or a misunderstanding of γάρ τέλος at the end of Mark 16:8. Burgon responded to the first explanation, "Codices in daily use, (like the Bibles used in our Churches), must by necessity have been of exceptionally

---

[32]Ibid., pp. 70-71.

[33]Ibid., p. 210.

[34]Ibid., p. 207. Burgon did not list the considerations by which one could infer the dating of the lectionaries back to an apostolic era.

brief duration; and Lectionaries, more even than Biblical MSS. were liable to injury and decay."[35] The second reason Burgon considered ℵ and B's abrupt ending at Mark 16:8, was because some ancient scribe "misapprehended the import of the solitary liturgical note τελος (or το τελος) which he found at the close of verse 8.[36] There is no evidence of a single codex in which τελος is written at the end of a Gospel, within the first six centuries. The subscription of the Gospel of Mark is either **ΚΑΤΑ ΜΑΡΚΟΝ** or **ΕΥΑΓΓΕΛΙΟΝ ΚΑΤΑ ΜΑΡΚΟΝ**.

According to Burgon, "An argument much relied on by those who deny or doubt the genuineness of this portion of S. Mark's Gospel, is derived from consideration of internal evidence."[37] This may be brought under the two categories of style and phraseology. Burgon responded to suggestions that the longer ending was a later appendage: (1) The longer ending may have been written long after the rest, therefore, its verbal peculiarities should not be troublesome; and (2) The longer ending may not have been written by Mark the evangelist after all.[38] Burgon dismissed these two theories by stating: "There is no appearance whatever of any such interval having been interposed between S. Mark xvi. 8 and 9,"[39] furthermore, "after cause has been shewn why we should indeed believe that not S. Mark but some one else wrote the end of S. Mark's

---

[35]Ibid., p. 215.

[36]Ibid., p. 226. See also p. 242.

[37]Ibid.

[38]Burgon, *The Last Twelve Verses*, p. 138.

[39]Ibid.

Gospel, we shall be perfectly willing to acquiesce in the new fact:--but not till then.''[40]

It is commonly argued that the longer ending was ''. . . abrupt, sententious (in) manner, resembling that of brief notices extracted from larger accounts and loosely linked together.''[41] He responded, "The style may indeed be exceedingly diverse, and yet the Author be exceedingly the same."[42] Such is the manner of the Second Gospel. According to Burgon, "Between S. Mark xvi. 9-20 and S. Mark i. 9-20, I profess myself unable to discern any real difference of style.''[43]

The second point of internal evidence that is often called upon to refute the authenticity of the longer ending is the phraseology of this section, in which text-critics[44] made assertions "that a certain word or phrase--(there are about twenty-four [sic Burgon lists twenty-seven] such words and phrases in all)--'occurs nowhere in the Gospel of Mark; with probability the alarming asseveration that it is 'abhorrent to Mark's manner.'''[45] Five types of phraseological problems constitutes the basis of the argument against the authenticity of the longer ending of Mark: (1) The Latinism of πρώτη σαββάτου

---

[40]Ibid.

[41]Ibid., p. 142.

[42]Ibid., p. 140. Two points of proof that Burgon offered is the dissimilar style of the Revelation of John and the Gospel of John and the style of the first five verses of the Gospel of John and the rest of the Fourth Gospel. Note that Burgon listed several similar points.

[43]Ibid., p. 143.

[44]See Alford, Davidson, Meyer, Tischendorf, and Tregelles, who argued that the verses of the longer ending of Mark are not authentic to the Evangelist, based on their peculiarity to the Second Gospel as a whole.

[45]Burgon, *The Last Twelve Verses*, pp. 145-146.

in verse 16:9; (2) Several phrases occur in this section which do not occur in the main of the Second Gospel; (3) The author of the longer ending used expressions that are not common with the ones used within the body of the Second Gospel; (4) There are several words in this section which do not occur anywhere else in Mark; and (5) There are words and typical syntactical features that are common to Mark missing in the longer ending.

Burgon responded to the above arguments: (1) Latinisms are a frequent phenomenon in the Second Gospel;[46] (2) Words and phrases occur in this section which do not occur in any other part of the Gospel, because the context of what is described is totally different from the rest of the Gospel;[47] (3) The same author used variety of expressions of style. An example of this is "the phrase παρ' ἧς ἐκβεβλήκει ἑπτὰ δαιμόνια which is attached to the name of Mary Magdalene, although she had been mentioned three times before without such appendix;"[48] (4) A large number of these words occurred also in an infrequent amount in the other three Gospels, therefore, it is not necessary to become alarmed over these occurrences, to the point of using these individual occurrences as proof that these

---

[46]See ibid., pp. 146-151. Burgon argued for a Roman origin of the Second Gospel, designated for a non-Jewish Hellenistic audience, based on these Latinisms. See also Vincent Taylor, *The Gospel According to St. Mark*, 2nd ed. Thornapple Commentaries (Grand Rapids: Baker Book House, 1981), pp. 45, 657-658.

[47]Ibid., p. 155. An example of this would be the phrase τοῖς μετ' αὐτοῦ γενομένοις. Burgon noted: "In no other . . . way could the followers of the risen SAVIOUR have been designated at such a time." Burgon went on to point out that the phrase τοῖς μετ' αὐτοῦ occurs twelve times in the Synoptic Gospels (including four times in Mark), which suggests that examples of this type are not legitimate evidence to disprove the authenticity of the longer ending of Mark.

[48]Ibid., p. 152. Other examples are: ἐκβεβήκει (verse 9) rather than the common ἐκβεβήκει ἀπό (p. 153), and ἐν τῷ ὀνόματί μου (verse 17) rather than the usual ἐπί. . . .

verses are not authentic to the Second Gospel;[49] (5) As to the absence of certain words and typical syntactical features common to Mark, which are missing in the longer ending, Burgon responded that this same phenomenon also occurred in the body of the Second Gospel as well. For example, the absence of the copulative in the longer ending of Mark suggests that these verses are not authentic, whereas Burgon responded that such of an assertion cannot be accurate if one did not prove the use of the copulative within other summary sections within the body of the Second Gospel.[50] Burgon also noted that the absence of εὐθέως and πάλιν (two favorite Markan words) are not valid arguments against the authenticity of the longer ending, because they are also absent from several chapters of the Second Gospel.[51]

Burgon concluded that of the twenty-seven points of internal evidence challenged by text critics, none of these points individually or collectively destroys the validity of the authenticity of the longer ending of Mark. Burgon affirmed that thirteen of the above points of internal evidence validated the authenticity of the longer ending[52] and he added fourteen other points of style and phraseology which he saw as vindicating the longer ending of Mark.[53]

---

[49]Burgon listed several examples in which this phenomenon occured.

[50]Burgon, *The Last Twelve Verses*, p. 167.

[51]Ibid., p. 169.

[52]Ibid., p. 170.

[53]Ibid., pp. 170-173.

Critique of John Burgon

John Burgon provided New Testament studies with an enormous amount of material in the field of textual criticism. It is not surprising that scholars of the twentieth century continued the argument for the authority, if not the authenticity of the long ending (see William R. Farmer, Edward Hills, and David Otis Fuller, below) based on the research of Burgon. Above all, Burgon is to be commended for his high view of scripture, through the preservation of the Holy Spirit.

Burgon maintained that as a basic premise the best and accurate text is preserved where there are the largest number of manuscripts, therefore, such numerical superiority revealed the providence of God in preserving the inspired original in the Byzantine text-type. Harry Sturz responded:

> To present preservation as a necessary corollary of inspiration, then to imply that preservation of the Scripture must be as faithful and precise as inspiration of the Scriptures, appears to be taking a position that is both unscriptural and impossible to demonstrate."[54]

Preservation and inspiration are related doctrines, yet they are distinct from each another, and there is a danger of making one the necessary corollary of the other.

Furthermore, Sturz responded to Burgon's approval of the Byzantine text being the "true text," (based on its numerical superiority) based on three objections: (1) In the West, Greek faded out in favor of Latin; (2) The Alexandrian texts multiplication were cut off in Egypt with the Moslem conquest in A.D. 642, whereas the Moslem conquest did not reach the Byzantine area until the fifteenth century with the fall of Constantinople in 1453; and (3) The Greek language dominated the Byzantine area, therefore, Greek manuscripts would

---

[54]Sturz, *The Byzantine Text-Type*, p. 37.

naturally multiply.[55] The result is obvious. Superior numbers of the Byzantine text does not guarantee its authenticity.

Burgon was quick to criticize the advocates of the short ending, who appealed to the testimonies of several of the Fathers,[56] that "these verses are missing in several of the better or most of the manuscripts."[57] Burgon's initial response was these Fathers were only quoting Eusebius and did not necessarily agree with his conclusions. The context of these "quotations" in the text of these Fathers, however, does not suggest that these Fathers disagree with Eusebius.

Burgon also offered an inconsistent argument about Eusebius' position on the longer ending of Mark. At times Burgon appeared to proceed with Eusebius as accepting the authenticity of Mark 16:8.[58] In other places he stated that Eusebius acknowledged a few manuscripts as ending at Mark 16:8, however, Eusebius often quoted from the longer ending of Mark, and accepted this section as authentic to the Second Gospel. Burgon continued, "If any one supposes that Eusebius has anywhere plainly 'stated that it (the longer ending of Mark) is wanted in many MSS.,' --he is mistaken. Eusebius nowhere says so."[59] Burgon continued,

> It is not even clear to me that the Verses in dispute were absent from the
> copy which Eusebius habitually employed. . . . Still less does that Father

---

[55]Ibid., pp. 47-48.

[56]See footnote 27 above.

[57]See pp. 60-62 above.

[58]See Burgon, *The Last Twelve Verses*, p. 131, where Burgon said, "What more have we learned when we have ascertained that the same Eusebius allowed no place to that subsequent portion (the longer ending) in his Canons."

[59]Ibid., p. 41.

anywhere say, or even hint, that in his judgment the original Text of S. Mark was without them.[60]

In other places Burgon pointed out that Eusebius' statement about the question of Marinus originated with Origen.[61] If that be the case, Eusebius was only quoting Origen and therefore, not making a statement about the ending of Mark. (Remember, Burgon was emphatic that six of the Fathers who are attributed to claiming that the short ending exists in many/most of the extant copies of the Second Gospel, were quoting Eusebius and were not making an independent statement of preference for the ending of Mark).[62] The questions often emerged, "Is Eusebius speaking for himself or is he quoting Origen? If Eusebius is speaking for himself about the ending of Mark, does he accept the long or short ending?" The inconsistency of Burgon's treatment of Eusebius weakened his argument against the Fathers who are accounted as denying the authenticity of the longer ending.

Burgon argued against the possibility the longer ending was a later addition by the same author. According to Burgon: "There is no appearance whatever of any such interval having been interposed between S. Mark xvi. 8 and 9."[63] As to the possibility that another author added the longer ending to Mark 16:8, Burgon replied: "After cause has been shewn why we should indeed believe that not S. Mark but some one else wrote the end of S. Mark's Gospel, we shall be

---

[60]Ibid., p. 41.

[61]Ibid., pp. 47, 235, and 238.

[62]See footnote 28 above.

[63]Burgon, *The Last Twelve Verses*, p. 133.

perfectly willing to acquiesce in the new fact: --but not till then.'"[64] Burgon was closed minded to any possibility that the longer ending, was not authentic to the Second Gospel. It is unfortunate that Burgon predated the great hermeneutical methods such as redaction criticism, for such a method may explain the need of an appendage to Mark 16:8 by the early church.[65]

Even though Burgon admitted that the style of an evangelist is singularly apt to be fallacious, especially when applied to a limited portion of scripture as Mark 16:9-20, he declared, "It becomes a fatal objection to such reasoning that the style may be exceedingly diverse, and yet the author be confessedly the same."[66] He then attempted to refute the argument of different authors, based on different styles by countering, "How exceedingly different in style are the Revelation of S. John and the Gospel of S. John,"[67] and they are authored by the same person. Contemporary scholarship acknowledged the authorship of the Revelation of John and the Gospel of John as a problem, and many maintained that these two works were written by two different authors.[68] If this is correct, it would prove to argue against Burgon's counterpoint.

In his critique of the text critics who opposed the authenticity of the longer ending and appealed to phraseological peculiarities, Burgon listed several passages

---

[64]Ibid.

[65]William R. Farmer (below) had the advantage of the knowledge of redaction criticism, and he argued for consideration of the authenticity of the long ending of Mark, but was not as dogmatic as Burgon.

[66]Burgon, *The Last Twelve Verses*, p. 144.

[67]Ibid.

[68]For a discussion of the controversy concerning the authorship of the Gospel of John and Revelation, see Werner Georg Kümmel, *Introduction to the New Testament*, 17th ed., trans. by Howard Clark Kee (Nashville: Abingdon Press, 1975), pp. 469-472.

that may be different from the body of the texts of each of the respective books. According to Burgon, "S. John also in his opening five verses seems . . . to have adopted a method which is not recognizable anywhere else in his writings."[69] Raymond Brown argued that the same author did not write both the prologue and the the body of the Fourth Gospel, for differences exist both in style and substance. (The textual apparatus of the UBS third edition of the Greek New Testament does not list textual support for Brown's argument).[70] Again, there is some question of Burgon's counterpoint.

Burgon emphatically stated that the twenty-seven phraseological points do not constitute enough evidence individually or collectively to challenge the authenticity of the longer ending.[71] If one considers that the other books of the New Testament have similar phraseological difficulties, one would have to agree with Burgon, however, no book in the New Testament has the number of phraseological as well as stylistic peculiarities in a select pericope as does the longer ending. Select words and or phrases may occur in the other Gospels in rare occurrences, but not with the frequency of the longer ending of Mark. Furthermore, it is ironic that Burgon did not one time argue against the short ending of Mark on the age old premise, "A manuscript, book, or even a chapter

---

[69]Burgon, *The Last Twelve Verses*, p. 141.

[70]Raymond Brown, *The Gospel According to John, I-XII.*, The Anchor Bible Vol. 29 (Garden City, N. J.: Doubleday and Co., 1966), pp. 18-23. According to Brown, both the prologue and the body originated out of the same matrix of wisdom material of the Old Testament and Apocrypha, therefore, the two should not be separated. Most scholars proposed that the prologue was originally a hymn composed and sung in the Johannine community which the evangelist adapted and affixed to his Gospel. The prologue served as the overture for the Johannine symphony, adumbrating themes later developed in the Gospel themes which are principally wisdom themes.

[71]See pages 64-66 above.

cannot end with γάρ!"[72]

Whether one agrees or disagrees with Burgon, everyone must admit that he has left a considerable amount of material for text critics to grapple with, in the attempt to find a conclusion to the question of the ending of Mark. Burgon's work provided the impetus of later scholars such as George Salmon and William Farmer.

George Salmon

George Salmon wrote three major works in Gospel studies which are pertinent to textual criticism, including: *A Historical Introduction to the Study of the Books of the New Testament: Being An Expansion of Lectures Delivered in the Divinity School of the University of Dublin;*[73] *Some Thoughts on the Textual Criticism of the New Testament;*[74] and *The Human Element in the Gospels: A Commentary on the Synoptic Narrative.*[75]

In the preface of *A Historical Introduction*, George Salmon described his methodology as seeking to discuss the "date and authorship (of the books of the New Testament) on purely historical grounds; and to examine . . . the various

---

[72]See the critique of George Salmon below, pp. 78-80 and the section on γάρ in chapter five, "The Use of γάρ in Ancient Writings: Canonical and Secular Literature."

[73]George Salmon, *A Historical Introduction to the Study of the Books of the New Testament: Being An Expansion of Lectures Delivered in the Divinity School of the University of Dublin* (London: John Murray, 1885).

[74]Idem., *Some Thoughts on the Textual Criticism of the New Testament* (London: John Murray, 1897). It is ironic that a book of this nature, discussed the supposed problem of the ending of Luke, but did not investigate the textual problem of the ending of Mark (see pp. 89-103).

[75]Idem., *The Human Element in the Gospels: A Commentary on the Synoptic Narrative* (New York: E. P. Dutton and Company, 1907).

theories on the subject advanced by modern schools of criticism."[76] He admitted that his method is apologetic in the sense that it agreed with "the traditional belief of the Church,"[77] however, this does not imply that the positions of contemporary scholarship will not be challenged, especially in the case of the ending of Mark.[78]

Salmon conceded that scripture contains the record of Divine revelation, however, it is necessary to inquire "whether these books have come down safely to us--how we are to remove all the errors which may have accumulated in the process of transcription during many centuries, and to restore the texts to their original purity."[79] Following the lead of Westcott and Hort, he sought to accomplish the investigation of the authenticity of the books of the Canon by applying the same critical methods one would with any ordinary book.[80]

Salmon prefaced his discussion as to the authenticity of the longer ending by discussing which Gospel was written first. He concluded that the Synoptic Gospels were independent of each other, drawing from a common source, however, Mark represents the most verbal exactness of that source.[81] According to Salmon, Markan priority is a point of question:

---

[76]Idem., *A Historical Introduction*, p. vi.

[77]Ibid., p. viii.

[78]By this time, the prominence of the short ending of Mark had begun to prevail.

[79]Salmon, *A Historical Introduction*, p. 2.

[80]Compare with Hills, "Introduction," pp. 40-42.

[81]Salmon, *A Historical Introduction*, p. 187.

Although in many places Mark's narrative, compared with the others, shows clear indications of priority, there are other places where I find no such indications, and where the hypothesis that Mark simply copied Matthew or Luke seems quite permissible.[82]

Salmon began his assessment of the validity of the longer ending based on the internal evidence of the text. He contended, "In Mark we have the Petrine tradition completed into a Gospel."[83] On the basis of a Petrine tradition, one should not expect a uniformity of style between verses that belong to this tradition and those which belong to the framework in which it is set. Salmon further added, "I should feel no difficulty in looking on this as a new section; for my theory being that the Gospel of Mark contains different recitations of the Petrine traditions delivered in the Christian assemblies."[84] He continued, "Arguments against the last twelve verses, drawn from a comparison of their language (syntax and philology) with that of other parts of the Gospel, at once lose their weight."[85] He acknowledged there is a resemblance between the last twelve verses of Mark and the first fifteen.

Burgon and Farmer limited their argument of internal evidence to the comparison of the language of the longer ending to the rest of the Gospel,

---

[82]Ibid., p. 188.

[83]Ibid.

[84]Idem., *The Human Element in the Gospels*, p. 528. On pages 530-531 Salmon commented on the longer ending: "Some have imagined that there was a different conclusion, and have hoped to recover it from the Gospel of Peter, or some other early document. I do not believe it is now possible to recover it. When this appendix was written no other conclusion to the Gospel was known. And the appendix is so early as to have been recognized by Irenæus. Therefore I conclude that if Mark ever put a different conclusion to his Gospel it was lost so early as to now be irrecoverable."

[85]Idem., *A Historical Introduction*, pp. 188-189.

however, Salmon included a theological comparison. He noted, "Three times in these concluding verses attention is called to the surprising slowness of the disciples to believe the evidence offered them (vv. 11, 13, 14)."[86] The motif of the disciples' slowness of heart and unbelief dominated throughout the Second Gospel:

> Thus, in the account of the healing of the man with the withered hand . . . Mark alone relates (iii. 5) that before commanding the man to stretch forth his hand our Lord looked round on the bystanders 'with anger, being grieved for the hardness of their hearts.' Again in Mark vi. 6 there is a note special to this Evangelist, 'Jesus marveled because of their unbelief.' And in the history of the tempest on the lake of Gennesaret . . . Mark (vi. 53) has . . . an expression of surprise at the stupidity and the hardness of heart of those who had not sooner recognized our Lord's true character.[87]

After considering several of the Fathers (as Burgon did), Salmon based his conviction of internal evidence in support of the longer ending on the early testimonies of Irenaeus, Justin, Papias, Celsus, Hippolytus, and "what seems a clear quotation of them (the verses of the longer ending) by a bishop at one of Cyprian's councils."[88] He responded to Hort's claim (that neither Tertullian nor Cyprian knew of the longer ending of Mark, for if they did, they would have quoted from it in their writings about baptism) by stating, "It is a very common experience with everyone who makes a speech or writes a book to find after he

---

[86]Ibid.. p. 189. See also idem., *Some Thoughts on the Textual Criticism*, p. 343.

[87]Idem., *A Historical Introduction*, p. 189.

[88]Ibid., p. 191.

has brought his work to a conclusion that he has omitted to use some telling argument which he might have employed."[89]

In the attempt to argue against the external evidence of short ending of Mark, Salmon dealt with the two great uncials B and ℵ. He conceded that the source of these two uncials is likely to have been as old as the second century, however, "the MSS are here not independent, the conclusion of St. Mark being transcribed by both in the same hand."[90] Salmon maintained that the conclusion was written in both Sinaiticus and Vaticanus on a cancel leaf, which takes the place of one containing more matter than the present text. The gap is covered in Sinaiticus by a spreading out the writing, whereas a blank is left in Vaticanus. Salmon concluded:

> There is, therefore, strong ground for suspecting that in this place these MSS. do not represent the reading of their archetypes, but the critical views of the corrector under whose hand both passed; and as they were both copied at a time when the authority of Eusebius as a biblical critic was predominant, we still fail to get distinctly pre-Eusebian testimony against the verses.[91]

The rejection of the longer ending forced the credibility of one of three views: (1) The original conclusion which Mark wrote in his Gospel was lost without leaving a trace of its existence; (2) The original ending of Mark was deliberately omitted; and (3) The Gospel of Mark never proceeded beyond verse 16:8. Salmon dealt only with the first and third option.

Salmon acknowledged it is possible the last leaf of the original manuscript became detached and perished. Such a hypothesis would explain the partial

---

[89]Ibid., p. 190.

[90]Ibid., p. 191.

[91]Ibid.

circulation of defective copies of a work. He concluded that in this manner, a local circulation of a defective family might originate, however,

> the total loss of the original conclusion could not take place in this way, unless the first copy had been kept till it dropped to pieces with age before anyone made a transcript of it, so that a leaf once lost was lost forever.[92]

Secondly, Salmon considered the hypothesis that the Gospel of Mark never had a formal ending, however, he also rejected this view. He was certain, "Long before any Gospel was written, the belief in the Resurrection of our Lord had become universal among Christians, and this doctrine had become the main topic of every Christian preacher."[93] If there were no doctrinal objections to the short ending, there would be the literary one; "That no Greek writer would give his work so abrupt and ill-omened a termination as ἐφοβοῦντο γάρ."[94]

He then recited two explanations for the absence of a suitable ending to Mark. The first explanation is that Mark the evangelist died before concluding his work. He maintained, "Even in the supposed case, that St. Mark, after writing verse 8, had a fit of apoplexy, the disciple who gave his work to the world would surely have added a fitting termination."[95] The second explanation was that Mark copied a source to which he was conscious to make an addition of his own. On the basis of this hypothesis, Salmon contended:

> . . . we must examine whether internal evidence supports the theory that Mark acted the part of a simple copyist, who did not attempt to set the previous tradition in any framework of his own; and that consequently,

---

[92]Salmon, *A Historical Introduction*, p. 192.

[93]Ibid.

[94]Ibid.

[95]Ibid., p. 189.

the second Gospel, as it stands now, was the source used by Matthew and Luke in the compositions of their Gospels.[96]

Salmon did not accept Markan priority, therefore, he thought it inconceivable that Mark's Gospel could have ended with ἐφοβοῦντο γάρ.

Salmon concluded his study on the ending of Mark with the opinion that the last twelve verses, just as much as the opening ones, belong to the original framework of the Gospel and have no internal difficulties whatever to encounter.[97] He was confident that the verses of the longer ending had such marks of antiquity that Tregelles, "who refused to believe them to have been written by St. Mark, still regarded them as having 'a full claim to be received as an authentic part of the Gospel.'"[98] If it was proved that these verses were not written by Mark, Salmon would next argue for the theory that these twelve verses "are clearly the work of one who wrote at so early a date that he could believe himself able to add genuine apostolic traditions to those already recorded."[99]

Critique of George Salmon
Salmon often contradicted himself and was inconsistent in his argument. Throughout his work *A Historical Introduction to the Study of the Books of the New Testament*, Salmon appeared as a staunch supporter of the authenticity of the longer ending, however, in his work *The Human Element in the Gospels: A*

---

[96]Ibid.

[97]Ibid.

[98]Ibid.

[99]Ibid., p. 193.

Commentary on the Synoptic Narrative, he questioned the existence of the authentic ending of Mark.[100]

Salmon responded to the suggestion that the evangelist died before completing his Gospel, "Even in the supposed case, that St. Mark had a brief fit of apoplexy, the disciple who gave his work to the world would have added a fitting termination."[101] In response to this statement made by Salmon, R. H. Lightfoot expressed the point more strongly:

> . . . in respect of all such theories as those of mutilation, whether deliberate or accidental, or the writer's sudden death or martyrdom or imprisonment, the question remains, why did not the local church, in which the gospel appeared, at once either restore the original ending or, if this had not been yet written or was not available, at least provide what could be regarded as a suitable conclusion?[102]

Salmon objected to the short ending of Mark based on two strands of internal evidence. The first strand of internal evidence is that the resurrection was left unmentioned in Mark 16:1-8.[103] It is apparent that Salmon was confused on this point. One must question whether he was saying that there is no account of Jesus appearing to the disciples in Mark 16:1-8, or does Salmon actually mean what he says: "A history of our Lord, in which this cardinal point (the resurrection) was left unmentioned may be pronounced inconceivable."[104]

---

[100]See idem., *The Human Element in the Gospels,* pp. 530-531.

[101]Idem., *A Historical Introduction,* p. 192. See note 95 above.

[102]R. H. Lightfoot, *The Gospel Message of St. Mark* (Oxford: Clarendon Press, 1950), p. 83.

[103]This statement is implied in Salmon, *A Historical Introduction,* p. 192, paragraph 1.

[104]See ibid.

In verse 16:4 there is evidence of some unusual thing in progress, because the stone was rolled away. In the next verse the three women meet a person described as νεανίσκον (a young man) and in verse 16:6 this young man announced the resurrection "he is risen." Mark 16:7 reported the "young man's reminder of Jesus' post-resurrection instructions as originally told in Mark 14:28: "But after I am raised I will go before you to Galilee."[105] It is ludicrous to suggest that there is no resurrection in Mark 16:1-8 for the message of the resurrection is the primary point of this pericope.

Secondly, Salmon's other point of internal evidence against the short ending was his rejection of a work ending with γάρ. According to Salmon, "if there were no doctrinal objection, there would be the literary one--that no Greek writer would give his work so abrupt and ill-omened a termination as ἐφοβοῦντο γάρ."[106] Several other scholars contended the rarity of γάρ ending sentences, however, Horst Balz confirmed that short sentences ending with γάρ are common.[107] Through research on the Ibycus Scholarly Computer (ISC), I found that γάρ ending sentences were common in ancient literature. We must reconsider the possibility of other endings to the Second Gospel other than the longer ending, for if a sentence or paragraph can end in γάρ, there is reason a document cannot end in the same way.

---

[105]See Mark 14:28 in Kurt Aland, Matthew Black, Bruce Metzger, and A. Wikgren eds., *The Greek New Testament*. 3rd. ed. (London: United Bible Societies, 1975), p. 185, which reads as, "ἀλλὰ μετὰ τὸ ἐγερθῆναί με προάξω ὑμᾶς εἰς τὴν Γαλιλαίαν."

[106]Salmon, *A Historical Introduction*, p. 192.

[107]See Horst Balz, "φοβέω," *Theological Dictionary of the New Testament*, vol. 9, trans. by Geoffrey W. Bromiley, ed. Gerhard Friedrich (Grand Rapids: Wm. B. Eerdmans Publishing Co., 1974), p. 211, n. 116. See also chapter 5 below, the section entitled, "The Use of γάρ in Ancient Writings: Canonical and Secular Literature."

William R. Farmer

Not since John Burgon had there appeared a defender of the authenticity of the longer ending of Mark as William Farmer. Farmer is most noted by his work *The Synoptic Problem: A Critical Analysis*[108] in which he called for a re-opening of the literary relationships between Matthew, Luke, and Mark. In this study, he called forth for the rejection of the priority of Mark and the idea of a second source (Q), employed independently by Matthew and Luke. Farmer's method called for a return to the Griesbach hypothesis (i.e., the theory that Matthew is the first of the three Synoptic Gospels, that Luke copied his Markan and non-Markan parallels from Matthew, and that Mark is a conflation of Matthew and Luke). Paralleling his attack on Markan priority, Farmer suggested that the case against the authenticity of the verses of the longer ending is not as strong as is popularly assumed.

Farmer's work, The *Last Twelve Verses of Mark*[109] was a response to an observation made by Kenneth Clark in his presidential address to the Society of Biblical Literature[110] and falls into three sections. The first section was a lengthy text-critical section which examined the external evidence, following closely to Burgon's methodology. He began with the Fathers and worked back to the manuscript evidence used to argue both for inclusion and omission of the verses of the longer ending.

---

[108]William R. Farmer, *The Synoptic Problem: A Critical Analysis* (New York: Macmillan, 1964).

[109]Idem., *The Last Twelve Verses of Mark*, Society for New Testament Studies Monograph Series (Cambridge: Cambridge University Press, 1974).

[110]See ibid., p. ix, where Farmer quoted Clark: '. . . the restoration of the traditional ending of Mark (in the RSV CE) is a wholesome challenge to our habitual assumption that the original work is preserved no further than 16:8. . . . Witnesses both for and against the CE restoration as genuine are early and impressive, and we should consider the question still open.'

Farmer attempted to explain the absence of the longer ending from the representatives of the Alexandrian family (Codex Vaticanus and Sinaiticus), and the widespread acceptance of these verses in other traditions, notably the Byzantine text. Farmer's basic thesis was, on textual grounds, verses 16:9-20 belonged to the autograph and was later excised by Alexandrian scribes. The key to this solution is connected with Origen and the alleged prior ecclesiastically sponsored scriptural activity in Alexandria.[111] The argument is twofold in that Farmer attempted to trace all the evidence for omission back to Alexandria and then he built a case for deliberate omission by a group of second-century Alexandrian scribes. Such an omission was the result of the textual tradition established in Alexandria, which did not accept with favor verse 9 or the series of promises which proposed that Christian believers could take up serpents and drink poison without being physically harmed. Some interpreters would have used a method of containment,[112] while others would have turned to allegory, however, in Alexandria the interpreter would have quietly deleted the troublesome verses.[113]

Farmer concluded this analysis of the external evidence on the verses of Mark 16:9-20 by stating:

> When the critic ponders the practical difficulties inherent in the teaching of these verses, it only serves to magnify the problem of comprehending in a convincing way how . . . the ending could have been

---

[111]Ibid., pp. 59-75.

[112]Ibid., p. 67. Farmer used the word "containment" to refer to a particular way in which the church incorporated disturbing passages. Even though the authenticity of a given passage may be accepted, the early interpreters frequently introduced other teachings from scriptures in order to nullify the normative character of the teaching of the controversial passage. By this methodology, "the peace and order of the church was maintained."

[113]Ibid., pp. 68-74.

added to copies of Mark and thereafter achieve the widespread acceptance attested by early patristic and versional witnesses. This problem, often overlooked, . . . poses an historical difficulty of considerable magnitude for any theory which presupposes that these verses were not original but added after the composition of the other Gospels.[114]

Farmer's tentative conclusion on the external evidence was that it enabled the scholar "to understand how the omission might have arisen, (however,) it does not provide the evidential grounds for a definite solution to the problem."[115] The major limitation of the study of the history of the text is "the evidence is divided and the decisive period, namely the second century, remains shrouded in obscurity."[116] Farmer confirmed that manuscripts which include the longer ending were in circulation in the second century, however, he was in doubt whether or not manuscripts ending with ἐφοβοῦντο γάρ were in circulation at this early period.[117]

In the second section, Farmer evaluated the internal evidence by conducting a linguistic comparison of Mark 16:9-20 and Mark 1:1-16:8. He concluded that verses 12, 14, and 16-19 may be considered as neutral, however, verses 9, 11, 13, 15, and 20 have definite indications of Markan composition. Verse 10 is the only verse that he considered as suspect of non-Markan authorship.

Farmer acknowledged that the connection between Mark 16:8 and the verses of the longer ending appeared to be awkward. This awkwardness was

---

[114]Farmer, *The Last Twelve Verses of Mark*, p. 74.

[115]Ibid.

[116]Ibid., p. 74.

[117]Ibid.

because of the change in the subject between verse 8 and 9 and the identification of Mary Magdalene, even though she has been mentioned before in Mark 15:47 and 16:1. Farmer attempted to remedy this awkwardness by noting, "the change in subject between verse 8 and 9 would occasion no comment were it not that Jesus as the subject of verse 9 is unexpressed."[118] Farmer concluded his syntactical comparison by commenting, "Abrupt transitions are not usual in Mark, and such awkwardness as may exist remains whether the evangelist or some later person added the verses concerned."[119]

Farmer concluded his work by presenting five alternative solutions to the problem of the origin of the last twelve verses of Mark:

> (1) Mark 16:9-20 was written *de novo* by the evangelist and belonged to the autograph of Mark. (2) Mark 16:9-20 represents redactional use of older material by the evangelist and belonged to the autograph. (3) Mark 16:9-20 existed virtually as we have it before the evangelist wrote his Gospel and has been used by him with little or no modification. (4) Mark 16:9-20 was written by a later writer who consciously sought to imitate certain features of Mark's vocabulary and syntax, as well as develop his conceptual use of certain terms. (5) Mark 16:9-20 is a later composition without linguistic or conceptual kinship to the rest of Mark.[120]

Critique of William R. Farmer

Farmer's work has received both positive and negative criticism. Gordon Fee considered this work "brilliantly conceived"[121] and Zahn Hodges revered

---

[118]Ibid., p. 103.

[119]Ibid.

[120]Ibid., p. 107.

[121]Gordon D. Fee, "Review of William R. Farmer, *The Last Twelve Verses of Mark*," *Journal of Biblical Literature*, 94 (1975), 462.

it "commendably thorough."[122] Farmer made a moderate claim "that the evidence, on balance, favors inclusion of the verses as originally Markan."[123] Such moderation is essential when assessing a text-critical problem which has often been dogmatized. Perhaps Farmer's greatest contribution is that he wrote from a perspective which challenged the opinions of a majority of Markan scholars. A second point of significant of this work is that it called for a re-examination of what so often is taken as proven without first-hand knowledge of the data.[124]

A majority of scholars have had major problems with Farmer's *The Last Twelve Verses of Mark*. J. N. Birdsall offered the most extensive and critical review of Farmer,[125] for he charged that Farmer's work "is marred by a remarkable lack of documentation and reference, as well as by the slender acquaintance which he shows with the implications of our present knowledge of the documents and history of the New Testament text."[126] This is a result of his dependence on Burgon, who did the same. Connected to this was Farmer's weak use of patristic evidence. Some of the more pertinent witnesses for inclusion were missing:

---

[122]Z. C. Hodges, "Review of William R. Farmer, *The Last Twelve Verses of Mark*," *Bibliotheca Sacra*, 133 (April, 1976), 178.

[123]Ibid.

[124]Fee, "Review", p. 463 and George R. Beasley-Murray, "Review of William R. Farmer, *The Last Twelve Verses of Mark*," *Review and Expositor*, 72 (Summer, 1975), 375.

[125]J. N. Birdsall, "Review of William R. Farmer, *The Last Twelve Verses of Mark*," *JTS*, 26 (1975), 151-160.

[126]Ibid., p. 158.

Asterius Sophista, *Hom.* 3 *in Ps.* 8, cites Mark 16:17; Didymus, *De Trinitate* 2.12 cites 16:16-17 as from Mark; Pseudo-Gregory Thaumaturgus, *De fide capitula* xii alludes to Mark 16:19; and the Clemetine *Epitome de gestis Petri* 141, cites Mark 16:16.[127]

Several of Farmer's (as well as Burgon's) supporting witnesses are doubtful, including Justin, Celsus, and Chrysostom.[128] Farmer noted the silence of several Fathers (including Tertullian, Athanasius, and Cyprian to name a few), however, he tended to play down the significance of their silence. Fee noted the "significance that key Fathers are silent precisely where the MS evidence favors omission (Tertullian and Cyprian with *k* in North Africa; Origen, Cyril with the Alexandrian MSS).[129]

Birdsall's primary concern was Farmer appeared "ill acquainted with most of the text-critical work of the last fifty years."[130] As alluded to above, Farmer was excessively dependent on Burgon and C. R. Williams, who wrote a monograph on these verses in 1915.[131] The major effect of Farmer's lack of acquaintance with the text-critical work of the last fifty years, was his neglect of Codex Bobbiensis (*k*). The main point about Bobbiensis is that it did not include

---

[127]Fee, "Review," p.463.

[128]Ibid. Fee offered an example with Chrysostom: "It is simply wrong to say of Chrysostom that he 'makes an unmistakable reference to Mk 16:9 (p. 34 of Farmer), when he could have just as easily be alluding to John 20:11-18 --more likely so, in fact, given that there is not a single quotation from 16:9-20 in the entire Chrysostom literature."

[129]Ibid.

[130]Birdsall, "Review," p. 153.

[131]In reference to Williams, see Clarence R. Williams, "The Appendices to the Gospel According to Mark: A Study in Textual Transmission," *Connecticut Academy of Arts and Sciences, Transactions*, 18 (New Haven, 1915), pp. 353-447.

Mark 16:9-20 and is the oldest witness textually to the Latin Bible.[132] Bruce Metzger confirmed the antiquity of the tradition behind *k* in that it "shows paleographical marks of having been copied from a second century papyrus."[133] Farmer responded by attempting to discredit Birdsall's use of the Bobbiensis.[134] He noted that Birdsall did not mention that Bobbiensis contained the shorter ending (the two verse ending which immediately follows Mark 16:8) which Williams successfully proved as Egyptian in origin.[135] This would have helped in Farmer's attempt to locate the manuscripts under the rubric of Alexandrian influence.

Farmer concluded his first section, "that the text tradition for inclusion, unlike that for omission (Alexandrian), cannot be traced to a particular ecclesiastical centre or geographical locale, nor to any singular text type or textual group."[136] Fee noted, "The whole argument that 'omission' spread out from

---

[132]Birdsall, "Review," pp. 153-154.

[133]Bruce M. Metzger, *The Text of the New Testament: Its Transmission, Corruption, and Restoration* (New York and Oxford: Oxford University Press, 1968), p. 73.

[134]See Dan R. Francis, "A Critical Survey of Contemporary Literature Concerning the Empty Tomb in Mark," Unpublished Th. M. thesis, The Southern Baptist Theological Seminary, Louisville, Kentucky, 1980, pp. 29-30. On these pages Francis cited an unpublished response of Farmer, William R. Farmer, "A Note on J. N. Birdsall's review of *The Last Twelve Verses of Mark* in *JTS* April, 1975."

[135]See ibid., where Francis referred to Farmer, "Note," p. 1. The major thesis of Farmer and Williams is that Bobbiensis has an Egyptian origin. This is vital for Farmer because the credibility of his thesis depends on being able to trace the evidence for the omission of the longer ending of Mark back to Egyptian influence.

[136]Farmer, *The Last Twelve Verses*, p. 74.

Alexandria can be turned on its head to show that inclusion spread out from Roman influence (Irenaeus, Tatian, Old Latin, etc.)."[137]

After attempting to revise his work with references to omissions as pointed out by Birdsall in reference to P. E. Kahle and F. C. Burkitt,[138] Farmer attempted to draw an analogy between the Alexandrian and Homeric critics of the Polemaic period. It is obvious that they had differing opinions based on various criteria about the authenticity of the certain lines of Homer and the ending of the *Odessey*, therefore, they invented diacritical signs and used them to mark suspect lines. It does not appear that these critics "had great influence upon the form in which the texts were transmitted."[139] According to Birdsall, "Farmer knows that in spite of the rejection of the ending of the *Odessey* by Aristarchus no manuscripts have come down to us which lack its present ending."[140] Birdsall continued:

> The Homeric text had far longer to become corrupted by accident or criticism than the text of Mark: and we have a far more numerous papyrus coverage for it than we have comparably early manuscripts for Mark: yet in spite of this, and of our certain knowledge of the opinions of the critics no evidence for the curtailment of the end of the Odessey [*sic*] is known in the tradition, whereas for Mark we have evidence from at least two independent sources (viz. the great codices and k) of the absence of verses 9-20 from early copies and no certain knowledge of any critical opinion.[141]

---

[137]Fee, "Review," p. 463.

[138]Birdsall, "Review," p. 156.

[139]Ibid., p. 155.

[140]Ibid., p. 156.

[141]Ibid.

The standards and procedures of both pagan and Christian Alexandrian philology was an act of preservation rather than the violent editorial changes which Farmer assumed. Birdsall concluded, "Farmer's hypothesis (of recension) fails, because it lacks historical probability in the light of the earliest history of the versions and the known nature of Alexandrian philological practices."[142]

A major concern in his second section dealing with "internal evidence" is the limited method by which Farmer dealt only with the linguistic comparison of the longer ending to the text of Mark 1:1-16:8. He readily discredited Morgenthaler's approach:

> Morgenthaler wishes to demonstrate that 'word-statistical research leads to clear results.' He assumes that his readers are convinced on textual grounds that these verses do not belong to Mark, and he believes that these readers will be impressed with the way in which his 'word-statistical research' supports this view, and will accordingly take 'word-statistical research' more seriously. Actually Morgenthaler only succeeds in demonstrating how misleading such statistical research can be.[143]

The troublesome issue of Farmer's criticism of Morgenthaler was that he chose the same method to defend the authenticity of the longer ending. It is also difficult to understand why Farmer limited his "internal evidence" to such a linguistic comparison. One must wonder why Farmer did not make a theological comparison between the longer ending and Mark 1:1-16:8.

Despite the above criticisms, Farmer's work is important in that he called for a re-examination of what so often is taken as proven without firsthand knowledge of the material. Whether Farmer's position is convincing or not, he did challenge the critics of the longer ending to evaluate his thesis by offering the

---

[142]Ibid., p. 157.

[143]Farmer, *The Last Twelve Verses*, p. 79.

sources necessary to do so. As Fee mentioned, many use these sources to refute his position.[144]

Recent Scholarship Which Supports the Authenticity
of the Longer Ending of Mark

From the time of William Farmer to the present day, few scholars have ventured to comment on, let alone write a defense of the authenticity of the longer ending of Mark. Of the books produced, two were in direct connection with Burgon's *The Last Twelve Verses of the Gospel According to St. Mark.* The first one was a reprint of Burgon's work with an extensive introduction by Edward Hills.[145] Hills took Burgon's defense of the Byzantine text one step farther by pointing out that the King James Version (KJV) was based on the Byzantine text.[146] The KJV did not place the longer ending of Mark in brackets, as did the 1946 edition of the Revised Standard Version (RSV).

A second work defending the longer ending of Mark was David Otis Fuller's *Counterfeit or Genuine: Mark 16? John 8?*[147] This work was produced because of the attack on scripture which Fuller said, "began in its modern form in the publication of the Revised Version (RV) of the Scriptures in 1881 in

---

[144]Fee, "Review," p. 463.

[145]See footnote 11 above.

[146]Hills, "Introduction," p. 67.

[147]David Otis Fuller, *Counterfeit or Genuine: Mark 16? John 8?* (Grand Rapids, Mich.: Grand Rapids International Publications, 1975). This work contained a condensed version of Burgon's *The Last Twelve Verses of the Gospel According to St. Mark* as well as a discussion Burgon's *Pericope de Adultera* which defends John 7:53-8:11.

England.''[148] In the RV several passages were called into question (including Mark 16:9-20) on the basis that they were omitted by the ''oldest and best'' manuscripts (primarily ℵ and B). Fuller concluded:

> Among the nearly one hundred versions available to today's readers, the one that is nearest to the original autographs is the King James Version. We repeat: Changes could and should be made to enhance the meaning . . . neither Mark 16:9-20 nor any other verse or verses need to be deleted for a moment.[149]

Chapter Summary

The Church eventually included the longer ending of Mark in its Canon and read these verses in public services, based on this pericope's antiquity, widespread manuscript support, and Patristic attestation. This, however, did not prove or dis-prove the authenticity of these verses.

The dominance of the manuscripts that include the longer ending influenced scholars of the past, however, within the past fifty years, a majority of scholarship has called into question the authenticity of the longer ending. John Burgon provided a strong defense of the authenticity of Mark 16:9-20, based on external evidence. Burgon made an honorable attempt to investigate most of the internal evidence and the external evidence that was known to him (note above, I said that excavations since Burgon's time have added more textual evidence to the question of the longer ending of Mark, especially the discovery of W). His method was simple: (1) Faith must be an element of the discipline of textual criticism, --a faith which trusts that God has worked in history to preserve the true biblical Greek text, and we can analyze history and find history testifying to the

---

[148]Fuller, *Counterfeit or Genuine*, p. 9.

[149]Ibid., p. 12.

accuracy of the Byzantine text; and (2) The approach of textual criticism with a recognition of the superiority of the Byzantine text, and use textual criticism as a tool only to determine the best readings from among the Byzantine text.

George Salmon highlighted the major points about the legitimacy of the longer ending of Mark and William Farmer produced a condensed version of Burgon's work *The Last Twelve Verses of Mark,* devoting most of his effort on the external evidence of the argument. Even though Salmon treated the external evidence in the same manner as Burgon (that the external evidence overwhelmingly supported the authenticity of the longer ending of Mark), he focused his internal evidence on the theology of Mark 16:9-20 and the argument that a document cannot end with γάρ. Farmer deemed the external evidence of manuscripts and Patristic witness as inconclusive, because most of these elements of external evidence post dated א and B. Farmer was supportive of the longer ending of Mark, however, he stated ". . . by the fifth century, possibly the fourth or even the third, . . . it could be said that the textual tradition ending Mark with ἐφοβοῦντο γάρ was strongly attested by contemporary manuscript evidence."[150]

Most scholars from the nineteenth century to the present day rejected the authenticity of the longer ending, whereas, they continued to view these verses as canonical.[151] Some scholars have held to the tradition that these verses

---

[150]Farmer, *The Last Twelve Verses,* p. 36.

[151]For an expanded discussion as to why some scholars held that the longer ending should be received as canonical even though it was not authentic to Mark, see Joseph Hug, *La finale de l'évangile de Marc (Mc 16,9-20)* (Paris: Gabalda, 1978). Hug accepted the canonicity of the longer ending and offered a valuable survey of the various positions taken on it (pp. 11-32), and he concluded this work by offering the possible sources of the longer ending (pp. 177-215). Hug concluded that the longer ending was appended in the late first century to the early second century.

originated from the Presbyter Aristion.[152] Metzger acknowledged the wide external evidence in support of the longer ending, however, he deemed it secondary on the basis of internal evidence. The philology and style, of the longer ending are non-Markan (note ἀπιστέω, Βλάπτω, Βεβαιόω, ἐπακολουθέω, θεάομαι, μετὰ ταῦτα, προεύομαι, συνεργέω, and ὕστερον are found nowhere else in Mark. θανάσιμον τοῖς μετ' αὐτοῦ γενομένοις, used as designations of the disciples occur nowhere else in the New Testament. The critique of George Salmon briefly pointed to the possibility of a document ending with γάρ, therefore, the internal evidence used by scholars that a document cannot end with γάρ has been nullified.[153]

The second point of internal evidence was the connection between verse eight and the longer ending is so awkward that it is difficult to believe that Mark the evangelist intended the longer ending to be a continuation of the Gospel. The subject of verse eight is the women, but the subject of verse nine is Jesus. Metzger noted the awkwardness of Mary Magdalene being identified again, even though she had been mentioned before in 15:47 and 16:1, and the absence of the other women in 16:1-8.[154] He further pointed to the use of ἀναστὰς δέ and the

---

[152]Hugh Anderson, *The Gospel of Mark*, The New Century Bible Commentary (Grand Rapids: Wm. B. Eerdmans, 1976), p. 358; William Lane, *Commentary on the Gospel of Mark*, The New International Commentary on the New Testament (Grand Rapids: Wm. B. Eerdmans, 1974), p. 605, n. 11; Eduard Schweizer, *The Good News According to Mark*, trans. by Donald H. Madvig (Atlanta: John Knox Press, 1970), p. 374; and Henry B. Swete, *The Gospel According to Mark* (London: Macmillan and Co., Ltd., 1924), p. civ. Metzger concluded that "the probability that an Armenian rubricator would have access to historically valuable tradition on this point is almost nil." See Metzger, *The Text of the New Testament*, p. 227.

[153]For a detailed discussion of the use of γάρ in ancient literature, see chapter 5 below, the section entitled, "The Use of γάρ in Ancient Writings: Canonical and Secular Literature."

[154]Ibid.

position of πρῶτον are appropriate at the beginning of a narrative, but they are ill-suited in a continuation of 16:1-8.[155]

Metzger concluded that all these features indicate that the longer ending was added by a person who was familiar of a form of Mark that ended with 16:8 and wished to provide a more appropriate conclusion.[156] In view of the differences between verses 1-8 and 9-20, it is unlikely that the long ending was written *ad hoc* to fill an obvious gap, but it is probable that the longer ending was taken from another document, dating from the first half of the second century.[157]

The acceptance of the canonicity of the longer ending has received objection from only a few scholars. Samuel Davidson rejected the canonicity of the longer ending based on this ending not being authentic:

> How persons who believe that the verses did not form a part of the original gospel of Mark, can say that they have a good claim to be received as a genuine part of the second gospel or of canonical scripture, passes comprehension.[158]

Farmer admitted, "Neither the external nor the internal evidence can be decisive,"[159] (in settling the question of the authenticity of the longer ending of Mark), however, he immediately followed, "Furthermore, to the extent that either on balance weighs for or against the originality of the present ending of Mark

---

[155]Metzger, *The Text of the New Testament*, p. 227.

[156]Ibid.

[157]Bruce Metzger et al., eds., *A Textual Commentary on the New Testament* (London and New York: United Bible Societies, 1976 corrected edition), p. 125.

[158]Samuel Davidson, *An Introduction to the Study of the New Testament: Critical, Exegetical, and Theological*, vol. 1, Second Edition (London: Longmans, Green, and Co., 1882), p. 577.

[159]Farmer, *The Last Twelve Verses of Mark*, p. 109.

. . . (the external and internal evidence) considered separately and taken together, argues for inclusion of these verses."[160] Because the most recent and independent scholar said, "Neither the external nor the internal evidence can be decisive,"[161] (even though he concluded in favor of the longer ending) it is necessary to continue the investigation of the ending of Mark. The next chapter will consider alternative endings to Mark other than the long and short endings.

---

[160]Ibid.

[161]Ibid.

CHAPTER 4

Theories on the Endings of Mark Other than the Short and Longer Ending

This chapter will discuss a variety of options to the ending of Mark, aside from the arguments for the authenticity of the longer ending and the intent of the evangelist in completing the Second Gospel with ἐφοβοῦντο γάρ. The format of this chapter will consist of three sections which calls for some type of appendage to ἐφοβοῦντο γάρ. The first section will discuss the scholarship that considered the unintentional ending of Mark's Gospel at 16:8. Such a proposal evolves from one of three possibilities: 1) a lost ending; 2) an incomplete Gospel; or 3) a suppressed ending. This section provides a transition from the scholarship which maintained the authenticity of the longer ending to those who deny it. The second section will survey the scholarship that calls for a "reconstructed" ending. Reconstruction demands weighty consideration because of its popularity and its own limitations. The third section will discuss both the "Freer Logion" and the "shorter" ending of Mark, which no one considered as authentic, but as appropriate supplements to the ending of the Second Gospel. Each of these sections will have a critique, except for Kurt Aland's response to Eta Linnemann, which will immediately follow Linnemann's proposal.

Mark 16:8: the Unintentional
Ending of Mark

Several scholars advocated that the longer ending of Mark was not the original ending, however, they also declined from accepting the short ending with ἐφοβοῦντο γάρ as the intended ending of the Second Gospel. J. J. Griesbach was one of the first critical scholars to argue that the longer ending of the Second Gospel was not authentic, still he did not suppose that Mark always ended at verse eight. According to Griesbach, "No one can imagine that Mark cut short the thread of his narrative at that place."[1] He was of the opinion that at some remote period, the original ending of the Gospel perished and an unknown editor substituted the longer ending in its place. Griesbach was confident that when the four narratives were collected into a volume and given the title "Gospel," (before the end of the second century), an unknown author supplemented Mark with the twelve verses that are in question, in order to remedy its incompleteness.[2]

In their *Introduction to the New Testament in the Original Greek*, B. F. Westcott and F. J. A. Hort maintained:

> the verbal abruptness (of Mark 16:8) is accompanied by a jarring moral discontinuity. When it is seen how Mt xxviii 1-7 is completed by 8-10, and Lc xxiv 1-7 by 8, 9, it becomes incredible not merely that St. Mark should have closed a paragraph with γάρ, but that his one detailed account of an appearance of the Lord on the morning of the Resurrection should end upon a note of unassuaged terror.[3]

---

[1] J. J. Griesbach, *Commentarius Criticus in Textum Graecum Novi Testamentl* (Ienae: Apvd J. C. G. Goepferdt, 1774/75), p. 197. The Latin reads: "Nemini autem in mentem venire poteft, Marcum narrationis fuae filum ineptiffime abrupiffe verbis."

[2] Ibid., p. 204.

[3] B. F. Westcott and F. J. A. Hort, "Notes on selected readings," *Introduction to the New Testament in the Original Greek* (New York: Harper Brothers, 1882), p. 47.

Bruce Metzger speculated that ἐφοβοῦντο γάρ of Mark 16:8 did not represent how the evangelist intended to end his Gospel. Whether Mark was interrupted while writing the end and subsequently prevented from completing his literary work, or whether the last leaf of the autograph was lost before other copies had been made, no one knows. Based on the above discussion, Metzger was sure "that the Gospel is a torso and (the Church) tried in various ways to provide a more or less appropriate conclusion."[4] Metzger concluded:

> Since Mark was not responsible for the composition of the last twelve verses of the generally current form of his Gospel, and since they undoubtedly had been attached to the Gospel before the Church recognized the fourfold Gospels as canonical, it follows that the New Testament contains not four but five evangelic accounts of events subsequent to the Resurrection of Christ.[5]

W. L. Knox was emphatically against the proposal of a gospel/work ending with, γάρ based on the dated assumption that only a few sentences in ancient Greek literature ended with γάρ. He refuted the supposition that Mark originally intended to end his Gospel with γάρ, for that would imply that he (Mark) was indifferent to the cannons of popular story telling, and by pure accident he happened to hit on a conclusion which suited the technique of a highly sophisticated type of modern literature.[6]

---

[4]Bruce M. Metzger, *The Text of the New Testament: Its Transmission, Corruption, and Restoration* (New York and Oxford: Oxford University Press, 1968), p. 228.

[5]Ibid., p. 229. Metzger's statement is based on the resurrection appearances of Matthew, Luke, John, Mark's intended conclusion, and the longer ending of Mark.

[6]W. L. Knox, "The Ending of Saint Mark's Gospel," *Harvard Theological Review*, 35 (1942), 21-22.

Étienne Trocmé rejected the ending with ἐφοβοῦντο γάρ, and likewise rejected the authenticity of the longer ending.[7] He contended that the ending with ἐφοβοῦντο γάρ did not belong to the evangelist, for "the author of Mark is usually more skillful than that."[8] Trocmé concluded that the 16:8 ending "must be the work of an editor more slavishly faithful than he to the letter of church tradition, who perhaps added an appendix to the Gospel without worrying too much about fitting it into the original version of Mark."[9]

Vincent Taylor agreed that Mark did not intend ἐφοβοῦντο γάρ as the conclusion of his Gospel. The reason for the disappearance of the ending after 16:8 is vague: "The mutilation of the original papyrus MS., Mark's premature death, and deliberate suppression have been conjectured."[10] He concluded by speculating the natural squeal to ἐφοβοῦντο γάρ "would be a μή clause . . . referring to the Jews or to the charge of madness . . . followed by appearances to Peter and to all the disciples."[11] Taylor did not advocate any theory as to the disappearance of the original ending of Mark.

The question of Mark 16:8 as an unintentional ending has been debated from the perspective of three theories. The first theory is that the "original" ending was lost. Reginald Fuller characterized this theory as the "mutilation

---

[7]Étienne Trocmé, *The Formation of the Gospel According to Mark*, trans. Pamela Gaughan (Philadelphia: Westminster Press, 1975), pp. 64-67.

[8]Ibid., p. 67.

[9]Ibid., pp. 67-68.

[10]Vincent Taylor, *The Gospel According to St. Mark*. 2nd ed. Thornapple Commentaries (Grand Rapids: Baker Book House, 1981), pp. 610.

[11]Ibid., pp. 609-610.

hypothesis," by citing both accidental and deliberate reasons for the ending's destruction.[12]

A Lost Ending

Several scholars advocated that the original ending of Mark was lost by accident, however, against such a theory is the argument:

> nearly all the documents from the first century are scrolls. Since the scroll would expose the beginning of the text it would be difficult to comprehend how this would be conducive to a theory that the end of Mark was accidentally lost.[13]

Peter Katz responded with a theory that the Gentile Christians in an early period adopted the codex form for their scriptures rather than using the scroll form, thus differentiating the use of the church from that of the synagogue.[14]

Westcott and Hort, after investigating the internal, external, and intrinsic evidence,[15] adhered to a theory that the authenticity of the longer ending has to be dismissed when considering a lost ending on the basis, "if the transition from v. 8 to v. 9 were natural, omission might be explained by a very early accidental

---

[12]Reginald H. Fuller, *The Formation of the Resurrection Narratives* (New York: Macmillan, 1971), p. 65.

[13]John Christopher Thomas, "A Reconstruction of the Ending of Mark," *Journal of Evangelical Theological Society*, 26 (1983), 415.

[14]Peter Katz, "The Early Christians Use of Codices Instead of Rolls, *Journal of Theological Studies*, 44 (1945), 63-65.

[15]Westcott and Hort defined intrinsic evidence (probability) as "what an author is likely to have written" in juxtaposition to transcriptional probability "having reference to the copyists." See Westcott and Hort, *Introduction to the The New Testament*, pp. 19-22.

loss of a leaf.''[16] They continued, ''Though the presence of these verses (Mark 9-20) furnishes a sufficient conclusion to the Gospel, it furnishes none to the equally mutilated sentence and paragraph (of 16:8).''[17] Westcott and Hort concluded, ''v. 9 (was) the initial sentence of a narrative which starts from the Resurrection,''[18] therefore,

> the true intended continuation of vv. 1-8 either was very early lost by the detachment of a leaf or was never written down; . . . a scribe or editor, unwilling to change the words of the text before him or to add words of his own, was willing to furnish the Gospel with what seemed a worthy conclusion by incorporating with it unchanged a narrative of Christ's appearance after the Resurrection which he found in some secondary record then surviving from a preceding generation.[19]

Rudolf Bultmann speculated that Mark originally went beyond 16:8, but he also denied the authenticity of the longer ending. Bultmann held that the original ending was lost.[20] Against the 16:8 ending, and without forming a reconstruction, Bultmann proposed, ''If ἐφοβοῦντο were such an excellent finish, giving the point of the story in the impression of the overpowering appearance and the words of the angel it would at least have been read: ἐφοβούντο καὶ οὐδενὶ οὐδὲν εἶπαν.''[21] He based this on the φοβοῦμαι appears with an object in half

---

[16]Westcott and Hort, ''Notes,'' pp. 50-51.

[17]Ibid., p. 47.

[18]Ibid., p. 49.

[19]Ibid., p. 51.

[20]Rudolf Bultmann, *History of the Synoptic Tradition*, Rev. ed. trans. John Marsh (New York: Harper & Row, 1976), p. 285, n. 2.

[21]Ibid.

of its appearances in Mark. Bultmann concluded, "Instead of this ἐφοβοῦντο (even if 'numinous effect' be meant) serves as a reason (γάρ) for οὐδενὶ οὐδὲν εἶπαν, and is therefore manifestly apologetic in character."[22]

Eduard Schweizer also maintained that the original ending of Mark was lost based on the argument that γάρ was an inappropriate ending. He reasoned, "Aside from any other argument, it is difficult to imagine that a book would have ended with the statements made in vs. 8, and with the little word because (γάρ)."[23] He continued that the original ending included a Galilean appearance, the first to Peter and then the eleven.[24] Schweizer concluded it is likely that the ending of Mark "was lost accidentally, since there are many examples of books with papyrus pages where the ending has been lost, and similar examples of incomplete scrolls."[25]

Charles J. Reedy advocated that the ending of Mark was lost, based on a textual analysis of the Gospel as a whole. He found in Mark 8:31-11:10 a pattern that the passion predictions followed while unfolding the messianic secret. Reedy's five point structure is as follows:

A. The Son of Man will be delivered (betrayed) to the authorities.
B. They will put him to death.
C. But he will rise from the dead.

---

[22]Ibid.

[23]Eduard Schweizer, *The Good News According to Mark*, trans. by Donald H. Madvig (Atlanta: John Knox Press, 1970), p. 366.

[24]Schweizer stated, "The disciples must have been in Galilee (sooner or later) because after this they lived in Jerusalem permanently." See ibid., p. 367.

[25]Ibid.

D. He is then seen teaching the true meaning of discipleship.

E. Finally he is depicted as being endowed with Messianic authority.[26]

He further pointed out that in Mark 8:31-11:10 "a pattern that in parts A, B, and
C, outlines the Marcan Passion account to its present end at 16:8,"[27] however,
the Markan resurrection narrative did not describe the final two points of the
messianic secret, as shown above. Reedy concluded:

> On the basis of the textual evidence in this study, it would not seem rash
> to suggest that the original Marcan [sic] Gospel went beyond 16:8
> including points D and E, that is, depicting the risen Jesus teaching his
> disciples, in some sort of Farewell Discourse, the nature of true
> discipleship and openly displaying his Messianic authority in fulfillment
> of (Mark) 9:9. For in the words of Anton Chekhov, 'If you hang a pistol
> on the wall in the first Act, you must fire it by the third.' We must hold
> Mark accountable to this literary principle.[28]

Mark Never Concluded His Gospel

The theory that Mark did not complete his Gospel has been advocated by
scholars of both the nineteenth and twentieth centuries. Samuel Davidson, a
renowned nineteenth century text critic who debated against John Burgon
concerning the authenticity of the longer ending, was sure "through some
unknown circumstance, the writer (of the Gospel of Mark) stopped without
concluding his work."[29] Davidson did not speculate why the evangelist left the

---

[26]Charles J. Reedy, "Mk. 8:31-11:10 and the Gospel Ending: A Redaction
Study," *Catholic Biblical Quarterly*, 34 (1972), 196-197.

[27]Ibid., p. 197.

[28]Ibid.

[29]Samuel Davidson, *An Introduction to the Study of the New Testament:
Critical, Exegetical, and Theological*, vol. 1, Second Edition (London: Longmans, Green,

Gospel incomplete, but he did suggest "another (writer) appended the paragraph (Mark 16:9-20) in the same century (the second) in which the gospel [sic] first appeared."[30]

A. E. J. Rawlinson was sure the ending of Mark did not survive, based on the mere fact that such of an ending never existed; for Mark never completed his Gospel.[31] He proposed that Mark broke off in the middle of the sentence (ἐφοβοῦντο γάρ) and never resumed. As to the reason behind the theory of an "incomplete Gospel," Rawlinson offered the following speculative questions: "Did he die? Was he suddenly arrested and martyred? Or did he leave Rome, where he was working, and for some reason never return?"[32] He concluded that there is no information available to resolve these questions, but "it is probable that even if the original autograph of the Gospel were damaged or torn, the missing portion would surely have been restored by the author himself, had he been living and accessible."[33]

A Deliberate Suppression

Some scholars argued that the original ending of Mark, whatever it may

---

and Co., 1882), p. 577.

[30]Ibid.

[31]Alfred Edwards John Rawlinson, *St. Mark*, Westminster Commentaries (London: Methuen and Co., Ltd, 1925), p. 270.

[32]Ibid.

[33]Ibid. In connection with the next section, Rawlinson was sure that if Mark continued past ἐφοβοῦντο γάρ there would have been a Galilean appearance. He continued, "appearances may have taken place both in Galilee and Jerusalem, but not to the same people: the Apostles and other more immediate disciples of the Lord will have stayed in Jerusalem." See ibid., p. 271.

have been, was intentionally omitted. Such conjecture was based primarily on twotheories: (1) The original ending was not harmonious with the other Gospel-resurrection accounts, therefore, it was possible for the sake of consistency, that the ending was omitted; and (2) Joachim Jeremias suggested that Mark ended where he did in order to prevent pagan readers from knowing the secrets of Christology:

> From then on out there are the secrets of Christology, which one does not dare to touch: No Gospel besides the heretical Gospel of Peter gives a description of the occurrence of Jesus' resurrection. Here lies, the solution of the abrupt ending of Mark at 16:8. The appearances of the resurrected (Jesus) composed a definite component of the doctrine, they belong to the sense for Mark to that material, which may not be laid in the hands of the heathen readers. The Markan story of the temptation (1:12f.) can be understood as corresponding (to this).[34]

According to Charles S. C. Williams, "There were two possible motives for suppressing the original Ending."[35] He maintained that Mark 14:28 and 16:7 implied the evangelist intended to recount a resurrection appearance in Galilee.[36] Williams continued, "If Jesus appeared in Galilee, then his disciples had

---

[34]Joachim Jeremias, *Die Abendmahlsworte Jesu* (Göttingen: Vandenhoeck & Ruprecht, 1967 rpt.), p. 125. The German reads as: Darüber hinaus gibt es Geheimnisse der Christologie, die man überhaupt nicht anzutasten wagt: kein Evangelium--ausser dem häretischen Petrusevangelium--gibt eine Schilderung des Vorgangs der Auferstehung Jesu. Hier liegt wahrscheinlich auch die Lösung des Rätsels, das in dem abrupten Schluss des Markusevangeliums mit 16,8 liegt: die Erscheinungen des Auferstandenen bilden zwar einen festen Bestandteil der Glaubenslehre, gehören aber für das Gefühl des Markus zu demjenigen Stoff, der nicht in die Hände heidnischer Leser gelegt werden darf. Entsprechend ist die markinische Versuchungsgeschichte (1,12f.) zu verstehen.

[35]Charles Stephen Conway Williams, *Alterations to the Text of the Synoptic Gospels and Acts* (Oxford: Basil Blackwell, 1951), p. 44.

[36]See also Adolf Jülicher, *An Introduction to the New Testament*, trans. Janet Penrose Ward (London: Smith, Elder, & Co. 1904), pp. 328-329.

disobeyed His command to wait in Jerusalem till they should be clothed in power from on high, Lk. xxiv, 49, thus a scribe would reason.''[37] On the other hand, Luke 24, John 20, and the longer ending of Mark account for resurrection appearance only in Jerusalem and the immediate area. In any event, Williams assumed, "It may have been felt necessary to correct any possibility of a misinterpretation of Mark's phrase that Jesus rose from the dead 'after three days,' cf. Acts x. 40.''[38] (A side by side perusal of the Gospel accounts of the resurrection would point out a discrepancy). Williams concluded:

> that the autograph copy of Mark was mutilated not of course by a Council but by an individual who believed . . . that the Apostles waited in Jerusalem for the Lord's . . . Spirit and who rashly assumed that if the Risen Lord appeared in Jerusalem, then He could not have appeared also to some disciples in Galilee who perhaps were offended by the phrase 'after three days.'[39]

Critique of the Arguments of Mark 16:8 as an Incomplete Ending

The proposal of Mark 16:8 not being the authentic and the intended ending has been the object of intense research for the past century, based primarily on the abrupt style of Mark as well as the unlikely event of a work in Greek literature ending with γάρ. There is no textual or patristic evidence which would suggest

---

[37]Ibid.

[38]Ibid. C. S. C. Williams was confident that the original ending of Mark was worded 'after three days' rather than 'on the third day,' as preferred by Matthew and Luke. On three other occasions Mark used 'after three days' whereas Matthew and Luke corrected these to 'on the third day.' Williams confirmed that the Caesarean scribes altered the Markan manuscripts in the same way.

[39]Ibid., p. 45.

that the ending of Mark was lost, incomplete, or suppressed. These proposals to the ending of Mark were based purely on conjecture.

Westcott and Hort did apply a logical reason for the addition of the longer ending by proposing that a scribe or editor, unwilling to change the words of the text before him or to add words of his own, was willing to furnish the Gospel with what seemed a worthy conclusion, by incorporating with it unchanged, a narrative of Christ's appearances after the resurrection, which he found in some secondary record then surviving from a preceding generation.[40] It is unfortunate that these two renowned text critics clinged to such conjecture rather than fact, in supposing "that the true intended continuation of vv. 1-8 either was very early lost by the detachment of a leaf or was never written down."[41]

Most of these scholars affirmed that the catastrophe of a lost ending took place at an early time, and that the longer ending was added in the second century. If that be the case, one must inquire "Why did the scribe/editor not consult another copy of Mark's Gospel?" Even if the Gospel of Mark was later considered as being secondary to Matthew, the manuscripts of Mark were not so rare in the early times, that the editor could not fill out the missing part from somewhere else. The possibility, that the copy ended thus, that the earlier copier did not notice its incompleteness, is very minimal, furthermore, oral tradition would have been another avenue for the recovery of the lost ending.

Only when one assumes that this lost page occurred very early, even with the author's own copy. has the theory of the lost pages as cause for the shortening of the Gospel of Mark, a possibility of existence. An explanation is that the short version of Mark was dominant in the early church. The text critic can bring no objections from his material against such a theory, rather only methodological

---

[40]Ibid.

[41]Westcott and Hort, "Notes," p. 50.

considerations. Since the first copyist was probably out of the author's own circle of friends, he would have missed the final leaf of the original, if the last line ended with ἐφοβοῦντο γάρ, if the short ending was not the authentic ending.[42] Then he would have reconstructed the missing part, or have written it himself. Whoever (with the original Mark) sets the text after 16:8, can only argue that he let this be stricken either before or at the production of the first copies. Then one must assume that the editor considered a rounding up of the new ending as not necessary or he was not able to do so.

The proposal of the ending of Mark being incomplete also has no textual or patristic support. The argument that Mark never completed his Gospel, because of persecution, would fail if one maintained the traditional view of an early date for the composition of Mark, yet a late date would make this theory more plausible, due to the persecution from the time of Nero to Augustine. The proposal that Mark died before completing his Gospel is also a plausible explanation, but there is no proof to support this conjecture.

As noted above, some scholars have adhered to the thesis that the ending of Mark was deliberately suppressed, on the basis that (1) it was offensive to the church, and (2) that Mark ended there in order to prevent pagans from knowing what followed. In response to the first proposal, one would have to conclude that such conjecture is ridiculous, for if the ending (whatever that may have been) was offensive to the church and therefore omitted, why was the Gospel of Mark as a whole not obliviated? The Gospel as a whole is offensive, for Mark portrayed the disciples, of whom the church patterned itself, as utter failures. Jeremias' approach was nothing short of ridiculous. The Gospel of Mark is an invitation to discipleship, therefore, before one becomes a disciple a conversion to Christianity

---

[42]Kurt Aland, ''Der wiedergefundene Markusschluss? Ein methodologische Bemerkung zur textkritischen Arbeit,'' *Zeitschrift für Theologie und Kirche*, 67 (1, 1970), 9.

is an imperative. Mark was not writing a Christian-gnostic Gospel which would be didactic in nature, but an evangelistic tract compelling people to become "true" disciples.

A Reconstructed Ending

Some scholars did not accept the possibility of a lost or suppressed ending of the Second Gospel, for they maintained that something could be known about its content. The proposal of a reconstructed ending to the Gospel of Mark is based on speculation rather than patristic or manuscript testimony.

Kirsopp and Silva Lake argued for a reconstruction on the basis of a lost ending. They suggested that Mark 16:8 was an incomplete sentence, based on "the fact that any one who mutilated the gospel [sic] on purpose would scarcely have left an unfinished half sentence."[43]

According to the Lakes, it is possible to recover the content of the original ending of Mark, for "Mark xiv.28 and the words of the young man at the tomb (xvi.6ff.) are clearly leading up to an appearance of the risen Jesus in Galilee."[44] On the basis of the emphasis put on Peter in 16:7, it is also probable that that he played a considerable part in the events of the post-resurrection. The Lakes were convinced that both Matthew and Luke were independent of the original Markan ending, however, they (Matthew and Luke) may have known Mark in a mutilated

---

[43]Kirsopp and Silva Lake, *An Introduction to the New Testament* (London: Christophers, 1938), p. 35. In the above paragraph, the authors suggested, "It is at least a question whether ἐφοβοῦντο does not require, or at least expect, an object, so that if translated according to the best probability, it should not be rendered 'For they were afraid,' but 'For they were afraid of--' and we should print γὰρ not γάρ."

[44]Ibid., p. 36.

form. They refered to the scholarship which argued "that John xxi (which is held by many to be non-authentic in origin) may be based on the lost conclusion and that the Apocryphal Gospel of Peter shows some traces of a knowledge of it."[45] The Lakes concluded "that the gospel [sic] (of Mark) originally contained the story of how the disciples went to Galilee and there saw the risen Jesus."[46]

Alfred Haefner suggested a reconstruction in which "Mark 16:8 originally continued with Acts 1:13-14, and that this in turn continued with Acts 3, 4, and 5 (the so-called Jerusalem A source of Acts)."[47] He suggested that the joining of Mark 16:1-8 with Acts 1:13-14 was linguistically cohesive: "This sentence (Acts 1:13-14) contains three verbs in the third person plural, none of which has its subject expressed. The present hypothesis understands 'the women' as the subject of the first two verbs."[48] Haefner pointed to Acts 1:13-14 as a link to

---

[45]Ibid., p. 37. See also Kirsopp Lake, *The Historical Evidence for the Resurrection of Jesus Christ* (New York: B. P. Putnam's Sons, 1907), pp. 137ff. and Paul Rohrback, *Der Schluss des Markusevangelium, der Vier-Evangelien-Kanon und die kleinasiatischen Presbyter* (Berlin: Georg Nauck (Fritz Ruhe), 1894), pp. 41ff.

[46]Lake and Lake, *An Introduction to the New Testament*, p. 37. In the next sentence the Lakes confirmed there is nothing to show whether the lost Markan resurrection followed "the Pauline view that the risen Christ was a spirit, or, more accurately, he had a body of spirit; or whether, like Luke and John, it represented him as appearing with a body of actual flesh."

[47]See Adolf Harnack, *The Acts of the Apostles*, trans. J. R. Wilkinson (London: Williams & Norgate; New York: G. P. Putnam, 1909), pp. 162-202, where Harnack classified the material in Acts 3:1-5:16 as Jerusalem A source. See also Alfred Haefner, "The Bridge Between Mark and Acts," *Journal of Biblical Literature*, 77 (1958), 67. See also F. Blass, *Philology of the Gospels* (London: Macmillan and Company, 1898), pp. 141ff.; p. 193; and C. A. Briggs, *New Light on the Life of Jesus* (New York: Charles Schribner's Sons, 1904), p. 135, who affirmed that Luke used the continuation of Mark as a source for the early chapters of Acts.

[48]Alfred Haefner, "The Bridge Between Mark and Acts," 69.

Mark's ending used in Acts 1:3-5.[49] He further maintained that the "last verse of Mark would allow for the possibility that the women rejoined the disciples . . . (and) they did not convey the young man's message to the disciples,"[50] therefore, the apostles never did leave Jerusalem. Haefner concluded:

> The proclamation of (the) message about Jesus and its development into a way of salvation, together with attention it received from the Jewish people, and the Jewish authorities, was reason enough for the disciples to continue in Jerusalem until persecution compelled them to leave.[51]

Another speculative ending of the Second Gospel has been offered by B. T. Holmes.[52] He stated that the original copy was written in 40 A.D. and consisted of Mark 1:1-16:8 connected by a couple of sentences with Acts 1:3-10:48. He concluded that this arrangement would have "made the gospel [sic] the approximate size of Matthew, Luke, and Acts and therefore, one may take this length as the standard roll available commercially to first century churches."[53]

There have been a few scholars who have offered reconstructed conclusions to Mark through words and phrases not verbatim in the New Testament.[54] Frederick W. Danker has conjured a reconstruction[55] through an

---

[49]Ibid., p. 68.

[50]Ibid., p. 69.

[51]Ibid., p. 70.

[52]B. T. Holmes, *The Word of God: Mark's Version* (Toronto: B. T. Holmes, 1962), p. 42.

[53]Ibid.

[54]Austin Farrar, *The Glass of Vision* (Great Britain: Dacre Press, 1948), pp. 136-146; idem., *A Study in St. Mark* (Great Britain: Dacre Press, 1951), pp. 172-181; idem., *St. Matthew and St. Mark* (Great Britain: Dacre Press, 1954), p. 150; and C. F. D. Moule, "St. Mark XVI. 8 Once More," *New Testament Studies*, 2 (1955-1956), 58-59.

error of faulty eyesight. Both of these types of reconstructions may be interesting, but they are only speculative in light of critical analysis.

Eta Linnemann

Eta Linnemann proposed a thesis that verses 16:15-20 of the secondary longer ending is original to the Second Gospel.[56] According to Linnemann, the original ending included Mark 16:1-8, followed by two verses preserved in Matthew 28:16-17, and Mark 16:15-20. She believed that those who opposed the longer redaction have all too readily justified their rejection of the longer ending on the premise that it was one piece of tradition. Indispensable to her theory was the dividing of the longer ending into two distinct strands of tradition, 16:9-14 and 16:15-20.[57] Linnemann held that Mark 16:15-20 posed none of the linguistic or stylistic problems as does 16:9-14,[58] furthermore, the ideas embedded in this second section of the longer ending are primitive.[59]

Moule suggested the addition of καὶ εὐθὺς λέγουσιν τοῖς μαθηταῖς περὶ πάντων ποὐτων after Mark 16:8.

[55]Frederick W. Danker, "Postscript to the Markan Secrecy Motif," *Concordia Theological Monthly*, 38 (1967), 27. Danker maintained "ΦΟΒΟΝ ΜΕΓΑΝ was originally written by Mark and that some copy, made after the addition of ΑΝΑΣΤΑΣ and the following words by haplography, perhaps because of the ending of ΜΕΓΑΝ and the beginning of ΑΝΑΣΤΑΣ; the cognates (ἐφοβοῦντοφόβον), and the similarity of ΓΑΡ and —ΓΑΡ."

[56]Eta Linnemann, "Der wiedergefundene Markusschluss," *ZTK*, 66 (3, 1969), 255-287.

[57]Ibid., pp. 258-260.

[58]Ibid., p. 264.

[59]Ibid., pp. 266-268.

Linnemann believed that Mark originally ended with vv. 15-20, but a later redactor inserted a summary of stories (Mark 16:9-14), changing certain sections for a smooth literary transition. This leaves the text critic with the task of finding the words taken from the original in order to show that Mark ended with verses 16:15-20, after the empty tomb story of 16:1-8. She further maintained that Matthew 28:18-20 and Luke 24:44-53 knew of Mark 16:15-20.

Linnemann's argument is best divided into three distinct proposals: (1) She attempted to overcome the text-critical problem by identifying the possibility that codices Sinaiticus and Vaticanus are defective. She called attention to the possibility that both Justin Martyr and Irenaeus appeared as familiar with 16:15-20 as the original ending of Mark.[60] (2) She demonstrated what she deemed as the weakness behind Robert Morgenthaler's statistical approach,[61] in that his conclusions have bearing mostly on Mark 16:9-14, which is not included in her reconstructed ending.[62] (3) She debated the positions held by Ernest

---

[60]Ibid., pp. 261f. Compare with Trompf's proposal that Justin Martyr was aware of the original verses between 16:8 and 16:15-20. See the section on G. W. Trompf below.

[61]Linnemann, "Der wiedergefundene Markusschluss," 262-264. See also Robert Morgenthaler, *Statistik des neutestamentlichen Wortschatzes* (Zürich: Gotthelf-Verlag, 1958), pp. 57-60.

[62]Ibid., 262f.

Lohmeyer,[63] E. Helzle,[64] and Vincent Taylor[65] concerning the ending of the Gospel of Mark.

Linnemann believed that the short ending was the result of the last page was lost as a result of the manuscript being torn. She maintained that the Gospels circulated by themselves in the earlier times, and on papyrus codices in which the outside leaves (despite envelops) were usually injured. From there she argued that the short ending belonged to one text group:

> א and B belong to one text group, and the sys[8] [sic] has close relationships to the same one. It stands firm that Origen, as long as he lived in Alexandria, used the manuscripts B and א, so one can suppose the same for Clement. One could assume the possibility, that the manuscripts that Eusebius and Jerome used, belonged to primarily one and the same text groups.[66]

---

[63]Ibid., pp. 264-266. See also Ernest Lohmeyer, *Das Evangelium des Markus*, 15th ed. (Göttingen: Vandenhoeck und Reprecht, 1959), pp. 356-360. Lohmeyer argued for the validity of the 16:8 ending of Mark.

[64]Linnemann, "Der wiedergefundene Markusschluss," 266-269. See also E. Helzle, "The Ending of the Gospel of Mark (Mark 16:9-20) and the Freer Logion (Mark 16:14W), Its Tendencies and Its Mutual Relationship, a Word-Exegetical Investigation," PhD Dissertation (Tübingen, 1959). Even though according to Linnemann's own declaration, she only refers to the three sections of the report of Helzle in *Theologische Literaturzeitung*, 85 (1960), 470-472, and failed to look into the 212 pages of the manuscript as follows: This method is in fact very efficient; for example, one could prove without anything else, that the Christmas story in Luke creates a literary unity with the ending of Mark.

[65]Linnemann, "Der wiedergefundene Markusschluss," 278-284. See Taylor, *St. Mark*, pp. 609-613. Taylor argued in favor of a late date for the longer ending found in his commentary.

[66]Linnemann, "Der wiedergefundene Markusschluss," p. 261. The German reads as follows: א und B gehören zu einer Textgruppe, und der sys[8] hat zu derselben enge Beziehungen. Steht es fest, dass Origenes, solange er in Alexandria lebte, die Handschriften B und א benutzte, dann kann man dasselbe mit einiger Wahrscheinlichkeit auch für Clemens annehmen. Die Möglichkeit, dass die Handschriften, die Euseb und Hieronymus benutzten, zumeist ein und derselben Textgruppe angehörten, wird man zugestehen können.

Linnemann cited Fredrick Kenyon who said "that Origen used manuscripts B and
א as long as he was in Alexandria."[67] She concluded that it is possible that in
a few examples of the Gospel of Mark the last page became lost, and subsequently
a later redactor inserted a summary of stories, changing certain sections for a
smooth literary transition. According to Linnemann, the development of the last
chapter went as follows:

> (1) The original ending of Mark: Mark 16:1-8 and an equivalent from
> Matthew 28:16f and Mark 16:15-20 in original place.
>
> (2) The loss of the page with the text after 16:8.
>
> (3) The revision of (1). Through the elimination of the equivalent of
> Matthew 28:16f and the addition of Mark 16:9-14 through the
> simultaneous oral revision of the original edition of 16:15-20.[68]

The task of the text critic, then, is to show that Mark ended with verses 15-20
after the tomb story.

Kurt Aland argued that Linnemann's hypothesis should be rejected on
grounds of faulty textual methodology. According to Aland, Linnemann was
wrong in her assessment that only one text group supported Mark 16:1-8 and she
appeared unfamiliar with some of the problems connected with the theory of the
lost folium.[69] In order to support her view, a three stage textual-tradition is not
needed, but a six-stage process:

---

[67]Ibid. The German reads as follows: dass Origenes, solange er in Alexandria
lebte, die Handschriften B und א benutzte." See also Frederic G. Kenyon, *The Text of the
Greek Bible* (London: Duckworth, 1937), pp. 73-75 and 128-131.

[68]Ibid., 286-287.

[69]Aland, "Der wiedergefundene Markusschluss?, 3-8.

(1) Mark 16:1-8.
(2) Mark 16:1-8 and 9-20 with text critical signs and commentary that recognizes the doubt of 9-20 originally belonging.
(3) Mark 16:1-8 and 9-20 as the continuing text.
(4) Mark 16:1-8 and the short ending.
(5) Mark 16:1-8, combination with the short ending and long ending.
(6) Mark 16:1-8 and 9-14, and the Freer Logion, and 15-20.[70]

Linnemann's appeal to patristic citations also lacks methodological accuracy. Aland noted that B and ℵ were written in the fourth century and Origen left Alexandria in 230-1 and he died in 253-4. Linnemann implied that Origen had used Alexandrian manuscripts from the type of B or ℵ.[71] Linnemann has erred in putting theological considerations above textual considerations. When her theory is considered, that ℵ, B, and the Sinaitic Syriac (which Clement and Origen used) along with the manuscripts known by Eusebius and Jerome, all belonged to one single group of texts, one can not explain the predominance of a whole group of texts through the short ending like Linnemann wants to.[72]

She believed the references of Justin,[73] and the quote of Irenaeus[74] "must not themselves refer to the longer ending, rather can refer very well to the

---

[70]Ibid., p. 10.

[71]Ibid., pp. 5-6.

[72]Ibid., p. 9.

[73]Justin Martyr, *Apologia 1*, Patrologiae Cursus Completus, Series Graeca, ed. Jacques Migne, vol. 6 (Paris: Seu Petit-Montrouge, 1857), p. 397. This reference is made on "ὃ ἀπὸ Ἰερουσαλὴμ, οἱ ἀπόστολοι αὐτοῦ ἐξελθόντες, πανταχοῦ ἐκήρυξαν."

[74]Irenaeus, *Contra Haereses, libre tertii*, PG, vol. 7, p. 879. The quote is: "In fine autem Evangelii ait Markus: 'Et quidem Dominus Jesus, postquam locutus est eis, recetus est in coelos, et sedet ad dexteram Dei'." See above chapter 2, p. 18, n. 11.

original ending of Mark,"[75] because she limited herself to Mark 16:15-20. The reference of Justin goes in fact to 16:20, and Irenaue to 16:19, however, such an argument is only possible when one does not know the existing references by the Fathers on Mark 16. Mark 16:9-14 provided nothing more than a short summary of the reports, which is complete in the other Gospels. For what reason would the Fathers go back to this compilation if they already had access to others? Even though dependent on other copies and self-reliant formulations, only Mark 16:15-20 gives the most meaningful content: 15 the commissionary commandments, 16 about the relationship of faith and baptism, non-faith depravity, 17-18 about powers given to the faithful, 19 about the ascension and the sitting of Jesus on the right side of God, 20 about the activity of the apostle.[76] When the church fathers quote from the long ending, normally they only use these verses.[77] The citations primarily of Mark 16:15-20 does not imply anything negative, only that their New Testament included Mark 16:15-20, since there where they also quoted Mark 16:9-20 surely can be supposed.

Linnemann made references to Kenyon, that Sinai-Syriac have "close relationships" to the described text groups ℵ and B.[78] Kenyon is less optimistic about the relationship between ℵ and B:

> The Old Syriac Gospels are to be classed as a whole neither with the Alexandrian (ℵ B type) nor with the Western (D Old Latin Texts).

---

[75]Linnemann, "Der wiedergefundene Markusschluss," 262.

[76]Ibid.

[77]See Appendix A.

[78]Kenyon, *The Text of the Greek Bible*, pp. 73-75 and 128-131.

. . . At the same time in minor variants there are frequent agreements with the Western D- Old Latin group.[79]

Aland maintained that Kenyon discounted Linnemann's opinion that the manuscripts, which Eusebius and Jerome used, mostly belonged to one and the same text group.

One pertinent argument against Linnemann that Aland failed to comment on was that she readily criticized Morgenthaler's statistical approach, but was ready to use this method to confirm 16:15-20 as the original ending of Mark.[80] The unity of the language of Mark 16:9-20 makes it difficult to uphold Linnemann's arguments that 15-20 can be treated separately when refuting Morgenthaler's linguistic points.[81]

G. W. Trompf

G. W. Trompf assumed that the longer and the shorter endings were secondary, "since both sit awkwardly after xvi 8, and because no amount of ratiocinative over-straining can convincingly explain away the non-Markan characteristics of either."[82] He maintained that the original ending of Mark, or at least a significant part of it, may be recovered in Matthew 28:1-10. It is obvious

---

[79]Ibid., p. 122.

[80]See James K. Elliott, "The Text and Language of the Endings of Mark's Gospel," *Theologische Zeitschrift*, 27 (1971), 256.

[81]Aland, "Der wiedergefundene Markusschluss," 13.

[82]G. W. Trompf, "The Markusschluss in Rescent Research," *Australian Biblical Review*, 21 (October, 1971), 15-16.

that Matthew closely followed Mark's passion narrative beginning from Jesus' quotation of Zechariah 13:7, and his prophecy that after the resurrection he would go before the disciples in Galilee (see Mark 14:26ff., Matthew 26:30ff., and Luke 22:39ff.), though supplementing the Markan material with his own aetiological and biblical arguments (see Matthew 28:3-10 and 28:11-15) and his special dramatic effects (see 27:51b-54a and 28:2-4).[83] Trompf continued, "Matthew followed Mark up to xvi. 7-8; he copied Mark's προάγει ὑμᾶς εἰς τὴν Γαλιλαίαν, ἐκεῖ αὐτὸν ὄψεσθε . . . word for word (xxviii.7) . . . and he reproduced (though softened) the women's fearfulness (xxviii. 8).''[84]

Since Matthew appropriated two Markan prophecies about Galilee (Mark 16:7/Matthew 28:7 and Mark 14:28/Matthew 26:32), it is not unreasonable to assume that in referring to Jesus' going to Galilee a third time (verse 10), Matthew followed an original ending of Mark, and this was a point which both evangelists originally wished to emphasize (as in the other threefold references, i.e. the women).[85] Trompf was confident that Matthew reproduced Mark's original ending in part, for it fits all the facts.[86] Several Matthean-type words and phrases in 28:9-10, such as καὶ ἰδού (Matt. 3:16; 7:4; 8:34; 9:2), προσεύνησαν αὐτῷ (Matt. 2:2, 8, 11; 4:9, 10), τότε, and probably κἀκεῖ, prevent scholars from accepting these two verses as a complete reproduction of Mark, despite the typical

---

[83]Idem., "The First Resurrection and the Ending of Mark's Gospel," *NTS*, 18 (1972), 316.

[84]Ibid.

[85]Ibid.

[86]Ibid., p. 317.

Markan κρατέω, φοβοῦμαι, ὕπαγε, ἀπαγγείλατε, and ὁράω.[87] The third reference of Christ going to Galilee points to a Markan origin, therefore, form critical and theological considerations favor this conclusion.

Certain scholars have questioned Mark's interest in the resurrection by maintaining that Mark 16:7 implied his identification of the resurrection with the parousia. Even though Mark anticipated an early parousia, his language clearly distinguished between "resurrection of the dead" (5:42; 8:31; 9:9-10, 27, 31; 10:34; and 14:58) and "the coming of the son of man" (8:34-9:1; 10:29-31; 13:5ff.; and 14:62).[88] The question remains, "If Mark stressed resurrection, why did he not 'clinch the point of his Gospel by appearance of the risen Lord, completely fulfilling the predictions of viii. 31, ix. 31 and x. 33-4.'"[89] There remains the unanswered question as to the characteristics and content of the original Markan resurrection pericope. Matthew 28:9-10 goes some way towards filling in the apparent lacunae, providing the divine words Χαίρετε and Μὴ φοβεῖσθε and the command to tell the disciples to go (with the Markan ὕπαγε) into Galilee.[90]

According to Trompf, "An appearance in the Markan original as suggested would also explain certain stylistic enigmas and blemishes in Matt. xxviii. 9-10."[91] Matthew's recording of μὴ φοβεῖσθε in 28:10 is problematic in two ways: (1) What is the need for this phrase if the women's fear is accompanied by

---

[87]Ibid.

[88]Ibid., p. 318.

[89]Ibid.

[90]Ibid., p. 320.

[91]Ibid.

"great joy;" and (2) Why should Matthew use this phrase twice when he could have used Mark's μὴ ἐκθαμβεῖσθε in the first instance to permit stylistic variation. Trompf was confident Mark's Gospel contained the variant expressions, though "Matthew's 'turgid repetition' resulted when he changed Mark's first words of comfort to his own μὴ φοβεῖσθε because . . . he disliked Mark's peculiar use of this thaumaturgic verb."[92]

There is also the question of Χαίρετε which was used in a derogatory manner on two previous occasions in the passion narrative of Matthew 26:49 and 27:29. A possible explanation for the use of Χαίρετε in Matthew is that it stood in the original ending of Mark in Aramaic, and Matthew replaced it with a Greek greeting out of sequence with the rest of the Gospel. The notion of an original ending of Mark lying in Matthew 28:9-10 implies that the fear of the women was cut short by the appearance of Jesus. Trompf continued, if Jesus' use of Χαίρετε is an aramaism, a translated שָׁלֹם is likely, because it would explain why such a greeting got into the resurrection traditions of John xx. 19, and Luke xxiv. 36 as εἰρήνη ὑμῖν.[93] He continued that Matthew's Χαίρετε apparently had christological implications in some Jewish Christian circles of the diaspora.[94] Following the greeting of the women, they came up and seized (ἐκράτησαν) and worshiped the risen Jesus, however, apart from the verb κρατέω, nothing could be considered Markan until Jesus' words of comfort and his reinforced command. Matthew's words of comfort countered the fear of the women (see Mark 4:38-39 and 5:35-36, etc.), furthermore, he had the strong tendency to reproduce Jesus' words from the Markan passion narrative. Matthew's concern for the place of

---

[92]Trompf, "The First Resurrection and the Ending of Mark's Gospel," 320.

[93]Ibid., p. 321.

[94]Ibid., n. 5.

appearance (Galilee) implied that he included 28:9-10 out of difference to Mark.[95] This third reminder about going into Galilee suits the Markan threefold emphasis.

Matthew's use of ἀδελφοί is possibly connected with the lost ending of Mark. Trompf noted that in Matthew 28:7, 10 "μαθηταί and ἀδελφοί, become synonymous, since the disciples/brethren do go to Galilee to see Christ there.''[96] He continued:

> But upon supposing a reference to the ἀδελφοί in the original Mark, we obtain an entirely different impression, for Mark xvi. 7 refers to the disciples καὶ τῷ Πέτρῳ . . . so that the list of names in Mark's ending would, if completed, read: τοῖς μαθηταῖς (xvi. 7), τῷ Πέτρῳ (xvi. 7), τοῖς ἀδελγοῖς (reconstructed from Matt. xxviii. 10).''[97]

Trompf suggested the following as a reconstructed ending of Mark: "And Jesus met them and said, peace; do not be afraid; (gap) Go, tell my brethren that I depart (or) I go into Galilee.''[98]

Matthew 28:9-10 satisfied the open and unresolved ending of Mark 16:1-8. Following Jesus' appeal to the women that they "be not afraid," Trompf constructed the conclusion of the original Mark, based on Matthew 28:10, where Jesus re-emphasized the message about Galilee. This is not required in terms of

---

[95]Ibid., p. 321.

[96]Ibid., p. 322.

[97]Ibid.

[98]Ibid. The Greek as presented by Trompf reads as: "ἐφοβοῦντο γάρ, ἀλλὰ Ἰνσοῦς ὑπήντησεν αὐταῖς λέγων, σαλώμ· μὴ φοβεῖσθε gap] ὑπάγετε ἀπαγγείλατε τοῖς ἀδελφοῖς μου either ἵνα ἀπέλθωσιν or ὅτι προάγω εἰς τὴν Γαλιλαίαν.''

his own Gospel, since Matthew made the women eager to carry the news after the
first injunction, however, it was necessary to do in terms of Mark and the present
form of Mark xvi. 8, if in Mark the women were not going to pass on the
message.

If the original ending of Mark survived long enough for any other
evangelist to use it, common sense would mandate that fragments of it would
show up in second century Christian literature prior to the shorter or the longer
ending. In *Quaestiones et responsiones ad orthodoxos*, Justin Martyr (the ascribed
author) quoted the New Testament, primarily from Mark, even though he once
began a quotation from Luke on the resurrection and then returned to Markan
phraseology without notice.[99] When explaining Jesus' resurrection, Luke wrote
of the fleshly aspect of the raised body and how Jesus confirmed ἴδετε, ἐγώ εἰμι
to his doubting disciples. Justin's quotation εἶπεν αὐτοῖς Οὔπω ἔχετε πίστιν,
ἴδετε ἐγώ εἰμι revealed two points: (1) The first half of this quotation did not
conform to key Lukan terminology; and (2) The second part left out important
references to Jesus' hands and feet (compare to Luke 24:39).[100] Justin's
quotation is decidedly Markan in terminology (note the terms οὔπω, ἔχετε
πίστιν, ἴδετε, ἐγώ εἰμι), therefore, Trompf maintained that this quotation came
from the lost ending of Mark.

With the inclusion of Justin's quotation in the reconstruction along with
the Matthean reference, the original Markan ending becomes more comprehensible
from both the form-critical and the theological points of view.[101] Trompf
proposed that in the original Markan ending Jesus spoke the divine word, quieted

---

[99]Ibid., p. 323. See also note 5 of this reference.

[100]Trompf, "The First Resurrection," 223-224.

[101]For Justin's reconstruction see ibid., p. 324.

the fear of the disciples, and acted in order to provide the divine presence and commands (see Mark 4:50b-51a and 9:8).[102] The themes of Jesus attempting to remove fear and misunderstanding from his disciples and his presence in their calamity are recurrent (see Mark 4:37-40; 8:14-21; 13:23-27; and 14:26-50).

According to Trompf, Mark apparently concluded his Gospel at Jesus' command to go to Galilee (even though the original ending included a Jerusalem appearance), therefore, such an ending was loaded with possibilities and elucidated further formation of resurrection traditions.[103] Trompf noted the first resurrection appearance to a member of Jesus' family, with no appearance to Peter or the apostles, presented difficulties which combined both factual inconsistencies among the Gospels, and was "very likely to have had 'political' repercussions in the early church."[104] Both of these facts were problematic to the original ending of Mark, therefore, subsequent Gospel writers transformed Mark's account in the interest of their own theology as well as the uniformity and the authority they accepted.[105] It is possible that the longer ending replaced the original ending in the interest of harmony and in this manner it stands as a resurrection synopsis. Based on this argument two questions remain: (1) "When and how did the longer ending of Mark (9-20) replace the original ending?" and (2) "Why do we not posses a copy of the original ending of Mark?" Trompf offered two answers to these two questions: "To the first, that the longer ending finishes a second edition

---

[102]Ibid.

[103]Ibid., pp. 326 and 327.

[104]Trompf, "The Markusschluss in Recent Research," 17. Trompf continued, "Such an appearance would have reinforced Jacobean claims for leadership (James being Jesus' brother and Mary's son), and detracted from the authority of the pro-Petrines."

[105]Idem., "The First Resurrection," 325.

of Mark . . . and to the next question, that we have no copies of the original ending of Mark because no first edition . . . is extant.''[106]

Trompf concluded that his proposed reconstruction ''goes some way towards filling the lacunae that Eta Linnemann cannot account for (i.e., the gap between Mark 16:8 and 15-20). Furthermore, if Linnemann's defense of the authenticity of 16:15-20 is valid, this could indicate that the ending of Mark was longer than many have previously surmised and that Mark's missionary message extended farther that Mark 16:7.[107]

Trompf's theory is not without problems. He appeared too dependant on Markan priority, therefore, his theory is only as strong as the proposal of Markan authority. A second hole in Trompf's thesis is the possibility that the evangelist intended the short ending be interpreted with a finalized ending by ellipsis. In this event, no ending would be necessary. A third problem of Trompf's theory concerns his proposal that Matthew and Luke changed the first appearance story from Mary to Peter. This suggests that Matthew and Luke were willing to replace fact with fiction in order to sooth socio-political difficulties.

Reconstructions Since Trompf

Reconstructions since Trompf have in essence reproduced the works of Linnemann and Trompf, however, Walter Schmithals and Grant Osborne added information which might be construed as validating the notion of reconstruction.

Walter Schmithals maintained ''Mark 16:8 cannot be the original ending of the Gospel of Mark''[108] based on its abrupt ending with ἐφοβοῦντο γάρ. He

---

[106]Ibid., p. 328.

[107]Ibid., p. 330.

[108]Walter Schmithals, *Einleitung in die drei ersten Evangelien* (Berlin and New York: Walter de Gruyter, 1985), p. 322. The German reads: ''Mk 16,8 kann nicht der ursprüngliche Schluss des MkEv gewesen sein.''

based his research on a consensus of New Testament scholarship which held that Mark had a narrative source of the passion and resurrection when he wrote his Gospel.[109] This narrative source (which was kerygmatic in nature) went on after the tomb story to relate both petrine and the group appearance accounts.[110] He maintained that this narrative source followed the pattern of 1 Corinthians 15:3ff.[111] According to Schmithals, Mark transferred the appearance narrative to the pre-resurrection setting of Mark 16:1-8. Because of Mark's use of messianic secret, he could not use these appearance accounts at 16:8, but by substituting the pointers of Mark 14:28 and 16:7, he relocated them.[112]

The petrine appearance, which originally related a total transformation of Jesus as a presentation of his divinity and then his disappearance, was relocated into the transfiguration.[113] The group appearance portrayed the call of the Twelve in (3:13-19).[114] The third account represented a messianic enthronement

---

[109]Idem., "Der Markusschluss, die Verklarungsgeschicte und die Aussendung der Zwolf," *ZTK*, 69 (1972), 379-411.

[110]See idem., *The Office of Apostle in the Early Church*, trans. by John E. Steely (Nashville and New York: Abingdon Press, 1969), pp. 72-73, where Schmithals pointed out that both Mark and Matthew did not refer to the disciples as apostles.

[111]Idem., "Der Markusschluss," 380.

[112]Ibid., pp. 381-384.

[113]Ibid., pp. 384-393. Compare with Mark 9:9f.; 2 Peter 1:16-18; The Revelation of Peter 1-14; and the synoptic parallels which appear to support this point.

[114]Ibid. pp. 398-403.

scene complete with the commissioning of the eleven as Easter witnesses and the summary of their mission (16:15-20).[115]

This latter scene is derivable from Matthew 28:18-20, which Matthew made use of the Markan original source preserved in Mark 16:15-20 (compare to Linnemann above) and from other Markan redactions. Schmithals concluded that the ending of the original Markan source is found in Mark 9:2ff., 3:13-19, and 16:15-20.

John E. Alsup acknowledged that Schmithals exegesis was creative, however, he had two major criticisms which may cast doubt on the viability of the whole: (1) It is an error to propose "that a consensus of New Testament research had a 'block source of Passion and Resurrection narratives at his disposal.'"[116] The foundation of Schmithals argument is based on this assumption. (2) Schmithals failed "to raise the probability question in terms of a form-critical comparison of his proposed appearance accounts with the accounts of other gospel traditions."[117] It is obvious that Schmithals' approach made

> exegetical leaps of considerable proportions to arrive at his group appearance and his reconstruction of the petrine appearance as presentation/translation story is no less problematical, although at least the elements suggesting possible Easter backgrounds here in general are more readily available.[118]

In his work *The Resurrection Narratives: A Redactional Study*, Grant Osborne proposed a reconstructed ending to the Second Gospel from a linguistic

---

[115]Ibid., pp. 403-408.

[116]John E. Alsup, *The Post-Resurrection Appearance Stories of the Gospel Tradition* (Stuttgart: Calwer Verlag, 1975), p. 143, n. 429.

[117]Ibid.

[118]Ibid.

perspective, based on the notion "traces of Mark's ending may exist in the other synoptic Gospels," (primarily Matthew).[119] The longer ending of Mark and Matthew 28:16-20 include similarities in both theme and structure. Osborne contended, "The Galilean setting and the great commission are both appropriate to the promise of Mark 16:7,"[120] furthermore, "Matthew's enthronement theme meshes nicely with Mark's royal motif, and Matthew's stress on universalism also follows a similar pattern in Mark (e.g., 7:24f, 31f; 11:17; 13:10; 14:9; 15:39)."[121] There have been arguments against Matthew's use of a lost Markan ending based on a thematic rather than linguistic approach. Osborne cited the pericope of Matthew 28:9-10 and observed that Matthew included several words that were common to Mark.[122]

Osborne contended that the message in Matthew 28:10 "might also be the perfect sequel to Mark 16:8, illustrating how the awestruck silence of the women was broken and their fear turned into joy."[123] He referred to Trompf, who claimed the three-fold emphasis on Galilee in Matthew also resonates with Mark's methodology (see pages 119-121 above and Mark 6:39f., 8:6f., and 15:61 for

---

[119]Grant Osborne, *The Resurrection Narratives: A Redactional Study* (Grand Rapids, Mich.: Baker Book House, 1984), p. 63.

[120]Ibid.

[121]Ibid.

[122]Ibid., p. 64. This list includes ἰδού (seven times in Mark, six of which are redactional); κρατέω (fifteen of forty-seven New Testament occurrences in Mark, of which nine are redactional); the historical present λέγει in Mark 16:6 (the historical present occurs 150 times in Mark, fifty-two with verbs of speaking); μὴ φοβεῖσθε (also in Mark 16:6. A form of the verb φοβέω occurs twelve times in Mark, eight of them redactional); ὑπάγετε (found also in Mark 16:7; ὑπάγειν occurs eight of fifteen times as redactional); and ἐκεῖ (six of eleven occurrences in Mark are redactional).

[123]Ibid., p. 64.

"Christ"; 1:11, 9:7, and 12:6 for "beloved," the passion predictions, etc.).[124] Osborne agreed with Trompf in that no one should say Mark did not include the appearances because he combined the resurrection and the parousia.[125]

Osborne confirmed, "It is therefore possible to construct (reconstruct) a Markan ending from his style, hints in his book, and parallels in Matthew."[126] This proposed reconstruction may have begun with καὶ εὐθέως (and immediately),[127] or ἀλλά (but),[128] however, καὶ ἰδοῦ (and behold) is best (as in Matthew) in light of Markan terminology. Nonetheless, verse 9 (of the authentic Markan ending) provided a change of scene and sets the stage for the joy motif.[129] Osborne continued his reconstruction with the risen Christ appearing to the women (using ὑπαντάω) highlighted by a command similar to that of Mark 16:7 (note that Matthew 28:10 followed Mark 16:7). Drawing on Trompf, Osborne assumed that Mark used ἀδελφοῖς "in imitation of the 1 Corinthian list since 'James' is mentioned in 15:40 and 16:1, and 'Peter' in 16:7."[130] The women

---

[124]Ibid. See also the section on Trompf, pages 119-126 above.

[125]Ibid. Trompf said that Mark clearly distinguished the two (5:42; 8:31; 10:34; 14:58 and 8:34f.; 10:29f.; and 13:5f.), for the messianic secret would cease after the resurrection (9:9) while a period of evangelization would take place prior to the parousia (8:35; 13:10, 26; and 14:9). See also the section on Trompf, pages 119-127 above.

[126]Osborne, *The Resurrection Narratives*, p. 64.

[127]Charles Francis Digby Moule, *The Gospel According to Mark*, The Cambridge Bible Commentary (Cambridge: University Press, 1965), pp. 58-59.

[128]Trompf, "The First Resurrection," 321-330.

[129]Osborne, *The Resurrection Narratives*, p. 64.

[130]Ibid. See the section on Trompf, pages 119-126 above.

"grasp" (based on the use of **κρατέω** in 1:31; 5:41; and 9:27) in "great joy" and ran to tell the disciples. Matthew 14:28 and Mark 16:7 revealed that Jesus appeared in Galilee. Osborne further speculated that the Markan form based on Matthew 28:9-10 would read:

> And behold Jesus met them and said, 'Greetings. Do not be afraid. Go, tell my brethren that I depart into Galilee; they will see me there.' And immediately they grasped his hand with great joy and ran to tell his brethren/disciples.[131]

Osborne concluded that Mark probably produced an ending which is hinted in Matthew 28:9-10 and possibly 28:16-20,[132] therefore, his proposed ending included the paradox of both fear and joy. The women who were struck silent by the words of the messenger, encountered the risen Lord, therefore, they were revitalized by his presence and announced the resurrection to the disciples.[133]

Critique on the Theories of Reconstruction

The reconstructed endings of the Gospel of Mark are based on conjecture, which depends on several immovable presuppositions. The first of these is that Mark the evangelist did, at one time, complete his Gospel and this ending was lost, because of a torn page, or was deliberately detached, because a later scribe deemed that the contents were offensive. Common sense would suppose a restoration of the original/authentic ending of Mark in the event that other copies existed. The notion of an incomplete Gospel would eliminate the proposals of the

---

[131]Ibid., pp. 64-65. The Greek reads as: "καὶ ἰδοῦ ὑπήντησεν αὐταῖς ὁ Ἰησοῦς καὶ λέγει Χαίρετε. Μὴ φοβεῖσθε; ὑπάγετε εἴπατε τοῖς ἀδελφοῖς μου ἵνα ἀπέλθωσιν εἰς τὴν Γαλιλαίαν; ἐκεῖ μέ ὄψονται."

[132]It appears that Osborne drew on a combination of Linnemann and Trompf to form his reconstruction.

[133]Osborne, *The Resurrection Narratives*, p. 65.

above reconstructionists, because each of these scholars based their theory on the existence on the proposal of an original Markan ending, which may be traced to Matthew, Luke, or even 1 Corinthians 15.

A second problematic issue for the proponents of a reconstructed ending is their dependence on Markan priority.[134] Matthean and Lukan priority are sill advocated by competent scholars, even though their number is a minority.[135] Markan priority is an essential element to the proponents of a reconstruction, for many of these scholars claim to find Mark's ending in the resurrection accounts in other works, therefore, if Mark was not written first, the reconstructionists' theory that Mark's ending was preserved is futile.

The advocates of a reconstructed ending, in a perverted way, have the textual and the patristic evidence that would support their argument, provided they were allowed to footnote that Mark continued after 16:8. The Fathers nowhere implicitly referred to a lost or incomplete ending. All that scholars have to support their conjecture is a similarity of vocabulary and a resemblance of syntax of the Gospel of Mark and those of Matthew and Luke. This is best explained by a common source, even if the Gospel writers wrote independently of each other.

---

[134]As noted above, I accept Markan priority, however, this has no effect on my final conclusions.

[135]Hugh Anderson, *The Gospel of Mark*, The New Century Bible Commentary (Grand Rapids: Wm. B. Eerdmans, 1976), p. 2, stated, "Mark's Gospel, it is generally held, is the earliest of the four in the NT." See Werner Georg Kümmel, *Introduction to the New Testament*, 17th ed., trans. by Howard Clark Kee (Nashville: Abingdon Press, 1975), pp. 38-79 and Wayne Ward, "Gospel Sources: A Reconsideration From the Perspective of Redactional Theology," *The Yearbook Annales* (1974-1975), 75-97, for a detailed discussion of the synoptic problem.

Two Other Optional Endings

Textual evidence supports two Markan endings other than the short and the longer endings, however, the Freer logion and the shorter ending have not received the support as did the other two endings.

The Expanded Long Ending: The Freer Logion

The longer ending existed with an appendage located after Mark 16:14 in selected Greek copies as shown by Jerome (see above chapter 2, pages 36-37):

> And they excused themselves saying, 'This age of lawlessness and unbelief is from Satan, who by means of unclean spirits does not allow the true power of God to prevail over unclean things of the spirits. Therefore reveal thy righteousness now.' They spoke to Christ, and Christ replied to them that 'the term of years for Satan's power has been fulfilled, but other terrible things draw near. And for those who have sinned I was delivered over to death, in order that they might turn to the truth and sin no more; that they might inherit the spiritual and incorruptible glory of righteousness which is in heaven.'[136]

The external evidence supporting the expanded long ending is limited.[137] This form was a mystery until the discovery of W (the Freer Logion) in 1906. Metzger

---

[136]This quote of the longer ending is from Aland, eds. et al., *The Greek New Testament.* 3rd. ed. (United Bible Societies, 1975), p. 197. The Greek reads as: "ἐπίστευσαν κἀκεῖνοι ἀπελογοῦντο λέγοντες ὅτι ὁ αἰὼν οὗτος τῆς ἀνομίας καὶ τῆς ἀπιστίας ὑπὸ τὸν Σατανᾶν ἐστιν, ὁ μὴ ἐῶν τὰ ὑπὸ τῶν πνευμάτων ἀκάθαρτα τὴν ἀλήθειαν τοῦ θεοῦ καταλαβέσθαι δύναμιν· διὰ τοῦτο ἀποκάλυψον σοῦ τὴν δικαιοσύνην ἤδη. ἐκεῖνοι ἔλεγον τῷ Χριστῷ, καὶ ὁ Χριστὸς ἐκείνοις προσέλεγεν ὅτι πεπλήρωται ὁ ὅρος τῶν ἐτῶν τῆς ἐξουσίας τοῦ Σατανᾶ, ἀλλὰ ἐγγίζει ἄλλα δεινὰ καὶ ὑπὲρ ὧν ἐγὼ ἁμαρτησάντων παρεδόθην εἰς θάνατον ἵνα ὑποστρέψωσιν εἰς τὴν ἀλήθειαν καὶ μηκέτι ἁμαρτήσωσιν· ἵνα τὴν ἐν τῷ οὐρανῷ πνευματικὴν καὶ ἄφθαρτον τῆς δικαιοσύνης δόξαν κληρονομήσωσιν. ἀλλά."

[137]Bruce Metzger eds. et al., *A Textual Commentary on the Greek New Testament* (London and New York: United Bible Societies, 1975), p. 124. See (4) on page 124 for an evaluation of the external evidence of the expanded form of the longer ending.

dated this manuscript "from the late fourth or early fifth century and, like codex Bezae, (it) contained the Gospels in the so-called Western order (Matthew, John, Luke, and Mark)."[138]

Metzger pointed out that the type of text in the Freer Logion (W) is variegated, as though copied from several manuscripts of different families of text:

> In Matthew and Luke viii. 13-xxiv. 53 the text is of common Byzantine variety, but in Mark i. 1-v. 30 it is Western, resembling the Old Latin; Mark v. 31-xvi.20 is Caesarean, akin to p[45]; and Luke i. 1-viii. 12 and John v. 12-xxi. 25 are Alexandrian.[139]

Henry Sanders explained this stratification of different types of texts, based on a theory that W goes back to a prototype made up of fragments from different manuscripts of the Gospels pieced together.[140]

William Lane surveyed the scholarship on the Freer Logion and supposed that this ending originated from a marginal gloss.[141] Some scholars challenged the opinion that this appendage was a gloss on the basis that without it, the narrative passes very abruptly from reproof of the disciples' unbelief (16:14) to the apostolic commission (16:15).[142] Theodore Zahn maintained that the logion appeared to supply a point of transition between verses 14 and 15, based on the

---

[138]Metzger, *The Text of the New Testament*, p. 56.

[139]Ibid. p. 57.

[140]Henry A. Sanders, "The Beginnings of the Modern Book," *Michigan Alumnus Review*, 54 (1938), 95-111.

[141]William Lane, *Commentary on the Gospel of Mark*, The New International Commentary on the New Testament (Grand Rapids: Wm. B. Eerdmans, 1974), p. 606. The contention that the logion is a gloss was accepted by B. Botte, "Freer (Logion de)," *Dictionnaire de la Bible Supplement III* (1938), col. 526f; Rawlinson, *St. Mark*, p. 248; Schweizer, *The Good News According to Mark*, p. 616; and Taylor, *St. Mark*, p. 615.

[142]Lane, *Commentary on the Gospel of Mark*, p. 606, n. 3.

context of Jerome's citation alone[143] (see above chapter 2 pp. 36-37), whereas, H. B. Swete appealed to the ease in which an obscure passage could be removed.[144] A. Harnack proposed that the logion was a gloss derived from the same source which supplied Mark 16:14-18, but the original compiler failed to include it in the longer ending.[145]

Lane concluded that the logion owes its existence to the intercalation of the text of the longer ending by some early reader whose attention was caught up by the charge of unbelief.[146] The occurrence of the logion in a single Greek manuscript suggests that it probably is an isolated logion embodying an isolated local tradition.[147]

---

[143]Theodore Zahn, *Geschicte des neutestamentlichen Kannons II* (Erlangen: 1896), p. 936 and idem., *Einleitung in das Neue Testament II* (Leipzig, 1900), p. 229. Lane, *Commentary on the Gospel of Mark*, p. 661, n. 22, errantly cited Zahn as accepting the logion as authentic to Mark. Compare with Zahn, *Einleitung in das Neue Testament II.*, p. 229. In a latter work of idem., *Introduction to the New Testament*, vol. 2, trans., Melancthon Williams Jacobus (Edinburgh: T. & T. Clark, 1909), pp. 467ff. Zahn affirmed that Mark cut off his Gospel from the resurrection traditions at 16:8.

[144]Lane, *Mark*, p. 611, n. 22, cited Henry Barclay Swete, *Zwei neue Evangelienfragmente* (Bonn: 1908), p. 10, and R. Dunkerley, *The Unwritten Gospel* (London: 1925), p. 197, as accepting the authenticity of the logion to Mark. It is unfortunate that I was not able to locate these two sources to confirm or deny Lane's statement.

[145]See A. Harnack, "Neues zum unechten Marcusschluss," *ZTK*, 33 (1908), 168-170. Haenack's thesis was accepted with minor modifications by H. Koch, "Der erweite Markussluss und die kleinasiatischen Presbyter," *Biblische Zeitschrift*, 6 (1908), 266-278. See also P. van Kasteren, Het slot van het Marcusevangelie," *Studien*, 86 (1916), 283-296; P. van Kasteren, "Nog een woord over het Marcusslot," *Std*, 87 (1917), 484-490.

[146]Lane, *Mark*, pp. 606-607, n. 3.

[147]Ibid., pp. 606-607. See also B. Botte, "Freer (Logion de)," *Dictionnaire de la Bible Supplement III* (1938), col. 526f.

Lane offered a brief theological study on the Freer Logion which pertained to the discipleship motif. He maintained that the key sentence of the logion was the phrase "the term of years for Satan's power has been fulfilled, but other terrible things draw near."[148] Preceding this verse, the disciples claimed that their present age was lawless and unbelieving, because of its being under the control of Satan. The hope of the disciples lies in the future, when Satan's power will be broken, the truth will be recognized. The statements of the disciples presuppose a dualism of "the present age" followed by "the age to come."

Jesus' response suggested an interval between the two poles. He confirmed that Satan's era in which he was allowed to exercise his authority has concluded, but "that does not mean that the age to come will immediately break into the time structure."[149] Jesus stated that other "terrible things" must occur.[150] Lane noted that the word δεινά is coupled with fear. (Note that the fear motif did not end with Mark 16:8, but continued with this appendage). According to Lane, δεινά "describes the fearful events which precede the judgment which accompanies the parousia of the Messiah."[151] He continued that this was

---

[148]Lane, *Mark*, p. 607. The Greek reads: "τῆς ἐξουσίας τοῦ Σατανᾶ, ἀλλὰ ἐγγίζει ἄλλα δεινά." For the sake of consistency, I have retained my translation of the logion. Lane's wording was slightly different in this phrase, "'the limit of the years of the authority of Satan has been fulfilled, but other terrible things are drawing near.'

[149]Ibid., p. 608.

[150]See ibid., where Lane stated that the phrase ἐγγίζει ἄλλα δεινά does not occur in any other place in the New Testament. Such a phrase is connected the the wisdom literature of the Old Testament.

[151]Ibid., p. 609.

"distinctly a Palestinian-Jewish concept, found in the rabbinic sources under the rubric "the birth-pangs of the Messiah."[152]

Lane concluded that the Freer Logion, with its periodization, was very similar to Acts 3:19-21, but, there are as many dissimilarities.[153] He concluded, "The Freer Logion and Acts 3:19-21 are independent witnesses to a tradition of the of inherited eschatological hopes by the early Palestinian Church."[154]

Critique of the Scholarship on the Freer Logion

The expanded long ending with its obvious and pervasive apocryphal flavor and the limited basis of evidence supporting it, condemns it as a totally secondary addition.[155] The internal evidence of the expanded ending is detrimental to its support, because the expansion contains several non-Markan words and expressions (ὁ αἰὼν οὗτος ἁμαρτάνω, ἀπολογέω, ἀληθινός, ὑποστρέφω) and several hapax legomenon to the New Testament (δεινός ὅρος and προσλέγω).[156]

---

[152]Ibid. This dates the logion at the earliest, sometime after 70 A.D. and probably later around 90 A.D. when Judaism was consolidated into Rabbinic Judaism after Jamnia. See Isidore Singer, eds. et al, "Jabneh," *The Jewish Encyclopedia*, vol. 7 (New York and London: Funk & Wagnall's Company, 1910), p. 18, and Michael Ani-Yonah, "Jabneh," *Encyclopedia Judaica*, vol. 9, Cecil Roth and Geoffrey Wigoder, editors in chief (Jerusalem: Keter Publishing House Ltd., New York: The MacMillan Co., 1971), pp. 1176-1177.

[153]See Lane, *Mark*, pp. 610-611.

[154]Ibid.

[155]Metzger, *The Text of the New Testament*, p. 227.

[156]See idem., eds. et al., *A Textual Commentary*, pp. 124-125.

External evidence also casts much doubt on the authenticity of the logion. As noted above, only one manuscript contained the logion, even though it can be logically argued that the logion once existed in a wider frame, the fact remains that only one Father addressed the logion. The problem of dating also points to a secondary addition. As noted above,[157] the logion contains several Rabbinic similarities which would date it after 70-90 A.D. C. R. Gregory suggested that the logion was written in the first half of the second century, based on its style and vocabulary.[158] He further noted that after 150 A.D. it became increasingly difficult to make additions to the Gospels. Lane suggested an early date of composition, based on "its Palestinian language, its emphasis on the significance of repentance as a condition for the Days of the Messiah, its use of ὁ Χριστός as a title of office, and its particular expression of periodization. . . ."[159]

Lane added another piece of external evidence by pointing out that the awkward transition of verses 15 and 16 is poorly overcome by this logion. He continued, "The words of the disciples are scarcely directed to the charge of unbelief, but rather reflect the difficulties they have encountered in their preaching."[160] The way in which these words have been attached to the rebuke by Jesus is sufficient to expose an interpolation.[161] It is obvious, that this addition was a later appendage, and further depended on a canonical acceptance of the longer ending in order that it may be considered for a practical use.

---

[157]See page 137, n. 152.

[158]C. R. Gregory, *Das Freerlogion* (Leipzig, 1908), pp. 64f.

[159]Lane, *Mark*, p. 611, n. 22.

[160]Ibid., p. 607, n. 3.

[161]Ibid.

The Shorter Ending

The abrupt ending of Mark 16:8 has led a few scholars to the task of providing a more appropriate conclusion to the Second Gospel which affords the most plausible explanation for the shorter ending: "But they reported briefly to Peter and those with him all they had been told. And after this Jesus himself sent out by means of them, from east to west, the sacred and imperishable proclamation of eternal life."[162] The shorter ending "was obviously written with the express purpose of providing the necessary conclusion to what its author took to be an otherwise incomplete Gospel."[163] The authenticity of the shorter ending has not been an issue, for it is obviously a later appendage, whose style and vocabulary "is most certainly not Mark."[164]

Westcott and Hort

Westcott and Hort confirmed that the shorter ending "was appended by a scribe or editor who knew no other ending to the Gospel than v. 8."[165] They maintained that the abrupt ending of Mark 16:8 was offensive, therefore, the scribe/editor "completed the broken sentence by a summary of contents of Lc

---

[162]The Greek reads as: "Πάντα δὲ τὰ παρηγγελμένα τοῖς περὶ τὸν Πέτρον συντόμως ἐξήγγειλαν. Μετὰ δὲ ταῦτα καὶ αὐτὸς ὁ Ἰησοῦς ἀπὸ ἀνατολῆς καὶ ἄχρι δύσεως ἐξαπέστειλεν δι' αὐτῶν τὸ ἱερὸν καὶ ἄφθαρτον κήρυγμα τῆς αἰωνίου σωτηρίας ἀμήν."

[163]Anderson, *Mark*, p. 361.

[164]Ibid.

[165]Westcott and Hort, "Notes," p. 44.

xxiv 9-12, and the Gospel by a comprehensive sentence suggested probably by Mt xxviii 19; Lc xxiv 47; Jo xx 21.''[166]

Westcott and Hort favored an early date of composition and appendage of the shorter ending based on the variety of its distribution.[167] They maintained that the prototype of *k* (Codex Bobiensis, the codex where the shorter ending stands alone as the ending of Mark) was early African or Cyprianic, therefore, either the early African text must have had the shorter ending or that the prototype must have been supplemented from another source. The shorter ending never would have been substituted for the longer ending, so it is probable that the prototype had neither of these endings and each of these two endings supplemented ἐφοβοῦντο γάρ of 16:8.

William Lane

The shorter ending stands in direct opposition to Mark 16:8b, "they said nothing to anyone," therefore, in joining the shorter ending to Mark 16:8 the phrase "they said nothing to anyone" was omitted in this manuscript.[168] The result of this redaction suggests that the women did leave the tomb with fear, however, they reported to Peter and to the rest of the disciples all the things they

---

[166]Ibid.

[167]Ibid. This distribution consisted of "Greek (including syr.hl [Harclean], which is virtually Greek), Latin, Memphitic, and Æthiopic the various lines of which must have diverged from a common original, itself (presupposes) a yet earlier MS or MSS which ended with verse 8." Following the lead of Westcott and Hort, Theodore Zahn speculated that the shorter ending had an early widespread circulation. Of the witnesses in which the shorter ending appeared, "Only in the Latin codex *k* . . . is B fully amalgamated with the text of xvi. 8; but in such a way, that the text of xvi. 8 is violently changed, in order to add the shorter ending without producing a contradiction." See Zahn, *Introduction to the New Testament*, p. 484.

[168]Lane, *Mark*, p. 602.

had been told. The shorter ending is found in combination with the longer ending in several uncial manuscripts of the seventh, eighth, and ninth centuries (L, Ψ, 099, and 0112); in a few minuscule or lectionary manuscripts (272^{mg} 579 $l^{961\ 1602}$); and a few ancient versions (sy^{hmg} sa^{mss} bo^{mss} aeth^{mss}).[169] It is important to understand that an early date of origin for the shorter ending, based on its primacy of position.[170] Lane affirmed that the shorter ending is now extant in only six Greek textual witnesses, but this is not a counter argument against its early origin.[171] He agreed with Aland's dating of the shorter ending as being in the middle of the second century.[172]

According to Lane, Codex Vaticanus (B) provided evidence for the existence of the shorter ending, based on the fact that after the conclusion of Mark in column 3 of folio 1303, a column is left free. This is a wholly singular phenomenon, for in Codex B a new book follows in the next column as soon as possible. The supposition that the scribe knew of a continuation after 16:8 best,

---

[169]Ibid. See also Metzger, *The Text of the New Testament*, p. 226; idem., eds. et al., *A Textual Commentary*, pp. 123-124; Westcott and Hort, "Notes," pp. 44-51; and Zahn, *Introduction to the New Testament*, vol. 2, pp. 468-469.

[170]Lane observed that "Codex Bobbiensis (*k*) was transcribed in the fourth or fifth century, . . . (however), the manuscript from which *k* was transcribed gives every appearance of going back to an earlier Greek text it is necessary to push the date back into the second century. This judgment is consistent with the increasingly established text-critical principle that all genuine textual alteration in normal cases goes back to the second century." See Lane, *Mark*, p. 603.

[171]Ibid.

[172]Ibid. and Kurt Aland, "Bemerkungen zum Schluss des Markusevangeliums," *NeoTestamentica et Semitica* (Edinburgh: T. & T. Clark, 1969), pp. 157-180.

explains the phenomenon of a free column after the conclusion of Mark. Space calculations indicate that this can only have been the shorter ending.[173]

Kurt Aland

Kurt Aland agreed with Westcott and Hort in that both the shorter and the longer ending of Mark were "not a part of the Gospel in its original form, although both may well be from the beginning of the second century"[174] and were placed in double brackets, noting that these two appendages were not authentic. He continued that this is best explained by the assumption the 16:8 ending was considered unsatisfactory as its use spread through all the provinces of the Church in its early decades.[175] The empty tomb story without a resurrection appearance was inadequate.

Aland concluded that the origin of the shorter ending was conceivable only with the hypothesis that the copy of Mark, which lay before the author, ended at 16:8, and that neither the longer ending or any other ending of the Gospel was known then.[176] In essence, this pointed out that the 16:8 ending existed in several text groups, therefore, defending authenticity of the 16:8 ending based on its widespread existence. He maintained that this shorter ending was used long after the longer ending became the approved ending of Mark,[177] being appended

---

[173]Ibid., p. 602, n. 1, and Zahn, *Introduction to the New Testament*, vol. 2, p. 469.

[174]Aland and Aland, *The Text of the New Testament*, p. 227. Aland noted that the longer ending of Mark is found in 99% of the Greek manuscripts as well as the rest of the tradition, (see pages 287).

[175]Ibid., p. 288.

[176]Kurt Aland, "Bemerkungen zum Schluss," 157-180.

[177]Aland and Aland, *The Text of the New Testament*, p. 288.

to the 16:8 ending by the early church through the 12th century, based on its wide geographical appeal.[178] When a manuscript contained both the shorter and longer endings, the shorter ending preceded the longer, based on its greater age and apparent higher authority.[179]

The brevity and clumsiness of style of the shorter ending reflects an early period of composition, a remote place of origin, and/or an awkward author. Aland continued that the author of the shorter ending made no attempt to create a link with the longer ending. The short ending might be considered a parallel construction with the longer ending, therefore, it is probable that the shorter ending and the longer ending originated in two separate geographical locations.[180]

Critique of the Shorter Ending

Even though Westcott and Hort affirmed an early date and use of the shorter ending, they maintained "it has no claim to be considered part of St, Mark's true text."[181] The language and contents have no internal characteristics that compensate for the textual authority. The vagueness and generality of the last

---

[178]Aland, eds. et al., *The Greek New Testament*, p. 196.

[179]Aland defended the temporal priority of the shorter ending over the longer ending, claiming that it had wider manuscript support than its competitors. As noted above, Aland did not conclude that this ending was the original one, however, he did stress the antiquity of its language, and he noted how it satisfactorily resolved the glaring openness of Mark 16:8 with its ἐφοβοῦντο γάρ. See Aland, "Bemerkungen zum Schluss," 161-162, 167-169, 173-174 and idem, "Der wiedergefundene Markusschluss?," 11-12.

[180]Aland and Aland, *The Text of the New Testament*, p. 288.

[181]Westcott and Hort, "Notes," p. 44.

sentence, "And after this Jesus himself sent out by means of them, from east to west, the sacred and imperishable proclamation of eternal life,"[182] is not parallel in the Gospel narratives. Westcott and Hort suggested the last phrase, "the sacred and imperishable proclamation of eternal life," as rhetorical, which differs from the style of Mark.[183]

Westcott and Hort assumed that the scribe/editor who appended the shorter ending to Mark 16:8 was not aware of the longer ending. They concluded: "The petty historical difficulty mentioned by Marinus as to the first line of v. 9 could never have suggested the substitution of 4 colourless lines for 12 verses rich in interesting matter."[184]

Metzger affirmed that the internal evidence for the shorter ending is against it being genuine. Besides containing a large number of non-Markan words, the rhetorical tone of the shorter ending differs totally from the simple style of Marks Gospel.[185] According to Metzger, "No one who had available as the conclusion of the Second Gospel the twelve verses 9-20 . . . would have deliberately replaced them with four lines of a colorless and generalized summary."[186] The shorter ending was an ineffective solution, because it was a very early stage of development and probably represented an outlying and undeveloped community.

---

[182]The Greek reads as: "Μετὰ δὲ ταῦτα καὶ αὐτὸς ὁ Ἰησοῦς ἀπὸ ἀνατολῆς καὶ ἄχρι δύσεως ἐξαπέστειλεν δι' αὐτῶν τὸ ἱερὸν καὶ ἄφθαρτον κήρυγμα τῆς αἰωνίου σωτηρίας ἀμήν."

[183]Westcott and Hort, "Notes," p. 44.

[184]Ibid. Bruce Metzger later adopted this view of Westcott and Hort, see Metzger eds. et al., *A Textual Commentary*, p. 126. See below n. 187.

[185]See ibid., p. 126, and Metzger, *The Text of the New Testament*, p. 228.

[186]Ibid., p. 126.

The longer ending was affective because it was formulated later than the shorter ending and it represents a more competent author.[187]

Chapter Summary

This chapter demonstrated the reluctance of the church and critical scholarship in accepting Mark 16:8 as the intended ending of the Second Gospel. Textual evidence suggested that the longer ending was appended by a scribe who made a composite of the resurrection stories as well as oral tradition in order to supply the ending. Textual evidence also supported the shorter ending and the Freer Logion. Each of these two endings are not considered authentic, but both were generally used in conjunction with the longer ending. The shorter ending preceded the longer ending in all the manuscripts which the shorter ending existed with the exception of (k) where it stood alone, whereas, the Freer Logion was appended to Mark 16:14.

Such additions proved to be useful to the church in varying degrees. The longer ending supplanted all other endings on the basis of its numerical superiority and the authority the church placed on it. The shorter ending was useful in that this ending enjoyed a widespread geographical spread even though it was inferior to the longer ending in manuscript quantities. The Freer Logion (W) probably existed on a more widespread basis that the textual evidence of one manuscript suggested. Jerome was acquainted with this text, however, (W) was not influential, for it existed in obscurity for some fifteen-hundred years.

Several scholars rejected both the intent of Mark ending at 16:8 and the authenticity of each of the above mentioned appendages. These scholars speculated various reconstructions which, as the name suggests, proposed an authentic ending

---

[187]Ibid., p. 288. The text of Mark 16:9-20 contains not only a summary account of the appearances of the resurrection of Jesus, but also the command to evangelize in a form more radical than that in Matthew, and also an account of the ascension of Jesus.

based on the redactional work of Matthew, Luke, John, Acts, and Paul. This proposal has no textual or patristic support.

Since the shorter ending and the Freer Logion are conceded as later appendages, the notion that Mark's ending was lost or never completed is only conjecture, therefore, the arguments of reconstruction are the only issues of debate concerning the authentic ending of Mark. Unlike the longer ending, as well as the later appendages, reconstruction and the idea of a lost or incomplete ending has no textual support (unless one attributes the texts that end Mark at 16:8 as supporting such a view) or patristic attestation. The next chapter will consider the scholarship which maintained the authenticity and intent of Mark ending at 16:8 with ἐφοβοῦντο γάρ.

CHAPTER 5

The Short Ending

Bruce Metzger confirmed that the earliest ascertainable form of the Second Gospel ended at 16:8,[1] however, he did not accept the note of fear of the women as an appropriate ending "to an account of the Evangel or as Good News."[2] He questioned the short ending from a stylistic point of view:

> To terminate a Greek sentence with the word γάρ is most unusual and exceedingly rare--only a relatively few examples have been found throughout all the vast range of Greek literary works, and no insistence has been found where γάρ stands at the end of a book.[3]

---

[1]Bruce M. Metzger, *The Text of the New Testament: Its Transmission, Corruption, and Restoration* (New York and Oxford: Oxford University Press, 1968), p. 228. The manuscripts that end with 16:8 belong to the most varied text groups and affirms that the literary dispersal of Gospel of Mark began with a text ending in 16:8. He added that it would be appropriate to add the manuscripts that end with the shorter ending as supporting the 16:8 ending, based on the acknowledgement of the shorter ending being an appendage.

[2]Ibid.

[3]Ibid. It is obvious that this originated before the production of the Ibycus Scholarly Computer (ISC). See below, 149-157 for the discussion of the use of γάρ in ancient literature.

Metzger maintained that it is possible that the evangelist used the verb ἐφοβοῦντο γάρ to mean "they were afraid of."[4] If ἐφοβοῦντο was intended as "they were afraid of" in 16:8, then it is obvious that something is missing.

This chapter will seek to answer the questions raised by Metzger by discussing the scholarship that argued "the Gospel of Mark ended with 16:8."[5] This chapter will consist of six sections. The first section will discuss the use of γάρ in the ending of clauses, sentences, and paragraphs in ancient literature, both biblical and secular. The importance of this section is the confirmation of γάρ ending sentences from the eighth century B. C. to the fourteenth century A. D.[6] The second section will survey three studies that discounted the textual evidence of all the options other than the short ending. The next three sections will approach the ending of Mark from three methodological approaches: (1) The third section will discuss select scholars who apply form-critical analysis to their conclusions; (2) The fourth section will discuss select scholars who apply redaction-critical analysis to their conclusions; and (3) The fifth section will discuss select scholars who apply literary-critical analysis to their conclusions. Each of these sections will have a sectional critique, with the exception of the first section. A chapter summary will conclude the chapter.

---

[4]Ibid. Metzger said that the evangelist used ἐφοβοῦντο to mean "they were afraid of" in four other places in the Second Gospel, but Metzger did not cite these references.

[5]Julius Wellhausen, *Einleitung in die drei ersten Evangelien* (Berlin: Druck und Verlag von Georg Reimer, 1903), p. 146. The German reads," Mit 16,8 endet das Evangelium Marci." See also Joachim Gnilka, *Das Evangelium nach Markus*, vol. 2 (Köln: Benziger, 1979), p. 350.

[6]See Appendix B for a listing of the use of γάρ in ending sentences in ancient literature.

The Use of γάρ in Ancient Writings:
Canonical and Secular Literature

Several works were produced that discuss the significance of the syntax of Markan ending(s) as well as the theological implications. The often debated syntactical question is whether γάρ can end a work or not.[7] Several scholars argued on a literary basis that Mark could not have ended his Gospel with γάρ,[8] for such an abrupt ending was not common at the time in which the Second Gospel was written.[9] Most scholars in recent years, however, have attested to the authenticity of the 16:8 ending, with γάρ concluding the Gospel.[10]

---

[7]It is unfortunate that the *Theological Dictionary of the New Testament* did not include an article on γάρ and its use. The only reference to γάρ was in the article Horst Balz, "φοβέω" *TDNT*, vol. 9 ed.. and trans Geoffrey W. Bromiley (Grand Rapids, Michigan: Wm. B. Eerdmans Publishing Company, 1984 rpt.), pp. 210-211.

[8]See H. B. Swete, *The Gospel According to St. Mark* (London: Macmillan and Company, Ltd., 1898), p. 399; B. H. Streeter, *The Four Gospels* (London: Macmillan and Company, Ltd., 1924), pp. 335-364; R. R. Ottley, "ἐφοβοῦντο γάρ, Mark XVI 8." *Journal of Theological Studies*, 27 (1926), 407-409; C. H. Kraeling, "A Philological Note on Mark 16:8," *Journal of Biblical Literature*, 44 (1925), 357; H. J. Cadbury, "Mark 16:8," *JBL*, 46 (1927), 344f.; W. L. Knox, "The Ending of St. Mark's Gospel," *Harvard Theological Review*, 35 (1942), 13-23; Vincent Taylor, *The Gospels* (London: The Epworth Press, 1938), p. 49f.; idem., *The Gospel According to St. Mark*, 2nd ed., Thornapple Commentaries (Grand Rapids: Baker Book House, 1981), p. 610; and Frederick W. Danker, "Postscript to the Markan Secrecy Motif," *Concordia Theological Monthly*, 38 (1967), 26.

[9]According to Taylor, Knox argued that there is no parallel in the beginning of Mark, in the conclusion of any other Markan pericope, or in Jewish and Hellenistic literature in general. Taylor, *Mark*, p. 609, stated that the hypothesis implies by pure accident Mark lighted on a conclusion which 'suits the technique of a highly sophisticated type of modern literature'. See also W. L. Knox, "The Ending of St. Mark's Gospel," *HTR*, 35 (1942), 13-23.

[10]See for example Hugh Anderson, *The Gospel of Mark*, The New Century Bible Commentary (Grand Rapids: Wm. B. Eerdmans, 1976); Thomas E. Boomershine and G. L. Bartholomew, "The Narrative Technique of Mark 16:8," *JBL*, 100 (2, 1981), 213-223; Werner Kelber, *Mark's Story of Jesus* (Philadelphia: Fortress Press, 1979), p.

Sentences in normal continual prose in Attic Greek are obligatory linked, 60 per cent of the time by three postpositive particles δέ, γάρ, adn σύν.[11] The word γάρ is a compound of γέ and ἄρα and is usually postpositive. According to A. T. Robertson, ἄρα was originally correspondence and later inference.[12] γέ, therefore, can function as an intensive particle in either one of these ideas. It is an error to approach the study of γάρ with the idea that it is always an illative and never a causal particle.[13]

The New Testament use of γάρ is generally in accord with that of the classic period. D. B. Monro exhibited γάρ as explanatory of something just mentioned; a usage that is common in Homer.[14] In such a manner, γάρ is in a subordinate or exceptional use: (1) in order to introduce an explanation,[15] or (2) as inversion, by which the clause with γάρ precedes the fact explained. By inversion, the writer states something that leads up to the main point.[16] D. B. Monro added, "γάρ serves to indicate the clauses in which it is used as a reason

---

85; Ed Meyer, *Ursprung und Anfange des Christentum*, vol. 1 (Stuttgart and Berlin: 1921-1923), pp. 13-18; and J. Wellhausen, *Einleitung in die drei ersten Evangelien*, 2nd ed. (Berlin: 1911), p. 137.

[11]F. W. Householder, "Ancient Greek," *Word Classes*, eds. A. J. B. N. Reichbing, E. M. Uhlenbeck and W. Sidney Allen (Amsterdam: North-Holland Publishing Company, p. 122.

[12]A. T. Robertson, *A Grammar of the Greek New Testament in the Light of Historical Research* (New York: Hodder & Stoughton, 1915), p. 1190.

[13]Ibid.

[14]See D. B. Monro, *A Grammar of the Homeric Dialect* (Oxford: The Clarendon Press, 1891), pp. 316-317.

[15]Ibid., p. 317.

[16]Ibid.

or explanation, usually of something just mentioned or suggested."[17] As a subordinate particle, γάρ introduces a mere explanation, which was a common usage in Attic Greek.

γάρ is often an exception to the rule that the subordinating conjunction stands at the beginning of the dependent clause. According to F. Blass and A. Debrunner: "In such cases elements belonging to the subordinate clause which are to be emphasized precede the conjunction."[18]

H. E. Dana and Julius R. Mantey stated that γάρ "is most frequently used in the illative sense introducing a reason."[19] They have concluded that γάρ is the regular connective for two coordinate clauses[20] which bear to each other some relation of cause and effect, or reason and conclusion.[21] The illative sense, therefore, appears as the best explanation in Mark 16:8.

Two points should be noted: (1) Some scholars contended the rarity of γάρ ending sentences, however, Horst Balz confirmed that short sentences ending with

---

[17]   Ibid, p. 316.

[18]F. Blass and A. Debrunner, *A Greek Grammar of the New Testament and Other Early Christian Literature: A Translation and Revision of the Ninth-Tenth German Edition Incorporating Supplementary Notes of A. Debrunner*, trans. Robert W. Funk (Chicago: the University of Chicago Press, 1961), p. 251.

[19]H. E. Dana and Julius R. Mantey, *A Manual Grammar of the Greek New Testament* (New York: The Macmillan Company, 1957 rpt.), p. 243.

[20]See also William Douglas Chamberlain, *An Exegetical Grammar of the Greek New Testament* (Grand Rapids, Michigan: Baker Book House, 1987 rpt.), p. 148. Chamberlain held that these two clauses are of equal rank of importance though the relationship between them may be different.

[21]Ibid., p. 153 and Dana and Mantey, *A Manual Grammar of the Greek New Testament*, p. 274.

γάρ were common.[22] Mark 16:8 is not the only sentence in the New Testament that ends with γάρ, for John 13:13 also ends with γάρ: ὑμεῖς φωνεῖτέ με Ὁ κύριος, καὶ καλῶς λέγετε, εἰμὶ γάρ (2) The use of γάρ with a question mark occurred in association with the relative pronoun ἤ, the interrogative pronoun τί, the interrogative adverb πῶς, and the negative adverb οὐ. In the research of γάρ ending sentences on the ISC,[23] I found that one thousand and five sentences end with γάρ followed by a period and roughly 500 sentences end with γάρ followed by a question mark.[24]

F. W. Householder stated, "γάρ occurs two thirds of the time or oftener, near the beginning of a sentence in second, third, or fourth position."[25] The ISC showed γάρ as postpositive in even farther positions at the end of sentences: there

---

[22]See Balz, "φοβέω," p. 211, n. 116.

[23]The ISC is a special-purpose computer with multilingual word processing capabilities. The ISC was designed for classicists and humanists who work with ancient texts, and allows users to search texts at a high rate of speed for multiple character strings.

[24]I gave the approximate number of sentences ending with "γάρ" because Αγαρ (Genesis 16:1), Σωγαρ (Numbers 7:23), and several examples of Ἀγαρ occasionally appear when the search command for "γάρ" is executed.

[25]Householder, "Ancient Greek," p. 121. Of the 1005 occurrences of sentences ending with γάρ catalogued in the ISC, 864 of these sentences that end with γάρ have γάρ postpositive in the second position. The ISC has cataloged seventy-five sentences with γάρ postpositive in the third position.

are eight examples in the fifth position,[26] six in the sixth position,[27] one in the seventh position,[28] and two in the eighth position.[29]

---

[26]See Alexis "Fragmenta," *Comicorum Atticorum fragmenta*, vol. 2, ed. T. Kock (Leipzig: Teubner, 1884), p. 95, and Alexis, "Fragmenta," *Fragmenta comicorum Graecorum*, vol. 3, ed. A. Meineke (Berlin: De Gruyter, 1970 rpt.), p. 1, "νὴ τὸν Δί᾽ ἦν γάρ ." See also Anonyma in Aristotelis Artem Rhetoricam Commentaria, "In Aristotelis artem rhetoricam commentarium," *Anonymi et Stephani in artem rhethoricum commentaria*, Commentaria Aristotlem Graeca, vol. 21, ed. H. Rabe (Berlin: Reimer, 1896), p. 241, "τὸ δὲ ἀντὶ τοῦ γάρ."; Athenaeus "*The Deipnosophistae*, vol.2, trans Charles Burton Gulick, The Loeb Classical Library (Cambridge, Massachusetts: Harvard University Press, 1987 rpt.), p. 108, "διαφέρει τῷ μαγείρῳ τοῦτο γάρ."; Eustathius "Commentarii ad Homer Iliadem (lib. Σ–Ω), *Eustathii archiepiscopi Thessalonicensis commentarii ad Homer Iliadem*, vol. 4, ed. G. Stallbaum (Leipzig: Weigel, 1830), p. 469, "οὕτως καὶ ἀπὸ τοῦ γάρ."; Menander, "Fragmenta longiora apud alios auctores servata," *Menandri reliquiae selectae*, ed. F. H. Sandbach (Oxford: Clarendon Press, 1972), p. 334, "οὐκ εἴρηκά σοι τουτὶ γάρ" and p. 397, "διαφέρει τῶι μαγείρωι τοῦτο γάρ."; and Menandri, "Comparatio Menandri et Philistionis," *Menandri Sententiae* (Leipzig: Teubner, 1964), p. 1, "ψυναῖκας οἱ θάπτοντες εὐτυχοῦσι γάρ."

[27]See Antiphanes, "Fragmenta," *Comicorum Atticorum fragmenta*, vol. 2, ed. T. Kock (Leipzig: Teubner, 1884), p. 26, and "Fragmenta," *Fragmenta comicorum Graecorum*, vol. 3, ed. A. Meineke (Berlin: De Gruyter, 1970 rpt.), p. 1, "ἐπὶ τὸ τάριχός ἐστιν ὡρμηκυῖα γάρ." See also Athanasius, "Expositions in Psalms," *Patrologiae Curseus Completus* (Series Graeca), vol. 27, ed. J. P. Migne (Paris: Migne, 1857), p. 197, "βαρύς ἐστιν ἡμῖν καὶ βλεπόμενος γάρ."; Athenaeus *The Deipnosophistae*, vol. 2, p.42, "διὰ δὲ τὸ κνισὸν κακοστομαχώτερος γάρ."; Athenaeus, *The Deipnosophistae*, vol. 4, LCL (Cambridge, Massachusetts: Harvard University Press, 1957 rpt.), p. 38, "ἐπὶ τὸ τάριχός ἐστιν ὡρμηκυῖα γάρ."; and Joannes, "In Aristotelis physicorum libros commentaria," *Ioannis Philoponi in Aristotelis physicorum libros octp commentaria*, Commentaria in Aristotelem Graeca, vol. 17, ed. M. Hayduck (Berlin: Reimer, 1888), p. 834, "ὁ δὲ 'δέ' ἀντὶ τοῦ γάρ."

[28]Eustratius, "In analyticorum posteriorum librum secundum commentarium," *Eustratii in analyticorum posteriorum librum secundum commentarium*, Commentariain Aristotelem Graeca, vol. 21, ed. M. Hayduck (Berlin: Reimer, 1907), p.188, "ὡς εἶναι τὸ δὲ ἀντὶ τοῦ γάρ."

[29]See Aelius Herodianus et Pseudo-Herodinus, "Περὶ Ἰλιακῆς προσῳδίας," *Grammatici Graeci*, vol. 3, ed. A. Lentz (Hildesheim: Olms, 1965 rpt.), p. 100, "κεῖται γάρ καὶ ὁ δὲ ἀντὶ τοῦ γάρ." This is technically two γάρ phrases, one γάρ in second

Single word sentences are a common phenomenon in the Greek language. Such sentences consist of verbs that have an understood subject (an example is λέγω "I say" where the subject is the understood first person singular pronoun located in the verb ending). Such sentences are grammatically correct and proper. It would be grammatically correct to have a two word sentence or phrase that was made up of a conjunction and a verb. ἐφοβοῦντο γάρ[30] (for they were afraid) would be a legitimate phrase or sentence as would καὶ ἐφοβοῦντο (and they were afraid). The point of this observation is if the Gospel of Mark ended with καὶ ἐφοβοῦντο, it is less likely that the question of the ending of Mark would have been as great of an issue as it now is with the particle ending the work in ἐφοβοῦντο γάρ. Since γάρ is usually a postpositive word, and single word phrases and sentences do exist, there is no rule of grammar to object to a sentence or phrase ending with γάρ.

If a sentence can end with γάρ, there is no reason that a paragraph, chapter, or work can end with γάρ. The ISC displayed γάρ on 74 occasions concluding paragraphs in selected ancient texts. It is obvious that some of these occurrences are questionable, but in a random selection, γάρ was the legitimate concluding word of select paragraphs. Note the following two examples:

Homer *The Odyssey XVIII*, 177-186

---

position and the other in sixth\eighth. By rule (postpositives cannot stand first in a clause) the second γάρ can be assumed in eighth position. See also ὥστε τὴν αὐτὴν ἄγε λαβὼν κάμὲ–δίκαιον γάρ in Lucian, "Hermontimus," *Lucian*, vol. 6, trans. K. Kilburn, LCL (Cambridge, Massachusetts: Harvard University Press, 1968 rpt.), p. 284. The hyphenated κάμὲ–δίκαιον places γάρ postpositive to δίκαιον in the translation, "So take and lead me too along the same path-that would be only right," there is no rule of grammar that would argue γάρ as postpositive to a hyphenated word or phrase as in this case.

[30]There are 354 examples of two word sentences ending in γάρ, in the literature of the canon of the ISC.

Τὴν δ᾽ αὖτε προσέειπε περίφρων Πηνελόπεια· "Εὐρυνόμη,
μὴ ταῦτα παραύδα, κηδομένη περ, χρῶτ᾽ ἀγλαΐπτεσθαι καὶ
ἐπιχρίεσθαι ἀλοιφῇ· ἀγλαΐην γὰρ ἐμοί γε θεοί, τοὶ Ὄλυμπον
ἔχουσιν, ὤλεσαν, ἐξ οὗ κεῖνος ἔβη κοίλῃς ἐνὶ νηυσίν. ἀλλά μοι
Αὐτονόην τε καὶ Ἱπποδάμειαν ἄνωχθι ἐλθέμεν ὄφρα κέ μοι
παρστήετον ἐν μεγάροισια· οἴη δ᾽ οὐκ εἴσειμι μετ᾽ ἀνερας·
αἰδέομαι γάρ."

    Ὣς ἄρ᾽ ἔφη, γρηῢς δὲ διὲκ μεγάροιο βεβήκει ἀγγελέουσα
γυναιξὶ καὶ ὀτρυνέουσα νέεσθαι. . . .[31]

Isocrates *To Demonicus*, 31-32

    Γίγνου πρὸς τοὺς πλησιάζοντας ὁμιλητυκός, ἀλλὰ μὴ
σεμνός· τὸν μὲν γὰρ τῶν ὑπεροπτικῶν ὄγκον μόλις ἄν οἱ δοῦλοι
καρτερήσριαν, τὸν δὲ τῶν ὁμιλητικῶν τρόπον ἅπαντεσ ἡδέως
ὑποφέρουσιν. ὁμιλητικὸς δ᾽ ἔσει μὴ δύσερις ὢν μνδὲ δυσάρεστος
υνδὲ πρὸς πάντας φιλόνικος, μηδὲ πρὸς τὰς τῶν πλησιαζόντων
ὀργὰς τραχέως ἀπαντῶν, μηδ᾽ ἄν ἀδίκως ὀργιζόμενοι τυγχάνωσιν,
ἀλλὰ θυμουμένοις μὲν αὐτοῖς εἴκων, πεπαυμένοις δὲ τῆς ὀργῆς
ἐτιπλήττων· μηδὲ παρὰ τὰ γελοῖα σπουδάζων, μηδὲ παρὰ τὰ
σπουδαῖα τοῖς γελοίοις χαίρων (τὸ γὰρ ἄκαιρον πανταχοῦ)· μηδὲ
τὰς χάριτας ἀχαρίστως χαριζόμενος, ὅπερ πάσχουσιν οἱ πολλοί,
ποιοῦντες μέν, ἀνδῶς δὲ τοῖς φίλοις ὑπουργοῦντες· μηδὲ φιλαίτιος
ὤν, βαρὺ γάρ, μηδὲ φιλεπιτιμητής, παροξυντικὸν γάρ.

    Μᾶλιστα μὲν εὐλαβοῦ τὰς ἐν τοῖς πότοις συνουσίας ἐάν
δὲ ποτέ σοι συμπέσῃ καιρός, ἐξανίστασο πρὸ μέθης. ὅταν γὰρ ὁ
νοῦς ὑπὸ οἵου διαφθαρῇ ταὐτὰ πάσχει τοῖς ἄρμασι τοῖς τοὺς
ἡνιόχους ἀποβαλοῦσιν· ἐκεῖνά τε γὰρ ἀτάκτως φέρεται
διαμαρτόντα τῶν εὐθυνούντων, ἥ το ψυχὴ πολλὰ σφάλλεται
διαφθαρείσης τῆς διανοίας. . . .[32]

---

[31]Homer, *The Odyssey*, vol. 2, trans. A. T. Murray, LCL (Cambridge,
Massachusetts: Harvard University Press, 1953), p. 210.

[32]Isocrates, *Isocrates*, vol. 1, trans. George Norlin, LCL (Cambridge,
Massachusetts: Harvard University Press, 1980), p. 22.

This is significant in that we are now arriving at a closer point of finding γάρ ending complete works. Plotinus concluded his thirty-second treatise (*Ennead* 5:5) with γάρ.

οὐδὲν ἔχον ἐν ἑαυτῷ, ἀλλὰ ἀμιγὲς πάντων καὶ ὑπὲρ πάντα καὶ αἴτιον τῶν πάντων. οὐ γὰρ δὴ κακοῦ τὸ καλὸν οὐδὲ τὰ ὄντα οὐδ᾽ ἐξ ἀδιαφόρων. κρεῖττον γὰρ τὸ ποιοῦν τοῦ ποιουμένου τελειότερον γάρ.[33]

Carl H. Kraeling observed that Pap. Oxy no. 1223, (a business document containing an order for certain goods, and quoting the rate of exchange) has a direct parallel to the end of Mark 16:8:

'Send and tell your people to hand over to me the remainder of the wine and one and a half units of the general account. ὁ ὁλοκόττινος νῦν μυ(ριάδων) βκ ἐστιν. Κατέβη γάρ. Do not neglect to send the boat or the sailor today. Fare-well.'[34]

According to Kraeling, the reference of the rate of exchange is parenthetical and the Κατέβη γάρ terminates the thought structure.[35] Kraeling stated: "Dr. Montgomery has kindly called my attention to the fact that it occurs also in the Peshitta . . . as . . . in John 13:13:

ܐܦܠܐ ܠܢ ܘܐܦ ܐܢܬܘܢ ܕܐܡܪܝܢ ܐܢܬܘܢ ܠܝ ܪܒܢ ܘܡܪܢ "[36]

---

[33]Plotinus, *Plotinus*, trans. A. H. Armstrong, LCL (Cambridge, Massachusetts: Harvard University Press, 1984), p. 196.

[34]Carl H. Kraeling, "A Philological Note on Mark 16:8," *JBL*, 44 (1925), 357.

[35]Ibid.

[36]Ibid.

The ISC did not list any ancient works that end with γάρ[37] except Mark 16:8 followed by 16:9-20 enclosed in the textual marks {{   }}.[38]

Textual Studies Which Discounted All but the Short Ending

The scholars who are surveyed in this section did not concentrate specifically on the ending of Mark, with the exception of J. K. Elliott.

Samuel Prideaux Tregelles

Samuel P. Tregelles was one of the earliest text-critics to argue that Mark ended his Gospel at 16:8, yet he did accept the verses of the longer ending as canonical.[39] Tregelles used the same Fathers that Burgon referred as used to denounce the authenticity and originality of the verses of the longer ending, with "later writers (especially Greeks), who, even though they copied from their predecessors, were competent to transmit the record of a fact."[40] He conceded that the testimony of Severus of Antioch may have been a "repetition of that already cited from Gregory of Nyssa; but if so, it is, at least, an approving quotation."[41]

---

[37]The reader should be aware that the canon of the ISC consists of corrected texts.

[38]This textual mark designates the enclosed passages as later additions to the text, but are also of evident antiquity and importance.

[39]Samuel Prideaux Tregelles, *An Account of the Printed Text of the Greek New Testament with Remarks on Its Revision Upon Critical Principles* (London: Samuel Bagster and Sons, 1854).

[40]Ibid., p. 247.

[41]Ibid., p. 249.

Tregelles correctly noted that both Eusebius and Victor of Antioch have τῇ μιᾷ in the place of πρώτῃ. He offered two explanations: (1) This usage may be accidental; or (2) These two Fathers may have commented on the longer ending without having the luxury of a copy before them, therefore, "they used τῇ μιᾷ as the more customary phraseology in the New Testament."[42]

Tregelles further sought to add Jerome's name to the list of those who supported the short ending, by denouncing the argument that Jerome used the verses of the longer ending in connection with another concluding passage, for "it is at least remarkable that we have no other trace of such an addition at ver. 14."[43]

The testimonies of the Fathers established as a historic fact that in the early church the twelve verses of the longer ending were not a part of the Gospel. After rehearsing the Fathers who accepted the longer ending in their canon, Tregelles, countered:

> The early citation and use of this section, (16:9-20) and the place
> that it holds in the ancient versions in general, and in the MSS.,
> sufficiently show, on historical grounds, that it had a place, and was
> transmitted as a part of the second Gospel.[44]

A question about the style of the verses of the longer ending has frequently been raised. Tregelles conceded that arguments of style are often very fallacious, and that by themselves prove nothing, but in conjunction with external evidence, these internal considerations, such as style, manner, verbal expression, and

---

[42]Ibid., p. 250.

[43]Ibid.

[44]Ibid., p. 253. This should not be interpreted that he accepted the longer ending as original to the Gospel of Mark.

connection, possess very great weight.[45] The phraseology of the evangelist possessed characteristics that did not appear in the longer ending. The longer ending has some peculiarities that distinguish it from Mark 1:1-16:8: (1) including the phrase πρώτῃ σαββάτου of verse 16:9 in comparison to τῇ μιᾷ τῶν σαββάντων of verse 16:2; (2) in both verse 16:10 and 14 sentences are conjoined without the copulative, which is contrary to Markan usage; (3) the abnormal use of ἐκεῖνος; and (4) the periodic structure of the last two verses is such as occurs only in Mark 14:38.[46] Tregelles also noted that several words, expressions, and constructions also occur in the longer ending that do not occur in any other part of the Gospel: "πορεύομαι (thrice), θεάομαι (twice), ἀπίστεω (twice) ἕτερος, παρακολουθέω, βλάπτω, ἐπακολουθέω, συνεργέω, βεβαιόω, πανταχοῦ, μετὰ ταῦτα, ἐν τῷ ὀνόματι, ὁ κύριος, as applied absolutely to Christ (twice)."[47] None of these points of phraseology alone, except for the first, posses much weight, however, these points of phraseology confined to twelve verses do possess much weight against Mark origin. Tregelles concluded, "By a comparison of other portions of St. Mark, it will be found that many chapters must be taken together before we shall find any list of examples as many . . . (as) in these few verses."[48]

As to the age-old objection that 16:8 could not be the intended ending, for γάρ was not a suitable ending, Tregelles responded, "Would this be transmitted as a fact by good witnesses, if there had not been real grounds for regarding it to

---

[45]Ibid., p. 256.

[46]Ibid.

[47]Tregelles, *An Account of the Printed Text*, p. 257.

[48]Ibid.

be true?"[49] It is obvious "such a peculiarity would have been invented"[50] by Mark.

In conclusion, Tregelles held that the longer ending should be viewed as canonical,[51] still, the fact remains "that the book of Mark himself extends no further than ἐφοβοῦντο γάρ, xvi. 8."[52]

Robert Morgenthaler

Robert Morgenthaler argued, based on textual grounds, that the verses 16:9-20 did not belong to Mark and he sought to demonstrate that word statistical research further supported this view.[53] He listed several words, expressions, and constructions that occurred in the longer ending that did not occur in any other part of the Gospel; notably πορεύεσθαι, which he concluded that it would be amazing for Mark to use this word three times in an uncompounded form in the longer ending, because he elsewhere used readily used compounds.[54]

Morgenthaler made several grammatical observations including: (1) Mark frequently used the dative plural αὐτοῖς, εἰ μή, and ἵνα, however, he found that αὐτοῖς appeared three times in the longer ending, while εἰ μή, and ἵνα were not

---

[49]Ibid.

[50]Ibid., p. 258.

[51]Arguments against this point were discussed in chapter 3, in the chapter summary.

[52]Tregelles, *An Account of the Printed Text*, p. 258.

[53]Robert Morgenthaler, *Statistik des neutestamentlichen Wortschatzes* (Zürich: Gotthelf-Verlag, 1958), pp. 58-60.

[54]Ibid., p. 59.

used. (2) Mark was fond of foreign words, but no foreign words occur in the longer ending. Morgenthaler acknowledged that the section was too short to decide on the authenticity of the longer ending. (3) The frequency of the occurrence of καὶ in the longer ending is half what it is in 1:1-16:8; δέ occurs twice as often in the longer ending as in the rest of Mark.[55] Morgenthaler was confident that with the longer ending "a style is written here completely different than appears anywhere else in Mark's Gospel."[56] Based on his word-statistic method, Morgenthaler concluded:

> Indications for authenticity are practically nonexistent. On the other hand the indications of unauthenticity are so numerous and so weighty, that one aught to draw the conclusion that Mk. 16:9-20, judged on word-statistical evidence, could never had been written by the same hand as the rest of the Gospel of Mark.[57]

James Keith Elliott

The most recent scholar who investigated the phraseological discrepancies between Mark 1:1-16:8 and both the longer, and the shorter endings, and the Freer logion was J. K. Elliott.[58] He provided a detailed list (with the help of the

---

[55]Ibid., pp. 59-60.

[56]Ibid., p. 60. The German reads: "Hier wird ein vollkommen anderer Stil geschrieben als sonst überall im Markusevangelium."

[57]Ibid. The German reads: "Jetzt erst haben wir den ganzen Abschnitt Mk. 16, 9-20 wortstatistisch nach allein Seiten hin auf seine Echtheit hin geprüft. Indizien für eine Echtheit finden sich praktisch keine. Hingegen sind sie die Unechtheitsindizien so mannigfaltig und so massiv, dass man den Schluss wird ziehen dürfen, dass Mk. 16, 9-20, nach den wortstatistischen Ergebnissen beurteilt, niemals von derselben Hand geschrieben sein kann wie das übrige Markusevangelium."

[58]James Keith Elliott, "The Text and Language of the Endings to Mark's Gospel," *Theologische Zeitschrift*, 27 (1971), 255-262.

Institute für neutestamentliche Textforschung in Munster) of textual evidence, which supported: (1) the longer ending, (2) the longer ending marked with asterisks, obeli, or with critical notes, (3) the shorter ending preceding the longer ending, (4) the shorter ending alone following 16:8, and (5) the short ending at 16:8.[59]

Elliott agreed with Linnemann that Morgenthaler's statistical methodology was vulnerable,[60] however, he continued, "Linnemann has selected a simple target because the evidence in the 'Statistik' for the secondary nature of the longer ending is by no means exhaustive."[61] Elliott concluded his critique of Linnemann, "If Linnemann had tried to argue against the full evidence (of language and style) it would have proved impossible to maintain that part of the longer ending belonged to the original gospel."[62]

The most pertinent part of Elliott's research in the question of the Markan ending was his detailed analysis of the language and style of the above mentioned endings compared to Mark and other New Testament writings, which concluded that these endings could not have been a part of the original Gospel of Mark.[63] Elliott found twenty words and nine phrases in the longer ending that did not occur elsewhere in Mark. As to be expected, he found six words and three phrases

---

[59]Ibid., pp. 255-256.

[60]Elliott listed a few examples of the problems that Linnemann found in the Morganthaler's method: (1) the number of examples of καί in the longer ending is lower than the average for the canonical Mark whereas the total number of occurrences of δέ is greater than in Mark, and (2) the longer ending is non-Markan, based on the absence of foreign words. See ibid., p. 257.

[61]Ibid.

[62]Ibid.

[63]Ibid., pp. 258-262.

in the shorter ending and eight words and one phrase in the Freer logion that did not occur in Mark 1:2-16:8.

Critique

Each of these scholars provided extensive studies showing the dissimilarities between Mark 1:1-16:8 and the optional endings that select manuscripts support other than the 16:8 ending (i.e., (1) the longer ending; (2) the shorter ending; and (3) the Freer Logion) based on stylistic and philological discrepancies. Both proponents and adversaries of such studies argued that by themselves these studies are fallacious, and prove nothing, however, the points style and philology used in conjunction with external evidence (i.e., Patristic and textual support) possess much weight, especially when one considers the confined space and large number of occurrences.

Especially damaging to these studies as arguments defending the short ending was, even though Tregelles definitely stated that Mark ended with 16:8,[64] he contended that the appendage of the longer ending should be considered as canonical. Morgenthaler and Elliott were also nullified by the argument that neither of these scholars blatantly claimed that 16:8 was the authentic ending of Mark. All that these latter two did, was to argue against the authenticity of the alternate appendages, especially the longer ending.

Tregelles cited several Fathers (including Eusebius, Victor of Antioch, and Jerome) as defending the shorter ending, who have also been cited as untrustworthy defenders of this portion.[65] As seen in chapter two above, each of

---

[64]Tregelles, *An Account of the Printed Text*, p. 258.

[65]John Burgon, *The Last Twelve Verses of the Gospel According to Saint Mark* (Oxford: James Parker and Co., 1871), pp. 38-69.

these, except for Jerome offered defensible positions for Tregelles' argument in favor of the short ending.

Morgenthaler's word-statistical method has received some negative criticism.[66] It is notable that some of those who have criticized Morgenthaler's approach have used his method to defend their point.[67]

Elliott's argument, which was more of a complete analysis of the longer ending than those of Morgenthaler or Tregelles, was more accurate than Morgenthaler's in the frequency of use of problematic words or phrases, and furthermore, was more inclusive of examples. He succeeded in proving his point of the discrepancy, between Mark 1:1-16:8 and the longer ending, of style and philology, yet his work, as did the ones preceding it, had its limitations: "there is . . . no thoroughgoing analysis of the language and style of these endings compared with New Testament language in general or with Mark's gospel in particular."[68] Such a project would either add credence to these studies or invalidate their testimony.

The studies of this section were helpful in defending the short ending by eliminating the three alternate appendages, however, on their own they did nothing to settle the question, "Was Mark 16:8 the authentic and intended ending of the Gospel?," for this section could easily be used as a basis for the argument for a lost, mutilated, or incomplete ending. The methods of the scholars of this section

---

[66]See above p. 162, n. 60.

[67]See William Reuben Farmer, *The Last Twelve Verses of Mark* (Cambridge: Cambridge University Press, 1974), pp.81-103; Eta Linnemann, "Der Wiedergefundene Markusschluss," *Zeitschrift für Theologie und Kirche*, 66 (3, 1969), 278-284; and Elliott, "The Text and Language of the Endings, 258-262.

[68]Elliott, "The Text and Language of the Endings," 257.

used in conjunction with the results of the previous section on γάρ endings (see above, pages 149-157) do make a strong argument for the short ending.

Form-critical Approaches to the Short Ending of Mark

The scholars who are surveyed in this section did not concentrate specifically on the ending of Mark, yet each applies the method of form criticism to arrive at a conclusion concerning the ending of Mark. The space dedicated to each of these scholars does not reflect the importance of one over the other, but instead reflects the material each scholar has produced that directly pertains to the subject of the present chapter.

Martin Dibelius

Martin Dibelius maintained that Mark the evangelist replaced the narrative of a post-resurrection appearance of Jesus to Peter "by the Legend of an empty grave, for this seems . . . to be the conclusion of Mark's gospel."[69] He assumed that the earliest Passion story contained at least one appearance of Jesus to the disciples.[70] He further assumed that 16:8 was the authentic conclusion to the Gospel of Mark, "therefore . . . the text as contained in the old MSS., Codices Vaticanus and Sinaiticus, as well as the Sinaitic Syriac, is complete."[71]

---

[69]Martin Dibelius, *Die Formgeschichte des Evangeliums* (Tübingen: Verlag J. C. B. Mohr (Paul Siebeck), 1933), p. 190. According to Dibelius, "There is a genuine legendary note in the story: concern about the stone; miraculous help in the fact that it is already rolled away; a divine interpretation of the whole given by the angels; the flight of the fearful women."

[70]This was based on the verses of Mark 14:28; 1 Cor. 15:5, which were probably written at an earlier date; Luke 24:34; John 21; and the Gospel of Peter. See also ibid., p. 181, where Dibelius confirmed that "the composition of the Passion was obviously earlier than Mark."

[71]Ibid. Dibelius stated that "the earliest Passion story must have had another conclusion than that now found in Mark, for the reference to the appearance of the Risen

Dibelius concluded that Mark 16:1-6, 8 belonged to a Legend, in that a secret miracle occurred, however, 16:7 did not belong to it, for it appears that at this point Mark joined the Legend of the grave with the traditions that were already present in the church.[72] The last words of the Gospel, "The women said nothing to anyone, for they were afraid," had a literary significance in "that the narrative of the empty tomb was still unknown in wide areas."[73] According to Dibelius, the purpose of the empty tomb tradition (that did not originate with Mark) was to confirm the resurrection by the mere fact of the empty tomb.[74] He continued, "The fact that the women are mentioned at the beginning, superfluously after xv,47, seems to prove that it was originally independent of this connection."[75]

Ernst Lohmeyer

Ernst Lohmeyer has defended the short ending based on both internal and external evidence. The external evidence which Lohmeyer appealed to, has often

---

Lord in Mark xiv, 28, seems strange. The Gospel does not tell of an appearance, but only refers to it again in Mark xvi, 7, 'You will see him there as he told you.' To a certain extent the Easter happenings in Galilee are by that put outside the book."

[72]Ibid., n. 1. See also John Dominic Crossan, "Empty Tomb and Absent Lord," *The Passion in Mark: Studies in Mark 14-16*, ed. by Werner H. Kelber (Philadelphia: Fortress Press, 1976), p. 138.

[73]Ibid., p. 190.

[74]Ibid. See also G. Mangatt, "At the Tomb of Jesus." *Biblebhashyam*, 3 (2, 1977), 91-96. Some scholars were diametrically opposed Dibelius view that Mark did not create the empty tomb tradition. See Neill Q. Hamilton, "Resurrection Tradition and the Composition of Mark," *JBL*, 84 (1965), 416. George Eldon Ladd opposed Dibelius' in that the empty tomb was never used to suggest the resurrection. See Ladd, *I Believe in the Resurrection of Jesus* (Grand Rapids: Wm. B. Eerdmans Publishing Co., 1975), p. 90.

[75]Dibelius, *Die Formgeschichte des Evangeliums*, p. 190.

been repeated, that both ℵ and B, the two oldest extant manuscripts, ended with 16:8 and that both Eusebius and Jerome testified to this phenomenon.[76] Lohmeyer added, "Matthew and Luke also knew of no continuation; since they followed the pattern of Mark more or less up to these sentences."[77]

Lohmeyer presented two frequently asked questions about the 16:8 ending:

If indeed the oldest tradition knew to talk about the appearances of the resurrected one (Jesus) [1 Cor. 15], how would it be possible that he didn't know or tell them? . . . 16:8 is not an ending according to its content; how can one close with the sentence: they said nothing to anyone, because they were afraid, how can the little word γάρ be the end of the Gospel?[78]

After listing several theories which answered the latter question negatively, Lohmeyer stated, "The questions have their important points answered in the explanation of 16:7f."[79] Lohmeyer maintained that the announcement of the angel in 16:7 did not announce the appearances of the resurrected one, which were pointed out by Paul and the Lukan reports, rather they announced "the near

---

[76]Ernest Lohmeyer, *Das Evangelium des Markus*, 15th ed. (Göttingen: Vandenhoeck und Ruprecht, 1959, pp. 358-359.

[77]Ibid., p. 359. The German reads, "Auch Mt und Lk haben keine Fortsetzung gekant; denn bis zu diesem Satz folgen sie, mehr oder minder frei, der Vorlage des Mk, von da ab führen ihre Erzählungen weit auseinander. See also Eduard Lohse, *Mark's Witness to Jesus Christ* (New York: Association Press, 1955), p. 92. Lohse earlier stated "Matthew and Luke, who both knew and used the Gospel of Mark, were acquainted with his narrative only up to this point," (Mark 16:8).

[78]Ibid. The German reads, "Wenn schon die älteste überlieferung von Erscheinungen des Auferstandenen zu reden wusste (I Kor 15:5 ff.), wie war es möglich, dass er sie nicht kannte oder nicht erzählte? . . . 6:8 ist seinem Inhalt nach kein Abschluss; wie kann man mit dem Satze schliessen: 'und sie sagten niemandem nichts; denn sie fürchteten sich' wie kann das Wörtchen γαιρ das Ende des Evangeliums sein?"

[79]Ibid. The German reads, "Die Fragen sind zu ihrem wichtigsten Teile bereits in der Erklärung von 16:7f beantwortet."

parousia of the Lord.''[80] The natural response to such a traumatic announcement would be that of silence and fear. Lohmeyer added that the reports of the appearances portray the crossing over from the "gospel of Jesus Christ" to the founding of the original church.[81] Where one sets the end of the "gospel of Jesus Christ" and the beginning of the church depends on the theological and historical opinions of the writer of the Gospel. Lohmeyer noted, "Paul had reckoned the appearances of the resurrected Jesus in 1 Cor 15:3-9 as κήρυγμα χριστοῦ,"[82] however, in other New Testament kerygmatic witnesses (i.e., Phil. 2:6; 1 Peter 3:18; and 1 Tim. 3:16) there was not mention of the appearances or of the resurrection. Even if these above mentioned formulations were written later, their witness is important, because it is not conceivable that the proofs for the resurrection should no longer have been important. The essence of the appearance stories lies in Jesus' words to Thomas in John 20:29, "Blessed are they who do not see and yet believe."[83] Lohmeyer continued, "is conceivable that a work that deals purely with 'the Gospel of Jesus Christ, the Son of God,' kept out the appearances of the resurrected one, of which Mark naturally knew, and ended with the heavenly announcement of the parousia of the Lord."[84]

---

[80]Ibid. The German reads, "die nahe Parusie des Herrn."

[81]Ibid.

[82]Ibid. The German reads, "Paulus hat mohl in I Kor 15:3-9 auch die Erscheinungen des Auferstandenen zum κήρυγμα χριστοῦ gerechnet."

[83]Ibid. Lohmeyer incorrectly cited John 20:30. Lohse confirmed the point by noting that with the words of the angel "He is risen," "is included everything that is essential to the faith of a Christian in His Lord." See Lohse, *Mark's Witness to Jesus Christ*, p 92.

[84]Ibid. The German reads, "ist es durchaus denkbar, dass ein Wert, das rein von "dem Evangelium Jesu Christi, des Sohnes Gottes" handelt, die Erscheinungen des Auferstandenen, von denen Mk selbstverständlich gemusst haben wird, ausschluss und in

The question arose, "Could there be an end of this work, which answers the content of the Gospel and the oldest ancient Christian beliefs?"[85] Lohmeyer continued that the appearances of the Lord were not the only argument for his resurrection, for "the story of the empty grave (with or without the appearances of the angel) served as the original Christians' proof for a long time."[86] In the context of a Markan silence on the post-resurrection appearances, it is notable that Acts is silent about the appearances of Jesus up to the ninth chapter, with the conversion and calling of Paul, and that the truth of these occurrences are covered with the implied phrase "of that we are witnesses."[87] Paul referred directly to the resurrection only once in Acts, (13:31) "(He) appeared to them over many days, who had come up from Galilee to Jerusalem with him." Lohmeyer concluded, "it is possible that the oldest Gospel only offered the proof of the empty tomb and does not report the appearances that belong to the history of the Apostles, although he knew of them," therefore, "with 16:8 the Gospel of Mark thus ends not only formally, but also in content."[88]

---

der himmlischen Ankündigung der Parusie des Herrn endete."

[85]Ibid. The German reads, "Könnte es einen Schluss dieses Werkes geben, der dem Inhalt des Evangeliums und dem ältesten urchristlichen Glauben reiner entspräche?"

[86]Ibid., p. 360. The German reads, "Gerade die Erzählung vom leeren Grabe (mit oder ohne Angelophanie) hat dem urchristlichen Glauben eine Zeit lang als vollgültiger Beweis gegolten."

[87]See Acts 2:32; 3:15; 5:32; and 10:39.

[88]Ibid. The German reads, "Mit 16:8 endet also das Mk-Evangelium nicht nur formal, sondern auch inhabtlich."

R. H. Lightfoot

R. H. Lightfoot proposed "that when copies of it (the Gospel of Mark) came into the hands of the first and third evangelists it ended at 16:8. 16:8 therefore is the oldest ending of the book we can trace."[89] For a period of time no special sanctity was attached to the texts of the books of the New Testament, therefore, both Matthew and Luke probably believed that their work would supersede the Gospel of Mark, since it lacked resurrection account.[90] Lightfoot was quick to point out "the message of the resurrection is indeed the cardinal content of Mark 16:1-8, especially verse 6."[91]

Lightfoot affirmed the "unlikely" absolute use of ἐφοβοῦντο, (for some argued that this verb needed a completing accusative or infinitive or a μή clause).[92] Several reconstructions regarded the women's fear due to the fear of the Jews or even the disciples' reaction to the news of their message. Lightfoot countered, "The whole tenor of 16:1-8 shows the amazement, flight, trembling, astonishment, and finally fear of the women to have been due to fear or dread of God, to fear caused by revelation."[93]

---

[89]Robert H. Lightfoot, *The Gospel Messages of St. Mark* (Oxford: Clarendon Press, 1952 rpt.), p. 80. See also idem., *History and Inter- pretation in the Gospels* (London: Hodder & Stoughton, 1934), p. 127.

[90]Lightfoot, *The Gospel Messages of St. Mark*, p. 83. The latter phrase of the above sentence is one of the primary arguments against the 16:8 ending, for some assumed that Mark 16:1-8 did not refer to the resurrection.

[91]Ibid., p. 84.

[92]Ibid., p. 86.

[93]Ibid., p. 88. The epiphany of Mark 4:35-41 parallels such divine fear as in Mark 16:1-8. See also John Paul Heil, *Meaning and Gospel Functions of Matt 14:22-33, Mark 6:45-52 and John 6:15b-21* (Rome: Biblical Institute Press, 1981), pp. 8-30; Rudolph Pesch, *Das Evangelium der Urgemeinde* (Freiburg: Herder, 1979), p. 219; and Wayne Stacy, "The Fear Motif in Mark" (Unpublished Ph.D. dissertation, The Southern

THE SHORT ENDINGS   171

Although fear and astonishment are usually the initial responses of humanity to a divine revelation, such fear and astonishment are not the purpose of revelation, and are undesirable for fear and astonishment occur because of a lack of understanding or insight. The Gospel of Mark consists of two parts: "In the first half of the book fear astonishment are caused more by . . . messianic acts, than by the teaching given,"[94] but in the second half the Gospel fear and astonishment are caused by messianic teachings (i.e., the confession at Caesarea Philippi). In the verses of Mark 16:1-8, the women were faced with both the action of his resurrection and by his divine teaching in verses 6 and 7; because of their imperfect faith and lack of understanding, the result was inevitable, "ἐφοβοῦντο γάρ." According to Lightfoot, the emphasis of 16:8 should not be the women conquering their fears, but the emphasis should be the "human inadequacy, lack of understanding, and weakness in the presence of supreme divine action and its meaning."[95]

Lightfoot maintained "that at Mark 16:8 the whole evangelic agreement ceases at one stroke (and this) may perhaps be additional evidence that the oldest gospel tradition did not necessarily include one or more accounts of a manifestation of the risen Lord."[96] The fact remains that Mark did give full expression to the resurrection in 16:1-8,[97] and he placed the three proclamations of the Passion with brief references to the resurrection. Mark 14:28 and 16:7

Baptist Theological Seminary, 1980), p. 155.

[94]Lightfoot, *The Gospel According to St. Mark*, p. 91.

[95]Ibid., p. 92.

[96]Ibid., p. 94.

[97]Ibid., p. 93. Also see p. 166, n. 74 above.

promise to the disciples a reunion with Jesus in Galilee.[98] Lightfoot contended, "An explanation of the passages is not unnatural, but is not necessary, and may be found to be only an assumption,"[99] for "Mark assumes throughout that his readers are acquainted with the root-facts of the Christian religion."[100] Mark 14:28 and 16:7 did not necessarily prepare for a story that must be told later, but represented the fact which the statement foretold.[101]

Lightfoot proposed that Mark's purpose in the ending was to emphasize the appropriateness, in response to God's revelation in the resurrection, of the awe or holy fear of God. He concluded, "The description of the reaction of the women throws into very strong relief the supremacy and greatness of the section's (16:1-8) central teaching, and that teaching is the . . . message of the Lord's victory and love."[102] Human failure and the need for understanding dominated the Gospel of Mark, however, "the divine foundation stands firm, and in this book has its final seal in the fact of the resurrection of the Lord."[103]

Critique

Form-critics portrayed Mark as an editor who pieced together Passion, the

---

[98]Ibid. See also Manfred Karnetzki, "Die galiläische Redaktion im Markusevangelium," *Zeitschrift für die neutestamentliche Wissenschaft*, 52 (1961), 256.

[99]Ibid., p. 95. See also Raymond E. Brown, *The Virginal Conception and the Bodily Resurrection of Jesus* (New York: Paulist Press, 1973), p. 123.

[100]Lightfoot, *The Gospel Messages of St. Mark.*, p. 95.

[101]Ibid. See also idem., *History and Interpretation in the Gospels*, p. 85, n. 1.

[102]Lightfoot, *The Gospel Messages of St. Mark*, p. 96.

[103]Ibid., pp. 96-97.

empty tomb, and early church traditions, while omitting post-resurrection appearances. These select scholars accepted the short ending based on the often cited textual support such as ℵ and B complimented by patristic support from Fathers such as Eusebius and Jerome. (The argument that Jerome was a legitimate defender of the short ending was raised in chapter two).[104] Markan priority was widely accepted by these form-critics. These same critics affirmed that the Gospel of Mark complete with 16:8, for the empty tomb was first hand proof of the resurrection.

The theories of these form-critics are not without problem. Both Dibelius and Lohmeyer argued that the empty tomb was proof of the resurrection. The skeptic could always respond that the disciples stole the body of Jesus' in order to make it appear that Jesus fulfilled his prophecy of his resurrection. Lohmeyer defended the empty tomb tradition by comparing its essence to that of John 20:29, that being faith.[105]

These critics raised many questions about Mark 16:7. Dibelius claimed that it was a part of the empty tomb tradition, Lohmeyer pointed that this verse was an announcement of the parousia, and Lightfoot held that it was a prediction of the resurrection. Dibelius did not give an explanation to his speculation. Lohmeyer's interpretation of 16:7 being an announcement of the parousia raises several questions. Such a theory would be dependent on the empty grave representing a post-resurrection appearance, for how could one talk of the parousia without including the resurrection in 16:1-8? Lightfoot understood 14:28 and 16:7 as prophetic to Jesus' meeting with the disciples in Galilee. Why could these verses not be interpreted as a narrator's hindsight to an event that he was aware

---

[104]See above chapter 2, pp. 34-37.

[105]See above p. 168, n. 83.

of? Based on these views of 16:7, Lightfoot's position is contextually more reasonable.

The value of form criticism in connection with the short ending, if we accept the empty tomb as without scandal, is that it called for one to accept 16:6-8 as the initial resurrection witness. The emphasis is an understanding of the resurrection by faith. Form criticism pointed out that the post resurrection appearances were profuse in traditions, to the point it became unnecessary to comment on since it was common knowledge. A second value of the form-critical scholars is that Markan priority is not essential to argument for the short ending. If Mark suppressed the appearance accounts of tradition, it is also obvious that he suppressed the appearance narratives of Matthew and/or Luke, according to their priority to Mark.

Redaction-critical Approaches to the Short Ending of Mark

The scholars of this section, as in the previous section, do not concentrate specifically on the ending of Mark, but each applies the method of redaction criticism to arrive at at a viable conclusion concerning the ending of Mark. Though these scholars are concerned with the evolution of traditional resurrection stories, the center of their interest lies in the authors' *sitz im leben* and how this affected the writing of the Gospel of Mark.

Willi Marxsen

Willi Marxsen has proposed that the primary motif in the ending of Mark is the tension between speech and silence. According to Marxsen, it is probable that Mark "appended 16:1-8 to the passion narrative furnished him by the tradition, since this pericope conflicts with 15:42-47 in many details."[106]

---

[106]Willi Marxsen, *Mark the Evangelist: Studies in the Redaction History of the Gospel*, trans. James Boyce, Donald Juel, William Poehlmann, and Roy A. Harrisville (Nashville: Abingdon Press, 1969), p. 76. See also Rudolf Pesch, *Naherwartungen:*

Marxsen contended that 16:7 did not belong to the report of the empty tomb and could easily be removed from the text.[107] Mark added the angel's commission to the women (16:7) in order to complete the motif of Jesus going before the disciples into Galilee (14:28). This complicated matters by implying that the ending emphasized the women's disobedience.[108] Marxsen concluded the point by noting, "the real difficulty in the text did not at all originate with the (Markan) alteration (of the traditional material) of vs. 8 , but with the insertion of vs. 7."[109]

Marxsen questioned whether the Galilean tradition of the resurrection narrative would have ever existed if Mark had not inserted 16:7 into 16:1-6, 8, since this verse formed the sole basis of the post-resurrection appearances in Galilee. According to Marxsen, if Mark inserted 16:7 into an already existing context, then we are dealing with the latest stratum reflecting Mark's own situation and time, therefore, "in Mark's context this passage can only refer to the expected Parousia."[110] If Mark intended 16:7 to prepare for the parousia, then

---

Tradition und Redaktion in Mk 13 (Düsseldorf: Patmos-Verlag, 1968), p. 233.

[107]Ibid. See also Frans Neirynck, "Mark 16:1-8: tradition et rédaction, pt. 1," *Ephemerides Theologicae Lovanienses*, 56 (1980), 68-72.

[108]Marxsen, *Mark the Evangelist*, p. 76.

[109]Ibid., p. 77.

[110]Marxsen, *Mark the Evangelist*, p. 85. See also David Blatherwick, "The Markan Silhouette?," *New Testament Studies*, 17 (1970), 18 and Tibor Horvath, "The Early Markan Tradition on the Resurrection," *Revue de l'Universite d'Ottawa*, 43 (3, 1973), 445-448.

its coming cannot be referred to after 16:8, because the phrase ὄψεσθε is future for Mark. The parousia is still to come.[111]

It is an error to say that Mark lacked Easter narrative, for "What is to prevent our understanding 16:1-6, 8 as an 'Easter narrative?'"[112] Marxsen contended that if we assume a polemic concerning the empty tomb, this Easter narrative is obvious.[113] The insertion of 16:7 mandated that the resurrection take on a provisional character, which will be consummated by the parousia. προάγειν (in both 16:7 and 14:28), was temporal, "He has set out before you toward Galilee," and should be interpreted from the perspective of the parousia.[114] Jesus' presence is hidden, yet it will soon take place through the experience of proclamation. Marxsen concluded the parousia motif by maintaining that a conclusion to the Gospel of Mark appended to Mark 16:8, which deals with the appearances, "extinguishes the hope that still informs Mark's ending."[115]

The women's response of silence is the reversal of an earlier Markan theme of messianic secret. The messianic secret was revealed in the resurrection and the angelic commission, only to be complicated again by the reversal of expectations of the women's silence. According to Marxsen,

> The injunctions to silence actually stimulate transgression, spreading of
> the news. In the Markan ending, the command to spread the news is

---

[111]Marxsen, *Mark the Evangelist*, p. 85.

[112]Ibid.

[113]Ibid., p. 86.

[114]Ibid. See also Robert H Stein, "A Short Note on Mark XIV. 28 and XVI. 7," *NTS*, 20 (1974), 448. For a study on the word προάγω see Christopher Francis Evans, "I Will Go Before You Into Galilee," *JTS*, 5 (1964), 4.

[115]Marxsen, *Mark the Evangelist*, p. 91.

inhibited by the women's flight and dread. Back of this common tension lurks an inner compulsion to spread the news which is also inhibited and restrained.[116]

Marxsen concluded that the messianic secret was centered on the issue of proclamation and was developed in the tension between disclosure and concealment, and therefore, "it is most typical of Mark to conclude his Gospel in this peculiar way."[117]

Theodore Weeden

Theodore Weeden maintained "that Mark intentionally ended his Gospel at 16:8, and by that intended his reader to take the full implications of 16:8b seriously."[118] He acknowledged that the debate over the so-called abrupt ending was based on linguistic and theological considerations that dealt with the negative ending of 16:8 and the lack of resurrection appearances, however, he chose not review these points in detail. Weeden scrutinized the argument that Mark intended to include post resurrection appearances because the early creeds referred to them, as "ungrounded generalization."[119]

The argument that 14:28 and 16:7 allude to post resurrection appearances and confirms the evangelist's intent to narrate them following the empty tomb story has been challenged by scholars who held that these two verses do not

---

[116]Ibid.

[117]Ibid. See also Jürgen Roloff, "Das Markusevangelium als Geschichtsdarstellung," *Evangelische Theologie*, 29 (1969), 73-93.

[118]Theodore J. Weeden, *Mark: Traditions in Conflict* (Philadelphia: Fortress Press, 1971), p. 45.

[119]Ibid.

allude to the resurrection appearance, but the parousia.[120] The argument that the evangelist must have followed the same or at least a similar procedure as the other Gospel writers "violates the integrity of Mark by forcing it to harmonize with its literary descendants."[121] Weeden further maintained that it would be "methodologically unsound to base an argument on the one-time existence of material for which absolutely no extant trace has been found."[122]

Weeden argued that internal evidence gives appropriate and adequate explanation for the abrupt ending at 16:8. He followed the redaction-critical conclusions of Ludger Schenke, that there existed "a pre-Markan narrative consisting of 16:2, 5, 6, 8a,"[123] and that the evangelist took this source and supplemented it with his remarks of 16:1, 3-4, 7, and 8b, which closed the Gospel.[124] Based on Schenke's conclusions, Weeden argued that if Mark 16:7 is a Markan addition to the pre-Markan story, then the emphatic point of this pre-Markan story must have been 16:6, therefore, the story of the women's awe

---

[120]See ibid., where Weeden argued for resurrection appearances. See also Lohmeyer, *Das Evangelium des Markus*, p. 356; Lohse, *Mark's Witness to Jesus Christ*, p. 91; and Marxsen, *Mark the Evangelist*, pp. 75ff.

[121]Weeden, *Mark*, p. 46.

[122]Ibid.

[123]Ibid., p. 47. See Ludger Schenke, *Auferstehungsverkundigung und leeres Grab. Eine traditionsgeschichtlich Untersuchung von Mk 16, 1-8* (Stuttgart: Katholisches Bibelwerk, 1969), p. 55, where Schenke stated, "In Mk 16,2.5.6.8a stehen wir vor dem ursprünglichen Text der Tradition vom Gang der Frauen zum Grabe."

[124]See Schenke, *Auferstehungverkundigung und leeres Grab*, pp. 47-53. Compare to Neirynck, "Mark 16:1-8," 72-76, 88, where Neirynck proposed that Mark 16:5-7 and 8cd were later additions by the evangelist.

(16:8a) must have been the natural conclusion.[125] Without 16:7 the women were only spectators to the supernatural event of the young man's message of the resurrection. The women's actions before 16:6 were not central to the story, yet with the addition of 16:7 the women "become active agents in the resurrection with responsibility to communicate the angel's (young man's) message."[126] Mark 16:8b became necessary to show that Jesus' command to go to Galilee (through the voice of the young man) was not carried out by the women because of their "cowardly" fear.[127]

Linguistic comparisons revealed elements of the pre-Markan narrative (ἔκστασις, [5:42 and 16:8a in the pre-Markan Material] and τρόμος [16:8a]) as well as identifying what was Markan (οὐδείς in combination with another negative in the indicative mood [16:8b] and the frequent Markan use of the third person plural imperfect passive indicative of φοβεῖσθαι [16:8b]).[128] Even more significant, however, is the presence of the intentional Markan abrupt and unexpected shifts in psychological emphasis and direction of thought by appending editorial comments to pre-Markan material.

Weeden contended that the evangelist intentionally joined 16:8b to 16:8a as a final editorial comment to his work. To some, the result of the words of 16:8b are offensive, because these words suggest that the disciples never heard the young man's message of Jesus' resurrection, therefore, they never met the risen Jesus and were never commissioned as apostles. This perspective of the disciples "is in complete harmony with Mark's attitude toward and treatment of the

---

[125]Ibid., pp. 54-55.

[126]Weeden, *Mark*, p. 48.

[127]Ibid.

[128]Ibid., p. 49.

disciples throughout the Gospel.''[129] Mark painted the disciples as hopeless men who were not perceptive and later opposed to the style and character of Jesus' messiahship.[130] Weeden concluded, "As the coup de grace, Mark closes his Gospel without rehabilitating the disciples.''[131]

Reginald Fuller

Reginald Fuller surveyed the scholarship which maintained that Mark 16:7 referred to the parousia and responded, "there is nothing *a priori* impossible in the use of (ὄψεσθε) for a resurrection appearance.''[132] Fuller countered Marxsen's position by stating:

> The decisive argument which proves (16:7) to be ... a resurrection rather than a parousia reference is the naming of Peter as well as the disciples, a circumstance which indicates that the Evangelist is alluding to the two appearances listed in 1 Corinthians 15:5.[133]

---

[129]Ibid., p. 50.

[130]According to Weeden, the Markan Jesus' Christology was that of a "suffering-servant" (see ibid., p. 52), whereas the disciples' Christology was that of a "*theos-aner* Christ . . . (who) display(ed) all the traits of a *theos-aner* discipleship" (see ibid., p. 64).

[131]Ibid.

[132]Reginald H. Fuller, *The Formation of the Resurrection Narratives* (New York: Macmillan, 1971), p. 63. Compare to Marxsen above and Norman Perrin, *Christology and a Modern Pilgrimage*, ed. by H. D. Betz (Missoula: Scholars Press, 1974), p. 26. Fuller said that this verb occurred also in 1 Cor. 9:1; Matthew 28:17; and John 20:18, 25, 29 as a part of resurrection accounts.

[133]Fuller, *The Formation of the Resurrection Narratives*, p. 63. See also idem., *A Critical Introduction to the New Testament* (London: Gerald Duckworth & Co. Ltd., 1971 rpt), p. 108. Fuller noted that Mark "certainly proclaim(ed) the resurrection (cf. the predictions, Mk 8:31; 9:9, 31; 10:34; and 16:6) and knows the tradition of appearances both to Peter and to the Twelve (14:28; 16:7)."

Accordingly, if 16:7 pointed toward the parousia, it is inconceivable why Peter and the twelve disciples were specifically named.

It may be assumed that Mark had appearance stories readily at his disposal, yet "the earliest church did not narrate resurrection appearances, but proclaimed the resurrection."[134] Fuller continued that at the time of the formulation of primitive creedal formulations, there is no proof that appearance stories were in circulation any more than Paul himself narrated his conversion. The resurrection was proclaimed (verse 6) and appended by the appearances first to Peter and then to the disciples (verse 7). According to Fuller, verse 7 "is a reference not to appearance narratives, but to an appearance list like the one in 1 Corinthians 15:5, . . . (therefore), Mark reinforced the proclamation of the resurrection by listing certain appearances."[135] Mark extended the pre-Markan device of the angel proclaiming the resurrection by "making him to allude further to the list of appearances."[136] Fuller added, "The silence of the women, which . . . was in the tradition an expression of the biblical reaction to angelophany, has been reinterpreted by Mark in connection with this special theory of the messianic secret."[137] Mark 9:9 suggested that the messianic secret would not be fully revealed until the resurrection, and then it is to be proclaimed by the disciples. This explained the women's silence, for "Mark would see no contradiction

---

[134]Fuller, *The Formation of the Resurrection Narratives*, p. 66.

[135]Ibid., p. 67.

[136]Ibid.

[137]Ibid., p. 64. According to Fuller, messianic secret entailed the consequence of combining isolated episodes of Jesus' life with the passion narrative. See idem., *A Critical Introduction to the New Testament*, p. 110. See above p. 170, n. 93.

between the angel's charge in verse 7 and the silence of the women in verse 8."[138] Fuller concluded that the charge to the women was simply a device pointing to the unveiling of the messianic secret in the resurrection appearances to Peter and the disciples.[139]

Critique

The redaction-critical studies of this section were divided as in the section on the form-critical approach, in that two conclusions were drawn concerning the interpretation of the ending of Mark and in particular verse 16:7: (1) Marxsen concluded that this verse must be interpreted as an announcement of the future event of the parousia, and (2) Weeden and Fuller concluded that this verse was connected with the post-resurrection appearances of Jesus. As did the form-critics Dibelius and Lohmeyer, the redaction-critics confirmed the empty tomb story as central to the resurrection motif.

Marxsen's claim that no pre-Markan Galilean resurrection accounts existed and his charge of their ever coming into existence was hypothetical. If no pre-Markan Galilean resurrection accounts existed, that would imply that both Matthew and John created their resurrection accounts independently, no matter how one views Markan priority. Based on the Matthean and Johannine accounts, it appears that at least two pre-Markan resurrection traditions existed.[140] A second problem of Marxsen's theory was an assumption that the scattering of the disciples (see Mark 14:50-52 and 14:66-72) could only refer to a period of tribulation before the parousia, therefore, 14:28 and 16:7 must be a reference to

---

[138]Fuller, *The Formation of the Resurrection Narratives*, p. 64.

[139]Ibid., p. 64.

[140]Note that Matthew 28:11-20 refers to a Galilean appearance and John 20:12-31 refers to a Judean appearance.

the parousia. Fuller correctly responded that if 16:7 was directed toward the parousia, it is inconceivable why Peter and the disciples were specifically named. The early church held a common conviction that after the passion, Jesus appeared to the disciples (see 1 Corinthians 15:3f.). The best interpretation of 14:28 and 16:7 might be a reference to a promise/fulfillment resurrection appearance of Jesus.

Weeden's treatment of the short ending hinged on the argument that the sudden and abrupt shifts were evidence of Mark's redactional work. The only way to confirm or deny this theory would be to investigate other Markan sections in the same manner of philology and style.

A second point that appeared inconsistent in Weeden's argument was the perpetual eternal silence of the women and the disciples' ignorance of a resurrection. If that be the case, it must be asked, "Why did Weeden not comment that the evangelist's negative perception of the disciples might also be considered as evidence of his redactional work?"

Fuller's argument, "The earliest church did not narrate resurrection appearances, but proclaimed the resurrection,"[141] is vague. How can the narration and the proclamation be separated?

These above redaction-critics have contributed to the question of the ending of Mark, on a whole, by confirming the resurrection based on the empty tomb story. From this point, the consensus of these redaction-critics have taken the empty tomb story and applied the motif of the reversal of the messianic secret, signifying the failure of the disciples. Fuller confirmed that ὄψεσθε is better interpreted in reference to an appearance, which furthers the progression of the consensus of the scholars of the last two sections, to a theological conclusion concerning the ending of Mark.

---

[141]Fuller, *The Formation of the Resurrection Narratives*, p. 66.

Literary-critical Approaches to the Short Ending of Mark

Recent literary methods of interpreting the short ending have lead to new possibilities for the explanation of the short ending in conjunction with the interpretation of the Gospel as a whole. As did the scholars who argued in favor of other theories on the ending of Mark, the scholars who advocated the 16:8 ending, based on a Markan literary technique, also began with the textual evidence that supported their view.

Robert P. Meye

Robert P. Meye defended the short ending of Mark based on four major points concerning this New Testament problem: the textual evidence, internal evidence, the abrupt ending, and the denial of a lack of resurrection appearances.[142] Meye maintained a conviction "that the history of Marcan and gospel studies has provided us with ample evidence to compel the conclusion that Mark 16:8 was indeed the original and intended ending of the gospel."[143]

As did several of his predecessors, Meye confirmed that both textual evidence and internal evidence supported 16:8 as the authentic conclusion to the Gospel. He accordingly held that the 16:8 ending posed two serious problems: (1) It is though improbable that a Gospel would end without including a resurrection narrative and 2) There is doubt about whether an evangelist would conclude in such an abrupt manner.[144] Meye responded to the first point by affirming "Mark

---

[142]Robert P. Meye, "Mark 16:8--The Ending of Mark's Gospel," *Biblical Research*, 14 (1969), 33-43. Meye later summarized this article in idem., "Mark's Special Easter Emphasis," *Christianity Today*, 15 (1970-1971), 4-6. James M. Robinson, *The Problem of History in Mark and Other Markan Studies* (Philadelphia: Fortress Press, 1982 rpt.) p. 53.

[143]Meye, "Mark 16:8," 33.

[144]Ibid., p. 34.

16:1-8 clearly articulates the resurrection of Christ."[145] He cited Hans Grass who confirmed that the words ἐφοβοῦντο γάρ are a typically Markan pericopal conclusion.[146] Hans Jürgen Ebeling concluded that such scenes show the contrast between the vividness of the divine deed or word and the darkness of human perception and response.[147] Accordingly, the ultimate fear and flight of the women were a sign that the women were at the scene of an ultimate mystery.[148]

In light of the Markan beginning and the Gospel in general, the 16:8 ending was not abrupt. Meye noted, "Markan clues are of crucial significance in the search for a solution to the Markan ending."[149] It is paradoxical that a solution to the ending question is suggested by the first verse of the Gospel: "The beginning of the gospel of Jesus Christ, the Son of God." The Gospel which was designated in Mark 1:1 is the Gospel of salvation contingent upon the death and resurrection of Jesus Christ. Julius Wellhausen pointed out the repeated passion (/resurrection) predictions of Mark 8:31; 9:31: and 10:32 as an anticipation of the

---

[145]Ibid., p. 35. Meye noted four factors that confirm the resurrection in the women's visit to the tomb: (1) The tomb was empty; (2) The interpretation of νεανίσκον at the tomb, supports this; (3) Verse 16:7 reports "He is going before you to Galilee; there you will see him as he told you;" and (4) The fear of the women. Fear is the human response to the divine deed; in this case the resurrection of Jesus. Note that Meye refrains from calling the resurrection an epiphany, yet, the characteristics of an epiphany and the resurrection event are very similar. See above p. 170, n. 93.

[146]Ibid. Meye quoted Hans Grass, *Ostergeschehen und Osterbrichte* (Göttingen: Vanderhoeck & Ruprecht, 1964), p. 16.

[147]Hans Jürgen Ebeling, *Das Messiasgeheimnis und die Botsschaft des MarcusEvangelisten* (Berlin: A Töpelmann, 1939), pp. 162, 168-169, 171, and 222-224.

[148]Meye, "Mark 16:8," 36.

[149]Ibid.

Christian Gospel.[150] If one considers ἀρχή as the "founding events" of the Gospel, then one can point to Mark 16:8 as the point at which the death and resurrection are accomplished events.[151]

A second supporting observation is the development of the resurrection motif. According to Meye, "The first official act of Jesus is the call of disciples" (1:16-20).[152] In Mark 3:14-15 the disciples were sent out to cast out demons and furthermore the commission was carried out in 6:7-13:30. Meye continued,

> The 'beginning of the gospel' is the outfitting of an apostolic body, chiefly by making them understanding witnesses of the Gospel-founding events, the death and resurrection of Christ. All beyond this was the period of proclamation. The time of the beginning is the time of the historical Jesus; beyond that lay the witness to a risen Christ, expressed first of all in the apostolic witness (16:6).[153]

Abrupt sectional endings are characteristic of the Gospel of Mark, still the introduction is abrupt as well.[154] Meye concluded the point by affirming that if the Markan beginning received the same scrutiny as is the ending, in comparison with the other Gospels, the Markan beginning would be equally problematic. Mark must be judged by his standards of narration, and no other. Once this happens, "Mark 16:8 is not as abrupt an ending when viewed in the light of the Marcan

---

[150]Wellhausen, *Einleitung in die drei ersten Evangelien*, p. 147.

[151]Meye, "Mark 16:8," 37.

[152]Ibid.

[153]Ibid., p. 37.

[154]See ibid., p. 38. Meye proved the abruptness of the Markan introduction: "In the beginning John suddenly appears in the wilderness (1:4), and is himself followed by Jesus, who suddenly appears out of Nazareth in Galilee." See also W. L. Knox, "The Ending of St. Mark's Gospel," *HTR*, 35 (1942), 14.

beginning or the Marcan narrative in general.''[155] Meye further argued ''the ending is not abrupt when viewed as a proclamation in the midst of a Christian community that had often heard the resurrection stories, and no doubt understood them as the sequel to Mark 16:8.''[156]

Meye contended, ''there is a further parallel between the Marcan conclusion and the Marcan prologue . . . . Prominent in both is the fulfillment of prophecy.''[157] After citing several examples of how Mark emphasized the word of Jesus (Mark 1:21-28; 4:1-9; 9:2-7; 8:35, 38; 10:29; and 13:31), he placed these as a backdrop to evaluating 16:1-8. In addition, are the series of passion and resurrection predictions that follow Caesarea Philippi (8:31; 9:31; and 10:32-34) along with Jesus' further prediction that after his death he would be raised and would go before his disciples into Galilee (14:27-28), with the additional words ''as he told you.'' The events that take place in these verses must be understood as the fulfillment of the word of Jesus.[158] The use of prophecy at the conclusion of the Gospel appears to have provided a transition between the time of the historical Jesus and the time of the church.[159]

---

[155]Meye, ''Mark 16:8,'' 39. See also N. B. Stonehouse, *The Witness of Matthew and Mark to Christ* (London: The Tyndale Press, 1944), pp. 116-118.

[156]Meye, ''Mark 16:8,'' 39.

[157]Ibid.

[158]Ibid. See also Anderson, *The Gospel of Mark*, p. 54; David Catchpole, ''The Fearful Silence of the Women at the Tomb,'' *Journal of Theology for Southern Africa*, 18 (1977), 3-10; William Lane, *The Gospel According to Mark*, The New International Commentary on the New Testament (Michigan: Eerdmans, 1974), p. 591; and Robert H. Smith, ''New and Old in Mark 16:1-8,'' *CTM*, 43 (1972), 525-527.

[159]Meye, ''Mark 16:8,'' 40.

According to Meye, one can theorize that a Markan extension would have included appearances to Peter and the disciples; the Gospel suggests that such of an appearance did take place. He concluded, "What is lacking . . . is any real evidence that Mark did, or intend to, extend that narrative beyond its note on the fear of the women."[160]

Norman Petersen

Norman Petersen interpreted the Gospel of Mark through literary criticism[161] and applied this methodology specifically to the ending of the Gospel of Mark.[162] He maintained, "The text-critical evidence indicates both that Mark's narrative text originally ended at 16:8 and that the text-critical problem is the result of readers' responses to that literary ending."[163] Petersen dealt with the ending of Mark in strictly literary terms, which he designated as "closure."[164] He sought to determine either the competency or incompetency of 16:8 as an ending for the narrative by considering its closure qualities.

---

[160]Ibid., p. 43.

[161]Norman R. Petersen, *Literary Criticism for New Testament Critics*, New Testament Series (Philadelphia: Fortress Press, 1978).

[162]Idem., "When is the End Not the End? Literary Reflections on the Ending of Mark's Narrative," *Interpretation*, 34 (April, 1980), 151-166.

[163]Ibid., p. 152.

[164]Ibid. Petersen defined closure as "a sense of literary ending derived from the satisfaction of textually generated expectations. . . . But a sense of an ending is also and at once a sense that the narration has terminated and a sense that in terminating it has reached its goal and been completed. To some degree the ending is therefore both the point towards which the narrator has been working and the point from which his narrative is to be construed." The criterion for the closure quality of the ending of Mark is "the closure congruity between textually generated expectations and satisfactions."

According to Petersen, "It is implied that when the women report to the disciples the disciples will make their way to Galilee and see Jesus."[165] Even though the text ends with Mark 16:8, the reader is compelled to respond to the narrator's unexpected withdrawal from communication. The literary work continues, for "the end of a text is not the end of the work when the narrator leaves unfinished business for the reader to complete, thoughtfully and imaginatively, not textually."[166]

Despite the variety of endings of Mark and the other Gospels, these endings are unified "in seeing that a proper sense of an ending hinges on the actions of the women."[167] The result of this is a disparity in that the narrator created "an expectation and then canceled it, leading the reader to wonder why he raised the expectation in the first place."[168] Such wonderment and disparity require that the reader solves the puzzle of the narrator's meaning. One must be careful to preserve the integrity of the author: "To solve it (the narrator's meaning of 16:8) by saying that he was incompetent is to deny not only any meaning to the apparent incongruity between 16:6-7 and 8, but also any coherence and integrity to the total narrative."[169] Petersen continued, "It is precisely the coherence and integrity of the narrative prior to 16:8 that renders 16:8 incongruous."[170] In order to understand what Mark affirmed with 16:8 the

---

[165]Ibid., p. 153.

[166]Ibid.

[167]Ibid.

[168]Ibid., p. 154.

[169]Ibid.

[170]Ibid.

reader must "follow one or both of two lines of inquiry--either to view everything before 16:8 in light of it or to view 16:8 in light of everything before it."[171]

Petersen continued, "Closure in narrative usually entails a plotted system of expectations and satisfactions that govern entire narratives."[172] This is the case in Mark where the principle plot device is one of prediction and fulfillment. The author of Mark generated expectation through prediction and through fulfillment he satisfied them. Two aspects of these predictions and fulfillments are significant for the interpretation of Mark 16:8: (1) The apparent incongruous closure of Mark 16:8 occurred in the context, even the climax of the greatest density of closural satisfactions in the entire narrative (Mark 14-16); and (2) The inconsistency of 16:8 with the narrator's previous style of emplotment renders its literal meaning suspect, based on what Jesus predicted up to this point has come about despite the intent and actions of other characters in the story.[173] Unlike the other characters of the narrative, only Jesus' words and actions have any finality about them, therefore, the "narrator leads us readers to expect something other than what we find in 16:8 and finding 16:8 to disbelieve that he means it."[174] The narrator's system of plotting and expectation has raised concern for the reader and therefore, provided the "reader's interpretive options--16:8 is either an intentional reversal of expectations or an ironic substitute for the obvious continuation of events implied by the narrator."[175]

---

[171]Ibid.

[172]Ibid., pp. 154-155.

[173]Petersen, "When is the End Not the End?," 155.

[174]Ibid., p. 156.

[175]Ibid.

In addition to the plotted narrative, it is important to understand the imaginative world in which the narrator depicts the actions of the characters of his story.[176] The narrative world is related to the narrative by plot devices; that is, by the ways the narrator arranges the knowledge he shows and tells. According to Petersen, "Mark's plotted narrative focuses on but a segment of a continuum of events known to him--on a segment that begins with John the Baptist and ends with the flight of the women from Jesus' empty tomb."[177] He continued:

> In terms of emplotment, the earlier events are, as if were, folded into the plotted segment of time through allusions or quotations, while the later events are folded into it through predictions whose fulfillment he does not emplot (e.g., Mark 13).[178]

One reason for the cause of disturbance about the 16:8 ending of Mark is the events of Mark 13 were communicated through prediction only. They have not come to pass, therefore, Mark 16:8 created a discontinuity in the temporal world which the narrator has shared with his reader. A secondary reason for disturbance is "that by ceasing to speak in 16:8 the narrator curiously obscures his implied location on the temporal continuum of his narrative word."[179] Through the narrator's emplotment of events in his narrative world, he required a reading of 16:8 in relation to both the narrator's plotted narrative and his narrative world.[180]

---

[176]Ibid. See also idem., *Literary Criticism for New Testament Critics*, pp. 73-80 and 91-92.

[177]Idem., "When is the End Not the End?," 157.

[178]Ibid.

[179]Ibid., p. 158.

[180]Ibid.

In the second section of this article, Petersen digressed to the question, "Does the narrator mean what he says in Mark 16:8?"[181] If he does, the reader must interpret 16:8 literally and interpret all the previous material in light of this verse, but if he does not the reader must interpret 16:8 as irony, and interpret Mark 1:1-16:7 in light of this verse.[182] The problem of interpretation is determining "which alternative provides a closure most congruent with the narrator's storytelling art."[183]

Petersen acknowledged that a literal reading of 16:8 would bring the total of the narrative to an immediate stop, furthermore, "the women's reaction to their experience at the empty tomb renders any further comment by the narrator as superfluous."[184] Though the narrator's work is completed, the reader's work has just begun. Petersen reviewed Theodore Weeden's literal approach, in which he agreed to some of the points, yet he noted that Weeden "established the character of the twelve as unreliable . . . (and) failed to identify the governing points of view and the effects of their inter-relations."[185] In essence, Weeden did "not consider the perspectival system in which the point of view of the twelve play(ed) but a relational part."[186]

---

[181]Ibid., p. 159.

[182]Ibid. See also David R. Catchpole, "The Fearful Silence of the Women at the Tomb: A Study in Markan Theology," *JTS*, 18 (1977), 3-10 and Robert H. Smith, "New and Old in Mark 16:1-8," *CTM*, 43 (1972), 525-527.

[183]Petersen, "When is the End Not the End?," 158.

[184]Ibid.

[185]Ibid., p. 160.

[186]Ibid.

Petersen showed that points of view in Mark's narrative are qualitatively divided into two ideological perspectives:

> For the narrator, whose ideological point of view is closely identified with Jesus', the perspective taken by Jesus is both right and reliable, while the perspectives taken by all other characters in the narrative (except God and the unclean spirits) are both wrong and unreliable--because they are to some degree contrary to Jesus' perspective.[187]

The literal interpretation of 16:8 impels the reader to loose faith in the restoration of the disciples, and therefore, form a similar conclusion as Weeden, that the disciples were utter failures. Even more damaging is the domino-effect of the literal interpretation would be that Jesus was deluded about the disciples, who eventually abandoned him, and the establishment eventually killed him, and the testimony of the young man at the empty tomb was nullified by his erroneous prediction about the meeting in Galilee. Throughout the Gospel, the narrator invited the reader to believe Jesus and to believe in both the narrator's and Jesus' imaginative word, therefore, a literal interpretation of 16:8 exposed the narrator as a "very nasty ironist" who misdirected the reader's affections and expectations.[188]

In the ironic reading of the narrator's closing sentence "the effect of the irony is to demand first the reader's acknowledgement of it and second the imaginative closure of the story which is temporarily suspended by it."[189] The reader recognized irony in Mark 16:8 and such recognition would redirect the reader's attention back to 16:6, where the young man announced "he is risen."

---

[187]Ibid., p. 161.

[188]Ibid.

[189]Ibid.

Petersen continued, "Hermeneutically, the acknowledgement of irony entails a deliterizing of the women's behavior which cancels its terminal finality."[190] This would facilitate the second effect of irony, because the reader's text ends, therefore, at this point the readers' task now begins. The words "he is risen" reminds the reader that though the women are unreliable, as were the disciples and the establishment previously in the story, Jesus has risen and is on his way to Galilee where the disciples will see him. Petersen concluded the section, "Because 16:8 is the bridge between the expectation (re)-generated in 16:7, . . . the implied satisfaction (is) provided by 'Galilee,' . . . because Galilee constitutes the imaginative resolution of the story's plot."[191]

Petersen called attention to the ramifications of the message suggested by the two consequences of the ironic bridge in 16:8:

> On the one hand, by leading us beyond plotted time the bridge establishes a continuity between story time--the time of Jesus--and discourse time--the time in which the narrator told his story to his implied readers, which is the time of the last events predicted by Jesus in Mark 13. . . . On the other hand, a further consequence of the ironic bridge in 16:8 is the creation of a discontinuity between the plotted story, including its imaginative closure in the episode in Galilee, and the unplotted times represented only predictively in Mark 13.[192]

Based on the above consequences, "the plot of Jesus' story thus center(ed) on a conflict of eschatological interpretation."[193]

---

[190]Ibid.

[191]Petersen, "When is the End Not the End?," 163.

[192]Ibid., pp. 163-164.

[193]Ibid., p. 164.

Mark's story and Jesus' story parallel one another, in their conclusions with the exception, "the continuum of Mark's narrative world, 'Galilee' did happen, whereas in Jesus' story the parousia will happen. . . ."[194] Petersen emphasized that there is no more finality to the claims of the false messiahs and prophets in chapter 13 than there were to the women's actions in 16:8.

Petersen confirmed, "The effect of chapter 13 is to minimize the significance of the disciples' abandonment of Jesus and to emphasize the expectation that they will soon abandon their mistaken point of view and return to Jesus."[195] Corresponding to the transformation of the disciples (from the role of antagonists to protagonists) there is also a transformation of their ideological point of view.[196] Mark 14:28 and 16:1-7 reinforced and focused respectively on the motif of the return of a remnant of the disciples, "with a certainty of its happening that guarantees the ironic interpretation of 16:8."[197]

Werner Kelber

Werner Kelber maintained that substantial manuscript evidence supports the argument of the short ending of Mark, furthermore, he added, "Almost as important as the manuscript evidence . . . is the narrative logic of Mark's

---

[194]Ibid., p. 165.

[195]Ibid., p. 166.

[196]Ibid., p. 165.

[197]Ibid., p. 166.

story.''[198] In the titular verse (Mark 1:1) the evangelist ''stated his intention to write what was only 'the beginning of the gospel.'''[199]

Kelber's method in interpreting the ending of Mark is a reader-response hermeneutic in which:

> the readers have relived the story of Jesus, their way must no longer concur with that of the Twelve. They know more than the disciples ever did, because Mark has given them the opportunity to learn from Jesus and his conflict with Peter and the Twelve. The readers, living after A.D. 70, have learned to understand the fall of the temple in connection with Jesus' life and death, and the demise of the Jerusalem church as a consequence of the abortive discipleship.[200]

He continued that the readers, based on a knowledge of the failure of the disciples, can transform from passive readers of the gospel of the kingdom to active participants in the kingdom of God. The fall of Jerusalem did not end the kingdom of God, for those who have read and believed the way is open to the new community, a community of faith.[201] This new and ongoing community was called into existence by Jesus and is open to all who responds to the gospel by faith.

The written Gospel ended with the narration of the abortive mission of the oral message. The three women were instrumental in the breakdown of oral transmission. Because of the fear of the women, the disciples who were absent at

---

[198]Werner H. Kelber, *Mark's Story of Jesus* (Philadelphia: Fortress Press, 1979), p. 85.

[199]Ibid., p. 93.

[200]Ibid., p. 94.

[201]Ibid.

the crucifixion, remained ignorant of the resurrection.[202] According to Kelber, "One reason the gospel ends in this 'incomplete' fashion is because the failure of the women is indeed not the last word on the story of the Kingdom."[203] The disciples were effectively eliminated as apostolic representatives of the risen Lord,[204] therefore, the readers (in Mark's time through the present) who understand the nature of the crisis, are invited to complete the journey of Jesus left incomplete by the disciples. He continued, "In this sense, reading the Gospel is but the beginning of the gospel's actualization in real life."[205]

With the demise of the disciples, "the structure of expectancy is finally and irrevocably reversed and the narrative has found its proper, parabolic ending."[206] Kelber stated, "The obvious conclusion to be drawn from the open ending is that it is meant to be inclusive."[207] Robert Funk confirmed Kelber's observation of the parable in that, 'the parable . . . does not have a conclusion.'[208] The reason for the absence of a conclusion "is because the

---

[202]Idem., *The Oral and Written Gospel* (Philadelphia: Fortress Press, 1983), p. 104.

[203]Idem., *Mark's Story of Jesus*, p. 94.

[204]Idem., *The Oral and Written Gospel*, p. 129.

[205]Ibid.

[206]Ibid.

[207]Ibid.

[208]Ibid. See Robert W. Funk, *Language, Hermeneutic, and Word of God: The Problem of Language in the New Testament and Contemporary Theology* (New York: Harper & Row, 1966; reprint Missoula, Mont.: Scholars Press, 1979), p. 196.

parable, far from inviting us to settle for the familiar, classical perspectives, shocks us out of them toward a new and unfamiliar logic."[209]

Boomershine and Bartholomew

Thomas Boomershine and Gilbert Bartholomew demonstrated the legitimacy of the short ending by identifying and comparing the specific narrative techniques of Mark 16:8 with those of the endings of stories earlier in the Gospel.[210] The 16:8 ending was probably the intended and original ending of Mark, based on the narrative style of the story endings of Mark. Boomershine and Bartholomew identified "three major narrative techniques in 16:8: (1) the use of extensive narrative commentary; (2) the use of intensive inside views; and (3) the use of short sentences."[211]

Boomershine and Bartholomew confirmed, "Narrative commentary is one of the major means by which a narrator varies his manner of address to his audience."[212] Narrative commentary takes place when the writer "interrupt(s) the reporting of the events of their stories in order to give brief notes of additional information, to translate a foreign word or to explain something that is surprising or confusing."[213] Narrative comments introduced by γάρ usually explain

---

[209]Kelber, *The Oral and Written Gospel*, p. 129.

[210]Thomas E. Boomershine and G. L. Bartholomew, "The Narrative Technique of Mark 16:8," *JBL*, 100 (2, 1981).

[211]Ibid., p. 214.

[212]Ibid. See also Wayne Boothe, *The Rhetoric of Fiction* (Chicago: University of Chicago, 1961) and Selomith Rimmon-Kenan, *Narrative Fiction: Contemporary Poetics* (London: Methuen, 1984 rpt.), pp. 98-100.

[213]Boomershine and Bartholomew, "The Narrative Technique of Mark 16:8," p. 214.

confusing or surprising events which were reported in the preceding sentence and serve as an answer to the anticipated questions of the reader/hearer.[214] Since the function of narrative comments is that of explaining an earlier statement, "these comments usually occur in the middle or at the end of literary units within a story,"[215] and look forward to what may happen in the future.[216]

The second type of narrative technique Mark used to write his Gospel was that of "inside view," in which "the narrator describes the perceptions, thoughts, or feelings of a character."[217] Such "inside view" takes the reader/hearer inside the character and describes the emotions of the which are unknown to an observer or participant within the narrative. Boomershine and Bartholomew classified the inside views of Mark into two types: the perceptions of the character and descriptions of emotions.[218] The words ἐφοβοῦντο γάρ are descriptive of the women's emotions and are therefore, a deliberate Markan characteristic.[219]

According to Boomershine and Bartholomew, "A survey of the endings of narrative units in the UBS Greek text of all four gospels shows that on several occasions in each gospel, a story ends with a simple and relatively brief

---

[214]Ibid., p. 215. See Mark 1:16, 22; 2:15, 3:21; 5:8, 28, 42; 6:17, 18, 20, 31, 48; 9:6, 34; 10:22; 11:13; 14:2, 40, 56; 15:10; 16:4, 8.

[215]Ibid.

[216]Note the parallels of the narrative commentary in the Markan pericopes 6: 45-52; 14:1-2; and 16:1-8.

[217]Boomershine and Bartholomew "The Narrative Technique of Mark 16:8,'', p. 218. See Percy Lubbock, *The Craft of Fiction* (London: Jonathan Cape, 1921), pp. 163-165, and 245-248 for a discussion of "point of view" in the modern novel.

[218]Ibid. See also note 11 of this article.

[219]Ibid., p. 219. Compare Mark's use of "inside views" in the ending of Mark pericopes 6:45-52; 9:30-32; 12:13-17 and 16:1-8.

sentence.''[220] This phenomenon appeared three times as often in Mark as it did in the other three Gospels, in spite of the comparative shortness of Mark. The ending of a story with a simple and relatively short sentence is probably a spontaneous and deliberate stylistic technique at work in the Gospel, in order to produce a combined effect of brevity and the final position with the purpose of bringing on maximum stress.

The punctuation of ἐφοβοῦντο γάρ has received much question and debate. Grammatical consideration does allow for the possibility of this phrase being a sentence, for in the Greek language, the subject is often implied from the parsing of the verb (in the case of 16:8, ἐφοβοῦντο, the subject is the implied third person plural "they" representing the women). Likewise, "a sentence may be related to what has gone before it either asyndetically or by means of a more or less ambiguous particle or conjunction.''[221] Secondly, Boomershine and Bartholomew contended, "The Gospel of Mark was composed to be heard rather than to be read in silence.''[222] This is problematic in that one must delineate the character of the pause which Mark and the readers employed before ἐφοβοῦντο γάρ.

Mark 16:8 contained two γάρ clauses that could end with a period as easy as it did with a colon or a semicolon. These two "narrative comments" explained the previous two statements, (that the women fled and they were silent), still these

---

[220]Ibid.

[221]Ibid., p. 221. Friedrich Blass and A. Debrunner, *A Greek Grammar of the New Testament and Other Early Christian Literature*, A Translation and Revision of the Ninth-Tenth German Edition Incorporating Supplementary Notes of A. Debrunner, trans. by Robert W. Funk (Chicago: University of Chicago, 1961), p. 241, cited οὖν, δέ and καί as such particles, whereas, Boomershine and Bartholomew added γάρ to this list.

[222]Boomershine and Bartholomew, "The Narrative Technique of Mark 16:8," p. 221.

two statements did not necessarily have to be a part of the preceding sentences. If the function of these two γάρ clauses was to explain these preceding sentences, "the probability is that the narrator made a full stop prior to the explanation."[223] It was an imperative that the narrator allowed the clause to come to a complete stop, because the force of the narrator's answers to the implied questions of the reader/hearer (Why did the women flee? Why were the women silent?) depended on the narrator allowing the reader/hearer enough time to ask the question themselves. Boomershine and Bartholomew concluded, "The final two-word sentence is a climatic use of a narrative technique which is present throughout the gospel."[224]

In a later article, Boomershine proposed that Mark 16:8 is the reversal of the messianic secret motif and that it emphasized the apostolic commission to proclaim the gospel, as did the endings of the other Gospels.[225] ἐφοβοῦντο γάρ was designed to be an experience of conflict between the silence of the women and the fear of proclamation. Boomershine continued that 16:8 appealed for the proclamation of the resurrection despite fear. In the silence surrounding the short statements of 16:8, and the ἐφοβοῦντο γάρ ending, "Mark invite(d) his audience to reflect on their response to the dilemma which the women faced,"[226] that of the commission to proclaim the gospel.

---

[223]Ibid., p. 222.

[224]Ibid.

[225]Thomas Boomershine, "Mark 16:8 and the Apostolic Commission," *JBL*, 100 (2, 1981), 225-239.

[226]Ibid., p. 237.

Critique

As did their predecessors, the literary critics cited the availability and antiquity of the texts which support the short ending. The empty tomb tradition remained an important element in the proof of a resurrection, but the question of the resurrection was not the primary issue of this method. The literary critics concentrated on the three women and their reaction the angel at the tomb and the ignorance of the disciples of the resurrection.

Meye spent no effort on the failure of the women in 16:1-8 and the continual failure of the disciples throughout the Gospel of Mark. He presented Gospel as a post-resurrection account of the disciples based on Mark 1:1, "the beginning of the Gospel of Jesus Christ," by extending from this verse to the call of the disciples (1:16-20), the apostolic commission (6:7-13:30), and to the future proclamation (13:10 and 14:9). Meye continued, "The time of the beginning is the time of the historical Jesus; beyond that lay the witness to a risen Christ expressed first of all in the apostolic witness (16:7)."[227] This argument appears as unrealistic, for no matter how one views the disciples in their work, they were failures in the Gospel of Mark, even in the time of Meye's so-called apostolic commission. Their hearts were hardened because of the absence of faith.

Petersen provided a more likely understanding of Mark 1:1 in connection with 16:1-8 by a reader-response hermeneutic in which 16:8 forced the reader to make a decision in response to God's call to discipleship. The beginning of the Gospel began with a call to discipleship in Jesus' ministry, yet the disciples of Mark 1:1-16:7 are perceived as utter failures, in spite of their promise and hope of redemption and gathering in 14:28 and 16:7. The reader must decide whether to accept or reject the call and commission of Jesus.

---

[227]Meye, "Mark 16:8," 37.

Petersen's work is a positive contribution to the argument for the 16:8 ending, but his characterization of genre, in order to arrive at this conclusion, is lacking. As many have errantly done, Petersen relied on the familiarity of the endings of the appendages to Mark as well as the other Gospels in order to form a characterization of the 16:8 ending. These appendages added to the problem of defining 16:8 as the authentic ending, because it promoted the idea of the necessity of the Gospel ending with the reporting of a resurrection appearance. This stressed the hermeneutical principle that Mark be interpreted based on Mark.

Kelber was more definitive than Petersen in defining the purpose of the ending of Mark concerning the reader response hermeneutic. He presented the reader response hermeneutic for a theological interpretation of Mark, where Boomershine and Bartholomew complemented Kelber's methodology by explaining the literary matrix of an interpretation. Their conclusion that Mark intended to be heard rather than read, added further validity to the literary critical method, via the reader response hermeneutic. This in turn explained the logic of ἐφοβοῦντο γάρ concluding the Gospel of Mark.

Chapter Summary

The short ending of Mark historically has had several advocates and also some antagonists.[228] This chapter confirmed that γάρ was frequently used to conclude sentences in Greek literature from the time of Homer (the eighth century B.C.) through the fourteenth century A.D., though only a couple of isolated documents end with γάρ, and the citation of these works is questionable, based on their genre. It was clearly proved that over a thousand sentences end with γάρ.

---

[228]It is unfortunate that several scholars who hinged their argument against the short ending, based on the unlikelihood of γάρ being used to end sentences, paragraphs, or works, did not have computers to aid in the investigation of works containing sentences that ended in this "unlikely" manner.

The logical conclusion to this point is if a sentence, by rules of syntax, can end in γάρ, there is no reason that sentence or any other sentence can end in γάρ.

The text-critics demonstrated that the appendages to Mark 16:8 were secondary, however, their method and conclusions were not the definitive answer to the question on the ending of Mark. It could be argued that there are parallels between the longer ending of Mark and Mark 1:1-16:8, as were there several differences. A second point of question was, even if the appendages were ruled out as authentic, these critics did not eliminate the possibility of a reconstructed ending. This leads to the need for a comprehensive study of Mark's style and vocabulary as a whole. From this, one may make a definite conclusion on the ending(s) of Mark, based on a comparison of style and philology.

The three sections that covered methodologies which provided New Testament studies with a logical strand of thought, in order to explain Mark 16:8 as the intended ending of the Gospel. The form-critics provided the empty tomb tradition as a proof of a resurrection of Jesus, therefore, it is in error when scholars refer to the 16:8 ending as lacking a resurrection as Salmon did above. The redaction-critics confirmed the theory of a proof of the resurrection by the empty tomb tradition. From this point the consensus of these redaction critics took the empty tomb story and applied the motif of the reversal of the messianic secret, signifying the temporal failure of the disciples. Fuller confirmed that ὄψεσθε (in 14:28 and 16:7) is better interpreted in reference to an appearance, which furthers the progression of the consensus of the scholars of the last two sections, to a theological conclusion concerning the ending of Mark. The literary-critics took the work of the preceding methodologies and applied a reader-response hermeneutic to the empty tomb tradition and the reversal of the messianic secret motif. These latter critics concluded that based on Mark 1:1 the Gospel of Mark discussed the history of the failure of the disciples and ἐφοβοῦντο γάρ calls for the hearer/reader to make a choice about becoming a disciple.

The next chapter will summarize the contents of this research, which offered a select study of the scholarship representing the various perspectives on the ending of Mark. From this summary, a proposal for further research in connection with this book will be offered.

CHAPTER 6
Conclusion

The proposal of this research was an attempt to survey and evaluate the scholarly views pertaining to the problems associated with the ending of Mark's Gospel.[1] Such a holistic approach may give insight to the modern interpreter in the consideration of the text. Central to each chapter of this book (chapters two through five) was the question about the possibility of a gospel ending in γάρ, a view that has been debated from the second century to the present day.

Summary

The Fathers provided much information on the traditions of the ending of Mark: (1) Several Fathers who advocated for the longer ending affirmed that there were some manuscripts that ended abruptly at 16:8 with ἐφοβοῦντο γάρ. Some of these Fathers traced the tradition which א and B follows, back to the third and even late second century.[2] (2) A majority of the Fathers affirmed the existence of the longer ending, but only three of these Fathers cited the longer ending as

---

[1]See page 1 above.

[2]William Reuben Farmer, *The Last Twelve Verses of Mark* (Cambridge: Cambridge University Press, 1974), p. 26.

authentic to Mark. It is important to remember that Tatian cited Mark as the author of the verses of the longer ending in the late second century. (We must remember that most of the Latin texts included the longer ending). (3) Jerome offered evidence that as early as the late second century there existed a third ending appended after 16:14 (the Freer Logion). This ending was not known until the twentieth century when Charles Freer discovered a manuscript (W) which included this ending.[3]

The Byzantine texts included the longer ending and were considered to be more reliable than the Alexandrian texts, which commonly ended with ἐφοβοῦντο γάρ.[4] It is obvious that the longer ending was in widespread use by the early part of the third century, still usage does not prove authenticity. Eusebius informed his audience that Mark preached in Alexandria and settled churches there.[5] From this, one may assume the priority of the Alexandrian texts rather than their inferiority.

From the sixth century to the end of the Reformation, the Latin texts were dominant, which in turn signaled the dominance of the longer ending. The value of the theologians of this time span were not helpful in a critical evaluation of the longer ending because of the widespread acceptance of the Latin traditions.

The second chapter confirmed that the early Fathers were aware of and concerned about the question of the authenticity of the longer ending. Based on

---

[3]Codex W is the only manuscript that is known to have this appendage after 16:14. Common sense would tell us that originally codex W was not the only manuscript to have ended in this manner.

[4]See chapter 2, p. 30, n. 57.

[5]Eusebius, *Historica ecclesiastica, lib. 2*, Patrologiae Cursus Completus, Series Graeca, vol. 20, ed. J. P. Migne (Paris, 1857), p. 173. Bede confirmed this point. See Bede, *Opera Historica*, vol. 2, The Loeb Classical Library Series, trans. J. E. King (London: William Heinemann and New York: G. P. Putnam's Sons, 1930), p. 337.

the result of the research of the works of the Fathers on this question, the result is inconclusive.

The Church eventually included the longer ending in its Canon and read these verses in public services, based on this pericope's antiquity, widespread manuscript support, and patristic attestation. Most scholars from the nineteenth century to the present day rejected the authenticity of the longer ending, whereas, they continued to view these verses as canonical. The canonicity of the longer ending, however, has received objection from a few scholars. Samuel Davidson rejected the canonicity of the longer ending based on this ending not being authentic.[6]

John Burgon provided a strong defense of the authenticity of Mark 16:9-20, based on external evidence. Burgon made an honorable attempt to investigate most of the internal evidence and the external evidence that was known to him (note above, that I said excavations since Burgon's time have added more textual evidence to the question of the longer ending, especially the discovery of W).

George Salmon highlighted the major points concerning the legitimacy of the longer ending, based on a similar investigation of the external evidence in the same manner as Burgon. He focused his internal evidence on the theology of Mark 16:9-20 and the argument that a document cannot end with γάρ. William Farmer deemed the external evidence of manuscripts and Patristic witness as inconclusive, because most of these elements of external evidence post dated ℵ and B. Farmer, though supportive of the longer ending, confirmed ". . . by the fifth century, possibly the fourth or even the third, where it could be said that the

---

[6]Samuel Davidson, *An Introduction to the Study of the New Testament: Critical, Exegetical, and Theological*, vol. 1, 2nd ed. (London: Longmans, Green, and Co., 1882), p. 577.

textual tradition ending Mark with ἐφοβοῦντο γάρ was strongly attested by contemporary manuscript evidence.''[7]

Bruce Metzger correctly concluded that these features indicate that the longer ending was added by a person who was familiar of a form of Mark that ended with 16:8 and who wished to provide a more appropriate conclusion. In view of the differences between verses 1-8 and 9-20, it is unlikely that the long ending was written *ad hoc* to fill an obvious gap, it is probable that 9-20 was excerpted from another document, dating from the first half of the second century.[8]

There is some reluctance by the church and critical scholarship in accepting Mark 16:8 as the intended ending of the Second Gospel. Textual evidence suggested that the longer ending was appended by a scribe who made a composite of the resurrection stories and oral tradition, in order to supply the ending. The shorter ending and the Freer Logion were not considered authentic, however, both were generally used with the longer ending.

Several scholars rejected the above argument and speculated various reconstructions which, as the name suggests, proposed an authentic ending based on the redactional work of Matthew, Luke, John, Acts, and Paul. Unlike the longer ending, and the other later appendages, the arguments for reconstruction and a lost or incomplete ending lacks textual and patristic support.[9]

---

[7]Farmer, *The Last Twelve Verses*, p. 36.

[8]Bruce M. Metzger, *The Text of the New Testament: Its Transmission, Corruption, and Restoration* (New York and Oxford: Oxford University Press, 1968), p. 227.

[9]This is true unless one attributes the manuscripts and Fathers testimony of Mark ending at 16:8 as supporting such a view.

The fifth chapter confirmed that γάρ frequently concluded sentences in Greek literature from the eighth century B.C. through the fourteenth century A.D., though only a couple of isolated documents end with γάρ and the citation of these works is questionable, based on their genre. The logical conclusion to this point is, if a sentence, by rules of syntax, can end in γάρ, there is no reason why the final sentence of a book or document can end with γάρ.

Some text-critics who argued for the short ending demonstrated that the appendages to Mark 16:8 were secondary, yet these critics did not eliminate the possibility of a reconstructed ending. This led to the need for a comprehensive study of Mark's style and vocabulary as a whole. Form criticism provided the empty tomb tradition as a proof of the resurrection of Jesus, therefore, it was an error when scholars maintained that Mark lacked resurrection account, if the Gospel ended at 16:8. Redaction criticism confirmed the proof of the resurrection by the empty tomb tradition. From this point the consensus of these redaction critics took the empty tomb story and applied the motif of the reversal of the messianic secret, signifying the temporal failure of the disciples. Literary criticism took the work of the preceding methodologies and applied a reader-response hermeneutic to the empty tomb tradition and the reversal of the messianic secret motif. These literary critics concluded that based on Mark 1:1, the Gospel of Mark discussed the history of the failure of the disciples and ἐφοβοῦντο γάρ calls for the hearer/reader to make a choice about becoming a disciple.

Proposed Research

This book is by no means the definitive answer to the ending of Mark. As stated in the first chapter, this research was intended to be a survey of select scholars who grappled with the issues concerning the ending of Mark. The results of this research calls for a further collection of the scholarship on the ending of Mark, primarily in the form of an annotated bibliography. Closely associated with this would be a series of works which presented an exhaustive account of the materials from each chapter (i.e., the longer ending; the shorter ending; the Freer Logion; the various reconstructions; and the short ending).

A second study that would help Markan scholars in the definition of the Markan ending would be a re-evaluation geographic origin of the Second Gospel. As noted above, Eusebius was familiar with the contents of the Second Gospel and how it ended. Eusebius also discussed the preaching of the evangelist: "But it is said this same Mark was the first to be sent to preach in Egypt the Gospel which he had also written, and was the first to establish churches in Alexandria itself."[10]

The external evidence is obvious. Since Mark preached "his Gospel" and settled several churches in Alexandria, one might expect the Alexandrian texts to be very accurate. Burgon maintained that the short ending dominated the Alexandrian texts, which he considered inferior to the Byzantine texts (which usually contained the longer ending).[11] Since the text of Mark was extant until Eusebius' day (according to Eusebius' testimony above) one would have to argue the superiority of the Alexandrian texts rather than their inferiority, therefore, the reliability of the short ending appears to be correct.

If one could prove the origin of Mark in Rome, it would be less than reasonable to suggest any other ending other than the longer ending, based on the geographic dominance of the longer ending in the provinces surrounding Rome. Likewise, if one could prove an Alexandrian origin (which would be possible, based on Eusebius' testimony that Mark ministered in Alexandria, and one

---

[10]Eusebius, *Historia ecclesiastica*, lib 2, PG, vol. 20, p. 173. The Greek reads as: "Τοῦτον δὲ Μάρκον πρῶτόν φασιν ἐπὶ τῆς Αἰγύπτου στειλάμενον τὸ Εὐαγγέλιον ὃ δὴ καὶ συνεγράψατο, κηρύξαι, ἐκκλησίας τε πρῶ ἐπ᾽ αὐτῆς Ἀλεξανδρείας συστήσασθαι."

[11]Edward F. Hills, "Introduction," John W. Burgon, *The Last Twelve Verses of the Gospel According to St. Mark* (Erlanger, Ky.: Faith and Facts Press, rpt.), pp. 21-30.

accepted Mark the disciple of Peter as the author of this Gospel) the short ending would be the logical ending based on the dominance of manuscripts with the 16:8 ending in the Alexandrian area. A third proposed area of the origin of Mark is Galilee. If this area was proved as the place of origin of the Gospel of Mark, a less definitive answer to the ending of Mark would be possible, because of a less dominance of the Byzantine texts in the area.[12]

A third proposed area of study is a comprehensive analysis and comparison of the style and philology of the appendages with each verse of the main of the Gospel (1:1-16:8). J. K. Elliott confirmed the need of such a study, "There is to my knowledge no thoroughgoing analysis of the language and style of these endings compared with New Testament language in general or with Mark's gospel in particular."[13] The variant readings of the manuscripts are seldom taken into a detailed account when considering the language and style of the Gospel of Mark.

The fourth and final proposed area of study is the various theories of Mark's Gospel ending other than the sixteenth chapter. Against these theories is the lack of textual support. Etienne Trocmé proposed a theory in which the original edition of the Gospel of Mark consisted of chapters 1-13.2[14] To this

---

[12]For a discussion of the place of origin of the Gospel of Mark, see Hugh Anderson, *The Gospel of Mark*, The New Century Bible Commentary (Grand Rapids: Wm. B. Eerdmans, 1976), pp. 26-29; Werner Kelber, *Mark's Story of Jesus* (Philadelphia: Fortress Press 1979), p. 13; Werner Georg Kümmel, *Introduction to the New Testament* (Nashville: Abingdon Press, 1984 rpt.), pp. 97-98; William Lane, *Commentary on the Gospel of Mark*, The New International Commentary on the New Testament (Grand Rapids: Wm. B. Eerdmans, 1974), pp 24-25; Dennis E. Nineham, *The Gospel of St. Mark*, The Pelican Gospel Commentaries (London: Adam and Charles Black, 1963), pp. 42-43; and Vincent Taylor, *The Gospel According to St. Mark: The Greek Text With Introduction, Notes, and Indexes*, 2nd ed., Thornapple Commentaries (Grand Rapids, Michigan: Baker Book House, 1966), p. 32.

[13]James Keith Elliott, "The Text and Language of the Endings to Mark's Gospel," *Theologische Zeitschrift*, 27 (1971), 255-262.

[14]Etienne Trocmé, *The Formation of the Gospel According to Mark*, trans. Pamela Gaughan (London: SPCK, 1975), pp. 248f. See also page 100 above.

original, "An anonymous ecclesiastic of the Roman community" attached chapters 14-16, which may have been based on a small document from Jerusalem and lent to the whole (chapters 1-16) the authority of Peter and the name of Mark.[15]

Alfred Haefner suggested a reconstruction in which "Mark 16:8 originally continued with Acts 1:13-14, and that this in turn continued with Acts 3, 4, and 5 (the so-called Jerusalem A source of Acts)."[16] Another speculative ending of the Second Gospel has been offered by B. T. Holmes.[17] He stated that the original copy was written in 40 A.D., and consisted of Mark 1:1-16:8 connected by a couple of sentences with Acts 1:3-10:48. He conclude that this arrangement would have "made the gospel [sic] the approximate size of Matthew, Luke, and Acts and therefore, one may take this length as the standard roll available commercially to first century churches."[18]

This book and the proposals of future research clarified that New Testament scholarship is only at the cutting edge in answering difficult questions concerning the Gospel of Mark. With the advent of new methods of interpretation,

---

[15]Ibid.

[16]See Adolf Harnack, *The Acts of the Apostles*, trans. J. R. Wilkinson (London: Williams & Norgate; New York: G. P. Putnam, 1909), pp. 162-202, where Harnack classified the material in Acts 3:1-5:16 as Jerusalem A source. See also Alfred Haefner, "The Bridge Between Mark and Acts," *Journal of Biblical Literature*, 77 (1958), 67. See also F. Blass, *Philology of the Gospels* (London: Macmillan and Company, 1898), pp. 141ff.; p. 193; and C. A. Briggs *New Light on the Life of Jesus* (New York: Charles Schribner's Sons, 1904), p. 135, who affirmed that Luke used the continuation of Mark as a source for the early chapters of Acts.

[17]B. T. Holmes, *The Word of God: Mark's Version* (Toronto: B. T. Holmes, 1962), p. 42.

[18]Ibid.

complemented by new archaeological finds, scholars may define the authentic Markan ending, and from there, be able to delineate the theological interpretations of the ending. Future scholarship will surely view the Gospel of Mark as a literary work rich with practical theological applications.

APPENDIX A

Fathers Who Quote From Mark 16:9-20

After assessing the value of the Father's opinion of a given text in the task of textual criticism, this research addressed the question of the Father's opinion on the original ending of Mark. It is obvious that this conclusion was based primarily on the Father's use of the last twelve verses of Mark compared to a lack of use of these verses. Attention was given to the location, date of the Fathers, and the references to the verses of the longer ending that the Fathers may have used. In the far right column is the Father's name, home, and date. The second column lists the works by the given Father, in which a reference to any of the verses of Mark 16:9-20 may be found. The columns that are to the right center are used to refer to the type of citation that this author made of the verses in question: A refers to a allusion to one of the verses in question; B refers to a quote of one of the verses in question; C is an attribute to Mark as the author of these verses; D is a reference of Mark 16:8 being the known ending of the Second Gospel. At the far right are the verses in question with which the Father mentions, with the corresponding letter as to the type of reference the Father makes. Note that some verses have two letters (A over B), this indicates that the verse is alluded to in one reference and the same verse is quoted in another reference.

a Papias			
b Heriapolis	Fragments of Papias	A	16:18
c 70-155			
a Justin Martyr			
b Rome	The First Apology of Justin	A	16:19-20
c 100?-165			
a Tatian			
b Rome	Diatessaron	A	16:9-20
c 2nd C.A.D			
a Irenaeus			
b Lyons, Gaul	Against Heresies	A	16:17-18
c 115-20		C	16:19
a Tertullian	An Answer to the Jews	A	16:15-16
b Rome	A Treatise on the Soul	A	16:9
c 150/5-220/5	On the Resurrection of		
	the Flesh	A	16:19
	Against Peaxeas	B	16:19
a Hippolytus	Concerning Gifts, and		
b Rome	Ordinations, and the		
c 170?-235	Ecclesiastical Canons	B	
		B	16:17-18
	Against the heresy		
	of one Noctus	A	16:19

a Cyprian			
b Carthage	Concerning the Baptism		
c 200-258	of Heretics	A	16:17-18
a Athanasius			
b Alexandria	Synopsis Scripture		
c 295-373	Sacrae	E	16:9-20
a Didymus	Expositio in Psalmos	A	16:19
b Alexandria	Fragmenta in Actus		
c 313-398	Apost.	A	16:19
a Epiphanius	Adversus Haereses, Lib.		
b Constantine	II. Tom. I. Haeres		
(Salamos)	LXII.	A	16:19
c 315-405			
a Various	Constitutions of the		
b Asia Minor	Holy Apostles		
c 3-4 A.D. Ignatius?	Book V.	A	16:9, 14
	Book VI.	B	16:16
Hippolytus,	Book VIII	B	16:17-18
a Aphraates	The Demonstration of		
(Aphrahat?)	Aphrahat, Demon-		
b Syria	stration I. Of Faith	B	16:16-18
c 4th C.A.D.			
a Ambrose	The Holy Spirit,		
	Book I.	B	16:15(2)
			-18

b Milan	On the Christian Faith		
	Book I.	B	16:15
c 337-397	Book III.	A	16:17-18
	Concerning Repentence,		
	Book I.	B	16:17-18
a Jerome	Against the Pelagians,		
	Book II.	A	16:14
b Rome	To Antonius, Monk of		
c 340-420	Haemona	A	16:9
a A Christian	The Gospel of Nicodemus		
Hellenistic Jew	Part I. The Acts of	A	16:16
c 4-5th C.A.D.	Pilate (1st and 2nd	B	16:15,
	Greek (form)		17-18
		A	16:16(2)
	Part II. The Descent		
	of Christ into Hell		
	(Greek Form)	A	16:16
	Part I. Acts of		
	Pilate (Latin Form)	B	16:
			15-18
a Chrysostom	Homilies on First		
b Constantinople	Corinthians		
c 345/7-407	Homily XXXVIII	A	16:9
	Homily attributed to		
	Chrysostom by his		
	Benedictine Editors	B	16:19-20
a Augustine	Harmony of the Gospels	C	16:9-20
b Hippo	Sermons on New Testa-		
c 354-430	ment Lessons, Lesson XXI.	B	16:16

	On Forgiveness of Sins		
	and Baptism	B	16:15.
			16(2)
	Against Two Letters		
	of the Palagians		
	Book I.	B	16:16
	On Baptism, Against		
	the Donatists	B	16:15-18
	Exposition on the Book	A	16:9
	of Psalms	C	16:19(3)
	On the Soul and its		
	Origen, Book II.	B	16:16,18
	Letters of St.		
	Augustine	A	16:12,14
a Nestorius	in a sermon published	A	16:20
b Antioch	in 429		
c 5th C.A.D.			
a Cyril of Alexandria	Adversus Nestorium,	B	16:20
b Alexandria	Libra. II.		
c 5th C.A.D.			
a John Cassian	The Institutes of the		
	Coenobia, Book VII.,	B	16:17
b Marseilles			
c ?-435			
a Leo the Great	Letter to Discorus,		
	Bishop of Alexandria	B	16:15
b Rome	Letter to Theodoret,		
	Bishop of Cyrus, on		

c 390/400-461	Preservation in the Faith	B	16:16
a Bede b British Isles c 672?-735	In Marci Evangelium Expositio. Lib. IV.	B	16:9-20
a John of Damascus b Damascus c 700?-753?	Barlaam and Ioasaph	A B	16:19-20 16:17
a Theophylact b Bulgaria c 11th C.A.D.	Enarratio In Marci Evangelium	B	16:9-20
a Euthymius b Constantinople c 12th C.A.D.	Comment. in Marcum	B	16:9-20

APPENDIX B

A Listing of Authors/Works Cited by Ibycus
that Have Sentences Ending in ΓAP

The ISC cited over one thousand references of sentences that end in γάρ. Below is a list of the authors, the geographical location, and the date of the reference of this phenomenon. The purpose of this appendix is to demonstrate γάρ is not limited to an era or geographic location. The dates and geographic references were taken from the works listed in the footnote below.[1]

Aelius Aristides	Smyrna (Ismir)	late second century A.D.
Aeschylus	Athens	525-456 B.C.
Aetius Amidenus	Amidenus	sixth century A.D.
Alexander	Aphrodisiensias	sixth century A.D.
Alexander	Tralles	sixth century A.D.
Alexis		fourth-third century B.C.
Ammonius	Alexandria	fifth century A.D.

[1]Luci Berkowitz and Karl L. Squitier, *Thesaurus Linguae Graecae Canon of Greek Authors and Works* (New York: Oxford University Press, 1986); Naphtali Lewis and Meyer Reinhold, eds. *Roman Civilization, Sourcebook I.: The Republic* (New York: Harper & Row, Publishers, 1987 rpt.); Naphtali Lewis and Meyer Reinhold, eds. *Roman Civilization, Sourcebook II.: The Empire* (New York: Harper & Row, Publishers, 1987 rpt.); and Colin Wells, *The Roman Empire* (Stanford, California: Stanford University Press, 1984).

Anonyma in Aristotelis Artem Rhetoricam Commentaria		varia
Anonymi in Librum Primum Analyticorum		
Posteriorum Commentarium		incert
Anonymi in Sophisticos Elenchos Paraphrasis		fourteenth century A.D.
Anonymus Londinensis		first century A.D.
Antigonus	Carystus	third century B.C.
Antiphanes		fourth century B.C.
Aretacus		second century A.D.
Aristophanes	Athens	fifth-fourth century B.C.
Aristophanes	Constantinople	third-second century B.C.
Aristotles Phil.	Stagirites, Pellacus, Athens	fourth century B.C.
et Corpus Aristotelicum		
Aristoxenus	Selinuntius	seventh-sixth century B.C.
Asclepius	Tralles	sixth century A.D.
Athanasius	Alexandria	fourth century A.D.
Athenaeus	Rome	early third century
Basil	Caesarea	A.D. 330-379
Clearchus		fourth century B.C.
Clement of Alexandria	Alexandria	A.D. 150-211/215
Comica Adespota, CGFPR		varia
Damascius Phil.	Damascenus	fifth-sixth century A.D.
David Phil.		sixth century A.D.
Democritus Phil.	Abderita	470-380 B.C.
Demosthenes Orat.	Athens	fourth century B.C.
Dio Cassius Hist.	Bithynia	A.D. 155-230
Dio Chrysostom	Prusa in Bithynia (Italy)	A.D. 40-120
Diogenes of Sinope (Laertius)	Sinope	400-325 B.C.
Dionysius Halicarnassensis	Rome	60-7 B.C.
Dromo Comic.		fourth century B.C.
Elias Phil.		sixth century A.D.
Empedocles Poet.		

Phil. Agrigentinum	(Sicily)	495-435 B.C.
Epicharmus Comic		
et Pseudepicharmea	Syracusanus	fifth century B.C.
Epictetus	Athens	A.D. 50-138
Epiphanius Scr. Ecc.	Constantine (Cyprus)	fourth century A.D.
Euclides Geom.	Alexandria	third century B.C.
Euripides	Athens	480-406 B.C.
Eusebius Scr. Eccl.	Caesarea	A.D. 260-339/340
et Theol.		
Eustathius Scr. Eccl.	Antioch	A.D. (?)-337
Eustratius Phil.	Nicaeensis	eleventh-twelth century
Flavius Philostratus	Arelatensis	second century A.D.
Galen	Pergamum	A.D. 130-200
Pseudo-Galen		post second century A.D.
Greek Anthology	Italy (?)	tenth century A.D.
Gregorius	Nazianzus	fourth century A.D.
Gregorius	Nyssa	after A.D. 330-394
Hermogenes *Rhetoric*	Tarsus	second-third century A.D.
Herodianus et	Alexandria/Rome	second century A.D.
Pseudo-Herodianus Gramm. et Rhet.		
Heron *Mech.*	Alexandria	first century A.D.
Hippiatrica		ninth century A.D.
Hippocrates Med.	Chius	fifth century B.C.
et Corpus Hipporcraticum		
Homer	Ioanian-Chio Smyrna	eighth century B.C.
Isaeus Orat.	Athens/Chaldea (?)	415/10-344 B.C. Isocrates
Orat.	Athens	436-338 B.C.
John Chrysostomus	Antioch/Constantinople	fourth-fifth century A.D.
Ecclesiastical Scrol		
John Philoponus Phil.	Alexandria	sixth century A.D.

Justin Martyr Apol.	Rome	A.D. -165 Pseudo-Justin
Martyr		fourth-fifth century A.D.
Libanius	Antioch/Constantinople/	
	Nicomedensis	fourth century A.D.
Lucianus	Samos	A.D. 120-180
Pseudo-Lucianus		post second century A.D.
<Macarius> Scr. Eccl.	Egypt	fourth century A.D.
Marcus Aurelius Antoninus	Rome	second century A.D.
Menander Comic.	Cephisus (Athens)	342/1-292/1 B.C.
Menandri et Philistionis Sententiae		Incert
Michael Phil.	Ephesus	eleventh-twelth century
New Testament	Palestine to Rome	first to second century
Nicostratus Comic		fourth century A.D.
Olympiodorus Phil.	Alexandria (Botthius)	480-524 A.D.
Origen Theology	Alexandria	A.D.182/5 -251/4
Palladius Med.	Alexandria	sixth century A.D.
Palladius Ecclesiastical Scr.		fourth century-fifth century
Paulus *Med.*	Aegineta	fourth century A.D.
Philo Judaeus	Alexandria	20 B.C.-40 A.D.
Philostratus Major Soph.	Lemnos	second-third century A.D.
Photius Scr. Eccl.	Constantinople	ninth century A.D.
Plato Phil.	Athens	427-346 B.C.
Plotinus	Rome	A.D. 205-270
Plutarchus Biogr. et Phil.	Chaeronea (Central Greece)	A.D. 46-126
Pseudo-Plutarch		post second century A.D.
Polybius History	Megalopolis (S. Greece)	200-117 B.C.
Polybius Rhet.	Sardis	Incert
Porphyry	Tyre/Rome	A.D. 233-304
Priscianus Phil.	Lydus	sixth century A.D.
Protagoras Soph.	Abderita	fifth century B.C. <Septem
Sapientes> Phil.	Rome (?)	late second century

Septuagint	Alexandria	250 B.C.
Sextus Empiricus Phil.		second-third century A.D.
Simplicus Phil.	Athens	sixth century A.D.
Sophocles	Athens	496-405 B.C.
Sophonias Phil.		thirteenth-fourteenth century A.D.
Stephanus Atheniensis	Damascius	seventh century A.D.
Stephanus Gramm.,	Constantinople	sixth century A.D.
Stephanus Gramm.,	Constantinople	twelth century A.D.
Strabo Geogr.	Amasia	first century B.C.-first century A.D.
Straton Comic		fourth-third century B.C.
Synesius Phil.	Cyrene	fourth-fifth century A.D.
Syriani Sopatri et Marcellini Scholia ad Hermogenis Status		post seventh century A.D.
Syrianus Phil.	Athens	fifth century A.D.
Thales Phil.	Miletus	624-554/48 B.C.
Themistius Phil. et Rhet.	Constantinople	fourth century A.D.
Theophilus Protospatharius	Athens	seventh century A.D.
Theophrastus Phil.	Eresius	fourth-third century B.C.
Timocles Comic		fourth century B.C.
Vita Aesopi		first century A.D.
Xenophon	Athens	429-357 B.C.
Zeno Phil.	Citium	336-263 B.C.

BIBLIOGRAPHY

I. PRIMARY SOURCES

Augustine

    De Consensu Evangelistarum

Bede

    Expositio in Marci

    Opera Historica

Eusebius

    Historia ecclesiastica

    Quæstiones evangelica ad Marinum

Euthymius

    In quatuon evangelia: In Marcum

Gregory of Nyssa

    In Christi resurrectionem

Irenaeus

    Contra hæreses

Jerome

    Epistola

Justin

    Quæstiones et responsiones ad orthodoxos

Origen

   Contra Celsum

   In Matthaeum

Tatian

   Harmonae Evangeliorum

Theophylact

   Enarratio in Evangelia: *In Marcum*

II. TEXTS AND TRANSLATIONS

A. Series

The Ante-Nicene Fathers, ed. Alexander Roberts and James Donaldson. 10 vols. Grand Rapids, Mich.: Wm. B. Eerdmans Publishing Co., 1908.

Berkowitz, Luci and Karl L. Squitier. *Thesaurus Linguae Graecae Canon of Greek Authors and Works*. New York: Oxford University Press, 1986.

The Loeb Classical Library. Cambridge, Mass.: Harvard University Press.

Nicene and Post Nicene Fathers, ed. Philip Schaff, Series 1. 14 vols. Grand Rapids, Mich.: Wm. B. Eerdmans Publishing Co., 1956.

Nicene and Post Nicene Fathers, ed. Philip Schaff, Series 2. 14 vols. Grand Rapids, Mich.: Wm. B. Eerdmans Publishing Co., 1956.

Patrologiae Cursus Completus. Series Graeca, ed. J. P. Migne. Paris, 1857-.

Patrologiae Cursus Completus. Series Latina, ed. J. P. Migne. Paris, 1844-.

B. Individual Works

Aelius Herodianus et Pseudo-Herodinus. "Περὶ Ἰλιακῆς προσῳδίας." Grammatici Graeci. vol. 3. Ed. A. Lentz. Hildesheim: Olms, 1965 rpt.

Alexis. "Fragmenta." Comicorum Atticorum fragmenta. vol. 2. Ed. T. Kock Leipzig: Teubner, 1884.

_____. "Fragmenta." Fragmenta comicorum Graecorum. vol. 3. Ed. A. Meineke (Berlin: De Gruyter, 1970 rpt.

Anonyma in Aristotelis Artem Rhetoricam Commentaria, "In Aristotelis artem rhetoricam commentarium," *Anonymi et Stephani in artem rhethoricum commentaria*, Commentaria Aristotlem Graeca, vol. 21, ed. H. Rabe Berlin: Reimer, 1896.

Antiphanes. "Fragmenta." *Comicorum Atticorum fragmenta*. vol. 2. Ed. T. Kock. Leipzig: Teubner, 1884.

_____. "Fragmenta." *Fragmenta comicorum Graecorum*. vol. 3. Ed. A. Meineke. Berlin: De Gruyter, 1970 rpt.

Eustathius. "Commentarii ad Homer Iliadem." (lib. Σ–Ω) *Eustathii archiepiscopi Thessalonicensis commentarii ad Homer Iliadem*. vol. 4. Ed. G. Stallbaum (Leipzig: Weigel, 1830.

Eustratius. "In analyticorum posteriorum librum secundum commentarium." *Eustratii in analyticorum posteriorum librum secundum commentarium*. Commentariain Aristotelem Graeca. vol. 21. Ed. M. Hayduck. Berlin: Reimer, 1907.

Joannes. "In Aristotelis physicorum libros commentaria." *Ioannis Philoponi in Aristotelis physicorum libros octp commentaria*. Commentaria in Aristotelem Graeca. vol. 17. Ed. M. Hayduck. Berlin: Reimer, 1888.

Menander. "Fragmenta longiora apud alios auctores servata. "*Menandri reliquiae selectae*. Ed. F. H. Sandbach. Oxford: Clarendon Press, 1972.

_____. "Comparatio Menandri et Philistionis." *Menandri Sententiae*. Leipzig: Teubner, 1964.

Plotinus. *Ennead*. V. Trans. A. H. Armstrong. Cambridge, Mass.: Harvard University Press. London: William Heinemann, 1984.

Tatian. *Evangeliorum Harmoniae*. Rome: 1888.

III. COMMENTARIES AND WORKS ON MARK

Achtemeier, Paul J. *Mark*. 2nd ed. Proclamation Commentaries. Philadelphia: Fortress Press, 1986.

Aland, Kurt. "Bemerkungen zum Schluss des Markusevangeliums." *NeoTestamentica et Semitica*. Edinburgh: T. & T. Clark, 1969.

_____. et al., eds. *Novum Testamentum Graece*. [*Nestle-Aland text*]. 26th ed. Stuttgart: Deutsche Bibelstiftung, 1979.

_____. *Synopsis of the Four Gospels: Greek-English Edition of the Synopsis Quattor Evangeliorum*. 3rd ed. United Bible Societies, 1979.

Aland, Kurt and Barbara Aland. *The Text of the New Testament: An Introduction to the Theory and Practice of Modern Textual Criticism*. Trans. Erroll F. Rhodes. Grand Rapids, Mich.: William B. Eerdmans, 1987.

Aland, Kurt, Matthew Black, Bruce Metzger, and A. Wikgren (eds.). *The Greek New Testament*. 3rd. ed. London: United Bible Societies, 1975.

Alsup, John E. *The Post-Resurrection Appearance Stories of the Gospel Tradition*. Stuttgart: Calwer Verlag, 1975.

Ambrozic, Aloysius M. *The Hidden Kingdom: A Redaction-Critical Study of the References to the Kingdom of God in Mark's Gospel*. The Catholic Biblical Quarterly Monograph Series, No. 2. Washington, D. C.: The Catholic Biblical Association of America, 1972.

Anderson, Hugh. "The Easter Witness of the Evangelists." *The New Testament in Historical and Contemporary Perspective*. (Fst. G. H. C. MacGregor, eds. Hugh Anderson and William Barclay). Oxford: Basil Blackwell, 1965, pp. 35-55.

_____. *The Gospel of Mark*. The New Century Bible Commentary. Grand Rapids: Wm. B. Eerdmans, 1976.

Ani-Yonah, Michael. "Jabneh," *Encyclopedia Judaica*, vol. 9, Cecil Roth and Geoffrey Wigoder, Editors in chief, Jerusalem: Keter Publishing House Ltd.; New York: The MacMillan Co., 1971.

Aquinas, Thomas. *Catena Aurea: Commentary on the Four Gospels Collected Out of the Works of the Fathers, St. Mark.* Oxford and London: James Parker and Co., 1874.

Balz, Horst. "φοβέω." *Theological Dictionary of the New Testament.* vol. 9. Trans. by Geoffrey W. Bromiley. Ed. by Gerhard Friedrich. Grand Rapids: Wm. B. Eerdmans Publishing Co., 1974, 189-219.

Bauer, Walter. *A Greek-English Lexicon of the New Testament and Other Early Christian Literature.* Trans. and Ed. by W. F. Arndt and F. W. Gingrich. Chicago: University of Chicago Press, 1957.

Bengel, Johann Jakob. *Gnomon Novi Testamenti.* vol. 1. Tubigin: Sumtibus Ludov Frid. Fues., 1850.

Best, Ernest. *Following Jesus: Discipleship in the Gospel of Mark.* Sheffield, England: JSOT Press, 1981.

_____. *Mark: The Gospel as Story.* Edinburgh: T. & T. Clark, 1983.

Blair, Peter Hunter. *The World of Bede.* New York: St. Martin's Press, 1970.

Blass, Friedrich W. *Phiology of the Gospels.* London: Macmillan and Co., 1898.

_____. and A. Debrunner. *A Greek Grammar of the New Testament and Other Early Christian Literature.* A Translation and Revision of the Ninth-Tenth German Edition Incorporating Supplementary Notes of A. Debrunner. Trans. Robert W. Funk. Chicago: the University of Chicago Press, 1961.

Blevins, James. *The Messianic Secret in Markan Research, 1901-1976.* Washington, D. C.: University Press of America, Inc., 1981.

Bode, Edward Lynn. *The First Easter Mourning: The Gospel Accounts of the Women's Visit to the Tomb of Jesus.* Analecta Biblica, 45. Rome: Pontifical Biblical Institute, 1970.

Boothe, Wayne. *The Rhetoric of Fiction.* Chicago: University of Chicago, 1961.

Botte, B. "Freer (Logion de)." *Dictionnaire de la Bible. Supplement III* (1938), col. 526f.

Bousset, Wilhelm. *Kyrios Christos.* Nashville: Abingdon Press, 1970.

Branscomb, B. Harvie. *The Gospel of Mark.* The Moffat New Testament Commentary. London: Hodder and Stoughton, 1937.

Briggs, C. A. *New Light on the Life of Jesus.* New York: Charles Schribner's Sons, 1904.

Brown, Raymond E. *The Gospel According to John, I-XII.* The Anchor Bible, vol. 29. Garden City, N. J.: Doubleday and Co., 1966.

_____. *The Virginal Conception and the Bodily Resurrection of Jesus.* New York: Paulist Press, 1973.

Browne, G. F. *The Venerable Bede: His Life and Writings.* London: Society for Promoting Christian Knowledge and New York: The Macmillan Company, 1930.

Bultmann, Rudolf. *History of the Synoptic Tradition.* Rev. ed. Trans. John Marsh. New York: Harper & Row, 1976.

Burgon, John. *The Causes of the Corruption of the Traditional Text of the Holy Gospels.* Ed. E. Miller, London: George Bell & Sons, 1896.

_____. *The Last Twelve Verses of the Gospel According to Saint Mark.* Oxford: James Parker and Co., 1871.

_____. *The Revision Revised.* London: John Murry, 1883.

_____. *The Traditional Texts of the Holy Gospels.* Ed. E. Miller, London: George Bell & Sons, 1896.

Burkitt, Francis C. *Christian Beginnings.* London: University of London Press, 1924.

Chamberlain, William Douglas. *An Exegetical Grammar of the Greek New Testament.* Grand Rapids, Michigan: Baker Book House, 1987.

Cranfield, Charles E. B. *The Gospel Acording to Saint Mark.* The Cambridge Greek Testament Commentary. Cambridge: University Press, 1966.

Crossan, John Dominic. "Empty Tomb and Absent Lord. " *The Passion in Mark: Studies in Mark 14-16.* Ed. by Werner H. Kelber. Philadelphia: Fortress Press, 1976, 135-152.

Dana H. E., and Julius R. Mantey. *A Manual Grammar of the Greek New Testament.* New York: The Macmillan Company, 1957 rpt.

Davidson, Samuel *An Introduction to the Study of the New Testament: Critical, Exegetical, and Theological.* vol. 1. 2nd. ed. London: Longmans, Green, and Co., 1882

Delorme, Jean. "Résurrection et Tombeau de Jésus: Mar 16, 1-8 dans la tradition evangelique." *La Résurrection de Christ et L'Exegese Moderne.* Paris: Les Editions Du Cerf, 1969.

Demarest, Bruce. *A History of Interpretation of Hebrews 7,1-10 from the Reformation to the Present.* Beiträge zur geschichte der biblischen exegese. Tübingen: J. C. B. Mohr (Paul Siebeck), 1976.

Dewey, Joanna. *Disciples of the Way: Mark on Discipleship.* Woman's Division, Board of Global Ministries, The United Methodist Church, 1976.

Dibelius, Martin. *Die Formgeschichte des Evangeliums.* Tübingen: Verlag J. C. B. Mohr (Paul Siebeck), 1933.

Die Bibel oder die ganze heilige Schrift des Alten und Neuen Teftaments nach der deutfchen uberfehung D. Martin Luther. New York: American Bible Society, 1816.

Dodd, Charles Harold. "The Appearances of the Risen Christ: An Essay in Form-Criticism of the Gospels." *Studies in the Gospels.* (Essays in Memory of R. H. Lightfoot, Ed. D. F. Nineham). Oxford: Basil Blackwell, 1957, 9-35.

Donahue, John R. *Are You the Christ? The Trial Narrative in the Gospel of Mark.* SBL Dissertation Series 10. Missoula: The Scholar's Press, 1973.

_____. "Introduction: From Passion Traditions to Passion Narrative." *The Passion in Mark: Studies in Mark 14-16.* Ed. by Werner H. Kelber. Philadelphia: Fortress Press, 1976, 1-20.

_____. *The Theology and Setting of Discipleship in the Gospel of Mark.* Milwaukee: Marquette University Press, 1983.

Dunkerley, R. *The Unwritten Gospel*. London: 1925.

Ebeling, Hans Jürgen. *Das Messiasgeheimnis und die Botsschaft des MarcusEvangelisten*. Berlin: A Töpelmann, 1939.

Elliott, J. K. *A Survey of Manuscripts Used in Editions of the Greek New Testament*. Leiden: E. J. Brill, 1987.

Ellis, Peter F. "Patterns and Structures of Mark's Gospel." *Biblical Studies in Contemporary Thought*. Ed. by Miriam Ward. Somerville, Mass.: Greeno, Hadden and Co., Ltd., 1975, 88-103.

Evans, Christopher Francis. *Resurrection in the New Testament*. Studies in Biblical Theology. 2nd Series, 12. Naperville, Ill.: Alec R. Allenson Inc., 1970.

Farmer, William Reuben. *The Last Twelve Verses of Mark*. Cambridge: Cambridge University Press, 1974.

_____. *The Synoptic Problem: A Critical Analysis*. New York: Macmillan, 1964.

Farrar, Austin. *A Study in St. Mark*. Great Britain: Dacre Press, 1951.

_____. *The Glass of Vision*. Great Britain: Dacre Press, 1948.

_____. *St. Matthew and St. Mark*. Great Britain: Dacre Press, 1954.

Friedrich, Gerhard. "εὐαγγέλιον." *Theological Dictionary of the New Testament*. vol. 2. Trans. by Geoffrey W. Bromiley. Ed. by Gerhard Kittel. Grand Rapids: Wm. B. Eerdmans Publishing Co., 1964, 721-737.

Fuller, David Otis. *Which Bible?* Grand Rapids: International Publications, 1970.

Fuller, Reginald H. *A Critical Introduction to the New Testament: Studies in Theology*. London: Duckworth, 1966.

_____. *The Formation of the Resurrection Narratives*. New York: Macmillan, 1971.

Funk, Robert W. *Language, Hermeneutic, and Word of God: The Problem of Language in the New Testament and Contemporary Theology*. New York: Harper & Row, 1966; reprint Missoula, Mont.: Scholars Press, 1979.

Gnilka, Joachim. *Das Evangelium nach Markus*. vol. 2 Köln: Benziger, 1979.

González, Justo L. *A History of Christian Thought*. 3 vols. Nashville: Abingdon Press, 1983 rpt.

Goodspeed, Edgar J. *New Solutions of New Testament Problems*. Chicago: University of Chicago, 1927.

Gould, Ezra P. *The Gospel According to St. Mark*. The International Critical Commentary. Edinburgh: T. & T. Clark, 1983 rpt.

Grant, Frederick C. "The Gospel According to St. Mark: Introduction and Exegesis." *The Interpreter's Bible*. Ed. by George A. Buttrick. New York: Abingdon-Cokesbury, 1952, 7: 627-917.

Grass, Hans. *Ostergeschehen und Osterberichte*. Göttingen: Vandenhoeck und Ruprecht, 1962.

Gregory, Caspar René. *Canon and Text of the New Testament*. New York: Charles Schribner's Sons, 1907.

_____. *Das Freerlogion*. Leipzig, 1908.

Griesbach, Johann Jakob. *Commentarius Criticus in Textum Novi Testamentl*. Ienae: Apud J. C. G. Goepferdt, 1774/1775.

Haenchen, Ernst. *Der Weg Jesu*. Berlin: Alfred Töpelmann, 1966.

Hargreaves, John. *A Guide to Saint Mark's Gospel*. London: SPCK, 1965.

Harnack, Adolf. *The Acts of the Apostles*. Trans. J. R. Wilkinson. London: Williams & Norgate; New York: G. P. Putnam, 1909.

Heil, John Paul. *Meaning and Gospel Functions of Matt 14:22-33, Mark 6:45-52 and John 6:15b-21*. Rome: Biblical Institute Press, 1981.

Hills, Edward F. "Introduction," John W. Burgon, *The Last Twelve Verses of the Gospel According to St. Mark*. Erlanger, Ky.: Faith and Facts Press, rpt.

Holmes, B. T. *The Word of God: Mark''s Version*. Toronto: Canada: B. T. Holmes, 1962.

Homer. *The Odyssey*, Vol. 2. Trans. A. T. Murray, LCL. Cambridge, Massachussetts: Harvard University Press, 1953.

Householder, P. W. "Ancient Greek." *Word Classes*. Amsterdam: North- Holland Publishing Company, 1967.

Hug, Joseph. *La finale de l'wvangile de Marc (Mc 16,9-20)*. Paris: Ĝabalda, 1978.

Isocrates, *Isocrates*, Vol. 1. Trans. George Norlin, LCL. Cambridge, Massachussetts: Harvard University Press, 1980.

Jeremias, Joachim. *Die Abendmahlsworte Jesu*. Göttingen: Vandenhoeck & Ruprecht, 1967 rpt.

Johnson, Sherman E. *The Gospel According to St. Mark*. Harper New Testament Commentaries. New York: Harper and Bro. Publ., 1960.

Jülicher, Adolf. *An Introduction to the New Testament*. Trans. by Janet Penrose Ward. London: Smith, Elder, & Co., 1904.

Kelber, Werner H. "Conclusion: From Passion Narrative to Gospel." *The Passion in Mark: Studies in Mark 14-16*. Ed. by Werner H. Kelber. Philadelphia: Fortress Press, 153-180.

_____. "The Hour of the Son of Man and the Temptation of the Disciples." *The Passion in Mark: Studies in Mark 14-16*. Ed. by Werner H. Kelber. Philadelphia: Fortress Press, 1976, 41-60.

_____. *The Kingdom in Mark*. Philadelphia: Fortress Press, 1974.

_____. *Mark's Story of Jesus*. Philadelphia: Fortress Press 1979.

_____. *The Oral and Written Gospel*. Philadelphia: Fortress Press, 1983.

Kenyon, Frederic G. *The Text of the Greek Bible*. London: Duckworth, 1937.

Kermode, Frank. *The Genesis of Secrecy: On the Interpretation of Narrative*. Cambridge, Mass.: Harvard University Press, 1979.

Kilpatrick, G. D. "Atticism and the Text of the Greek New Testament." *Neutestamentliche Aufsätze*. Festschrift für Prof. Josef Schmid. ed. by J. Blinzler, O. Kuss, and E. Mussner. Regensburg: Puster, 1963.

Kingsbury, Jack Dean. *The Christology of Mark's Gospel*. Philadelphia: Fortress Press, 1983.

Kümmel, Werner Georg. *Introduction to the New Testament.* 17th ed. Trans. by Howard Clark Kee. Nashville: Abingdon Press, 1975.

Ladd, George Eldon. *I Believe in the Resurrection of Jesus.* Grand Rapids: Wm. B. Eerdmans Publishing Co., 1975.

_____. *The New Testament and Criticism.* Grand Rapids, Mich.: William B. Eerdmans Publishing Company, 1978 rpt.

Lake, Kirsopp. *The Historical Evidence for the Resurrection of Jesus Christ.* New York: B. P. Putnam's Sons, 1907.

Lake, Kirsopp and Silva Lake. *An Introduction to the New Testament.* London: Christophers, 1938.

Lane, William. *Commentary on the Gospel of Mark.* The New International Commentary on the New Testament. Grand Rapids: Wm. B. Eerdmans, 1974.

Lehmann, Helmut T., eds et al. *Sermons, II.* Luther's Works. vol. 51. Philadelphia: Fortress Press, 1974.

Lewis Naphtali and Meyer Reinhold, eds. *Roman Civilization, Sourcebook I.: The Republic.* New York: Harper & Row, Publishers, 1987 rpt.

_____. *Roman Civilization, Sourcebook II.: The Empire.* (New York: Harper & Row, Publishers, 1987 rpt.

Liebermann, Saul. "Jewish and Christian Codices." *Hellenism in Jewish Palestine.* New York: Jewish Theological Seminary of America, 1950.

Lightfoot, Robert H. *The Gospel Messages of St. Mark.* Oxford: Clarendon Press, 1952 rpt.

_____. *History and Interpretation in the Gospels.* London: Hodder & Stoughton, 1934.

_____. *Locality and Doctrine in the Gospels.* New York: Harper, 1937, 1-23.

Linnemann, Eta. *Historical Criticism of the Bible: Methodology or Ideology? Reflections of a Bultmannian turned Evangelical.* Trans. by Robert W. Yarbrough from *German Wissenschaff oder Meinung.* Grand Rapids, Mich.: Baker Book House, 1990.

Lohmeyer, Ernest. *Das Evangelium des Markus.* 15th ed. Göttingen: Vandenhoeck und Ruprecht, 1959.

Lohse, Eduard. *Mark's Witness to Jesus Christ.* New York: Association Press, 1955.

Lubbock, Percy. *The Craft of Fiction.* London: Jonathan Cape, 1921.

Luccock, Halford E. "The Gospel According to St. Mark: Exposition." *The Interpreter's Bible.* New York: Abingdon-Cokesbury, 1952.

Lucian. *Lucian*, Vol. 6. Trans. K. Kilburn, LCL. Cambridge, Massachussetts: Harvard University Press, 1980.

Luther, Martin. *Church Postil, Gospels: Epiphany, Lent, and Easter Sermons.* Minneapolis, Minn.: Lutherans in all Lands Co., 1906.

Macmillan, Earle. *The Gospel According to Mark.* The Living Word Commentary. Texas: Sweet Publishing Co., 1973.

Mann, Christopher Stephen. *Mark.* The Anchor Bible. vol. 27. Garden City, N. Y.: Doubleday and Co., Inc., 1986.

Marxsen, Willi. *Mark the Evangelist: Studies in the Redaction History of the Gospel.* Trans. James Boyce, Donald Juel, William Poehlmann, and Roy A. Harrisville. Nashville: Abingdon Press, 1969.

Matera, Frank J. *Passion Narratives and Gospel Theologies: Interpreting the Synoptics Through Their Passion Stories.* New York: Paulist Press, 1986.

McNeil, John T. ed. *Calvin: Institutes of the Christian Religion.* 2 vols. Philadelphia: Westminster Press, 1960 ed.

Metzger, Bruce M. *The Text of the New Testament: Its Transmission, Corruption, and Restoration.* New York and Oxford: Oxford University Press, 1968.

_____. Et al., eds. *A Textual Commentary on the Greek New Testament.* London and New York: United Bible Societies, 1976 corrected edition.

Meye, Robert P. *Jesus and the Twelve: Discipleship and Revelation in Mark's Gospel.* Grand Rapids: Wm. B. Eerdmans Publishing Co., 1968.

Meyer, Ed. *Ursprung und Anfange des Christentum.* Stuttgart and Berlin, 1921-1931.

Michaelis, Wilhelm. "ὁράω." *Theological Dictionary of the New Testament.* vol. 5. Trans. by Geoffrey W. Bromiley. Ed. by Gerhard Friedrich. Grand Rapids, Mich.: Wm. B. Eerdmans Publishing Co., 1967, 315-382.

Mill, John. *Novum Testamentum Graecum* (1907).

Minear, Paul S. *Gospel According to Mark.* Epworth Preacher's Commentaries. London: Epworth Press, 1957.

Monro, D. B. *A Grammar of the Homeric Dialect.* Oxford: Clarendon Press, 1891.

Morgenthaler, Robert. *Statistik des neutestamentlichen Wortschatzes.* Zürich: Gotthelf-Verlag, 1958.

Moule, Charles Francis Digby. *The Gospel According to Mark.* The Cambridge Bible Commentary. Cambridge: University Press, 1965.

Moulton, William Fiddian. and Alfred S. Geden, eds. *A Concordance to the Greek Testament: According to the Texts of Westcott and Hort, Tischendorf and the English revisers.* Edinburgh: T. & T. Clark, 1980 rpt.

Neirynck, Frans. *Duality in Mark.* Louvain: Louvain University Press, 1972.

Nineham, Dennis E. *The Gospel of St. Mark.* The Pelican Gospel Commentaries. London: Adam and Charles Black, 1963.

Osborne, Grant R. *The Resurrection Narratives: A Redactional Study.* Grand Rapids: Baker Book House, 1984.

Perrin, Norman. *Christology and a Modern Pilgrimage.* Ed. H. D. Betz. Missoula: Scholars Press, 1974.

_____. *The New Testament: An Introduction.* New York: Harcourt Brace Janovich, Inc., 1974.

_____. *The Resurrection According to Matthew, Mark, and Luke*. Philadelphia: Fortress Press, 1977.

Pesch, Rudolph. *Das Evangelium der Urgemeinde*. Freiburg: Herder, 1979.

_____. *Naherwartungen: Tradition und Redaktion in Mk 13*. Düsseldorf: Patmos-Verlag, 1968.

Petersen, Norman R. *Literary Criticism for New Testament Critics*. New Testament Series. Philadelphia: Fortress Press, 1978.

Ramsey, Arthur Michael. *The Resurrection of Christ*. London: Lowe and Brydone Ltd., 1945.

Rawlinson, Alfred Edwards John. *St. Mark*. Westminster Commentaries. London: Methuen and Co., LTD, 1925.

Rhodes, David and Donald Mitche. *Mark as Story: An Introduction to the Narrative of a Gospel*. Philadelphia: Fortress Press, 1982.

Richardson, Alan. *Introduction to the Theology of the New Testament*. Great Britain: SCM Press Ltd., 1958.

Rimmon-Kenan, Sclomith. *Narrative Fiction: Contemporary Poetics*. London: Methuen, 1984 rpt.

Robertson, A. T. *A Grammar of the Greek New Testament in the Light of Historical Research*. New York: Hodder & Stoughton, 1915.

_____. *An Introduction to the Textual Criticism of the New Testament*. Nashville, Tenn.: Sunday School Board of the Southern Baptist Convention, 1925.

Robinson, James M. *The Problem of History in Mark and Other Markan Studies*. Philadelphia: Fortress Press, 1982.

Robinson, James M. and Helmut Koester. *Trajectories Through Early Christianity*. Philadelphia: Fortress Press, 1971.

Rohrback, Paul. *Der Schluss des Markusevangelium, der Vier-Evangelien-Kanon und die kleinasiatischen Presbyter*. Berlin: Georg Nauck (Fritz Ruhe), 1894.

Salmon, George. *A Historical Introduction to the Study of the Books of the New Testament*. London: John Murray, 1885.

_____. *The Human Element in the Gospels: A Commentary on the Synoptic Narrative*. New York: E. P. Dutton and Company, 1907.

_____. *Some Thoughts on the Textual Criticism of the New Testament*. London: John Murray, 1897.

Schaff, Philip, ed. *A Select Library of the Nicene and Post-Nicene Fathers*. Series 1. Grand Rapids, Mich.: Wm. B. Eerdmans Publishing Company, 1956.

Schenke, Ludger. *Auferstehungsverkundigung und leeres Grab: Eine traditionsgeschichtliche Untersuchung von Mk. 16: 1-8*. Calver Verlag, 1968.

Schmithals, Walter. *Einleitung in die drei ersten Evangelien*. Berlin and New York: Walter de Gruyter, 1985.

_____. *The Office of Apostle in the Early Church*. Trans. by John E. Steely. Nashville and New York: Abingdon Press, 1969.

Schniewind, Julius. "Das Evangelium nach Markus." *Das Neue Testament Deutsch*. Göttingen: Vandenhoeck und Ruprecht, 1949.

Schweizer, Eduard. *The Good News According to Mark*. Trans. by Donald H. Madvig. Atlanta: John Knox Press, 1970.

Selby, Donald J. *Introduction to the New Testament*. New York: The Macmillan Co., 1971.

Singer, Isidore eds. et al. "Jabneh." *The Jewish Encyclopedia*, vol. 7, New York and London: Funk & Wagnall's Company, 1910.

Sodon, Hermann Freiherr von. *Die Schriften des Neuen Testaments in ihrer ältesten erreichbaren Textgestalt, I Teil, Untersuchen, i, Abteilung, Die Textzeugen*. Berlin, 1902.

Stein, Robert H. *The Synoptic Problem: An Introduction*. Grand Rapids: Baker Book House, 1987.

Stemberger, Günter. "Galilee-Land of Salvation?" *The Gospel and the Land*. Ed. W. D. Davies. Berkeley: University of California Press, 1974.

Stock, Augustine, OSB. *Call to Discipleship: A Literary Study of Mark's Gospel*. Wilmington: Michael Glazier, Inc., 1982.

Stonehouse, Ned Bernard. *The Witness of Matthew and Mark to Christ*. 2nd ed. Grand Rapids: Wm. B. Eerdmans Publishing Co., 1958.

Streeter, Burnett Hillman. *The Four Gospels*. London: Macmillan and Co., Ltd., 1924.

Sturz, Harry A. *The Byzantine Text-Type and New Testament Textual Criticism*. Nashville: Thomas Nelson Publishers, 1984.

Swete, Henry B. *The Gospel According to Mark*. London: Macmillan and Co., Ltd., 1924.

_____. *Zwei neue Evangelienfragmente*. Bonn: 1908.

Tagawa, Kenzo. *Miracles et Évangile: La Pensée personelle de L'évangliste Marc*. Paris: Presses Universitaires de France, 1966.

Talbert, Charles H. *What is a Gospel?* Philadelphia: Fortress Press, 1977.

Taylor, Vincent. *The Gospel According to St. Mark*. 2nd ed. Thornapple Commentaries. Grand Rapids: Baker Book House, 1981.

_____. *The Gospels*. London: The Epworth Press, 1938.

Telford, William, ed. *The Interpretation of Mark*. Philadelphia: Fortress Press, 1985.

Throckmorton, B. H. "Philosophy." *The Interpreter's Dictionary of the Bible*, vol. 3, et al., eds. Nashville: Abingdon Press, 1962.

Tischendorf, Constantine von. *Novum Testamentum Graece*. Editio ovtava critica maior. 3 Vols. Lipsae: Giesecke and Devrient, 1869.

Torrance David W. and Thomas F. Torrance, eds. *A Harmony of the Gospels Matthew, Mark and Luke Volume III. and the Epistles of James and Jude*. Trans. A. W. Morrison. Grand Rapids, Mich.: Wm. B. Eerdmans Publishing Company, 1972.

Tregelles, Samuel Prideaux. *An Account of the Printed Text of the Greek New Testament with Remarks on Its Revision Upon Critical Principles.* London: Samuel Bagster and Sons, 1854.

Trocmé, Etienne. *The Formation of the Gospel According to Mark.* Trans. Pamela Gaughan. Philadelphia: Westminster Press, 1975.

Via, Dan O. *Kerygma and Commedy in the New Testament.* Philadelphia: Fortress Press, 1975.

Von Campenhausen, Hans. "The Events of Easter and the Empty Tomb." *Tradition and Life in the Church.* Philadelphia: Fortress Press, 1968.

Walker, Williston. *A History of the Christian Church.* 3rd edition. New York: Charles Schribner's Sons, 1970.

Wallace-Hadrill, D. S. *Eusebius of Caesarea.* London: A. R. Mowbray & Co. Limited, 1960.

Weeden, Theodore J. "The Cross as Power in Weakness." *The Passion in Mark: Studies in Mark 14-16.* Ed. by Werner Kelber. Philadelphia: Fortress Press, 1976, 115-134.

_____. *Mark: Traditions in Conflict.* Philadelphia: Fortress Press, 1971.

Weiss, D. Bernhard. *A Commentary On the New Testament.* vol. 1, Trans. George H. Schodde and Epiphanius Wilson. New York and London: Funk & Wagnalls, 1906.

_____. *das Neue Testament.* vol. 1. Leipzig: J. C. Hinrichs'sche Buchhandlung, 1905.

_____. *Lehrbuch der Einleitung in das Neue Testament.* Berlin: Verlag von Wilhelm Hertz, 1897.

Wellhausen, Julius. *Einleitung in die drei ersten Evangelien.* 2nd ed. Berlin, 1911.

Wells, Colin. *The Roman Empire.* Stanford, California: Stanford University Press, 1984.

Westcott, Brook Foss and Fenton John Anthony Hort. *The New Testament in the Original Greek.* London: Macmillan and Co., Ltd., 1881.

Wettstein, J. J. *Novum Testamentum Graecum*. 2 Vols. Amsterdam, 1751.

Wikenhauser, Alfred. *New Testament Introduction*. New York: Herder and Herder, 1963.

Wilchens, Ulrich. *Resurrection*. Trans. by A. M. Stewart. Atlanta: John Knox Press, 1978.

_____. "The Tradition-History of the Resurrection of Jesus." *The Significance of the Message of the Resurrection for Faith in Jesus Christ*. Ed. by C. F. D. Moule. Great Britain: Robert Cunningham and Sons, Ltd., 1968.

Williams, Charles Stephen Conway. *Alterations to the Text of the Synoptic Gospels and Acts*. Oxford: Basil Blackwell, 1951.

Williams, Clarence R. "The Appendices to the Gospel According to Mark: A Study in Textual Transmission." *Connecticut Academy of Arts and Sciences, Transactions*. 18 New Haven, 1915.

Wrede, William. *The Messianic Secret*. Trans. by J. C. G. Grieg. Greenwood, S. C.: Attic Press, Inc., 1971.

Zahn, Theodore. *Einleitung in das Neue Testament*. 2 vols. Leipzig, 1900.

_____. *Geschicte des neutestamentlichen Kannons*. 2 vols. Erlangen: 1896.

_____. *Introduction to the New Testament*. 2 vols. Trans., Melancthon Williams Jacobus, Edinburgh: T. & T. Clark, 1909.

Zwingli, Huldreich. *Commentary on True and False Religion*. Eds. Sammuel Macauley Jackson and Clarence Nevin Heller. Durham: The Labyrinth Press, 1981 rpt.

IV. ARTICLES AND ESSAYS

Achtemeir, Paul. "Mark as Interpreter of the Jesus Traditions." *Interpretations*, 32 (1978), 339-352.

Aland, Kurt. "Der wiedergefundene Markusschluss? Ein" methodologische Bemerkung zur textkritischen Arbeit." *Zeitschrift für Theologie und Kirche*, 67 (1, 1970), 3-13.

_____. "Luther as an Exegete." *Expository Times*, 69 (1957), 46-48.

Barrett, Charles Kingsley. "Review of William R. Farmer, *The Last Twelve Verses of Mark* ." *Durham University Journal*, 36 (December, 1974), 104-106.

Bartholomew, Gilbert L. "The Narrative Technique of Mark 16:8." *Journal of Biblical Literature*, 100 (1981), 213-223.

Bartsch, H. W. "Der Schluss des Markus-Evangeliums: Ein überlieferungsgeschichtliches Problem." *Theologische Zeitschrift*, 27 (4, 1971), 241-254.

Bater, Robert R. "Towards a More Biblical View of the Resurrection." *Interpretation*, 23 (1964), 47-65.

Beare, Francis Wright. "Review of William R. Farmer, *The Synoptic Problem: A Critical Analysis*." *Journal of Biblical Literature*, 84 (1965), 295-297.

Beasley-Murray, George R. "Review of William R. Farmer, *The Last Twelve Verses of Mark*." *Review and Expositor*, 72 (Summer, 1975), 375.

Best, Ernest. "Mark: Some Problems." *Irish Biblical Studies*, 1 (1979), 77-98.

Bickermann, E. "Das leere Grab." *Zeitschrift für die neutestamentliche Wissenschaft*, 23 (1924), 281-292.

Birdsall, J. N. "Review of William R. Farmer, *The Last Twelve Verses of Mark*." *Journal of Theological Studies*, 26 (1975), 151-160.

Blatherwick, David. "The Markan Silhouette?" *New Testament Studies*, 17 (1970), 184-192.

Blevins. James L. "The Christology of Mark." *Review and Expositor*, 75 (4, 1975), 505-517.

Boobyer, G. H. "Galilee and Galileans in St. Mark's Gospel." *Bulletine of the John Rylands Library*, 35 (1953), 334-348.

Boomershine, Thomas. "Mark 16:8 and the Apostolic Commission." *Journal of Biblical Literature*, 100 (2, 1981), 225-239.

_____. and G. L. Bartholomew. "The Narrative Technique of Mark 16:8." *Journal of Biblical Literature*, 100 (2, 1981), 213-223.

Bornhäuser, Karl. "The Present Status of Liberal Theology in Germany." *American Journal of Theology*, 18 (1914), 191-204.

Cadbury, Henry J. "Mark 16:8." *Journal of Biblical Literature*, 46 (1927), 344-350.

Catchpole, D. R. "The Fearful Silence of the Women at the Tomb: A Study in Markan Theology." *Journal of Theology for South Africa*, 18 (1977), 3-10.

Crossan, John Dominic. "A Form For Absence: The Markan Creation of Gospel." *Semeia*, 12 (1978), 41-53.

_____. "Mark and the Relatives of Jesus." *Novum Testamentum*, 15 (1973), 81-113.

Culpepper, R. Alan. "An Outline of the Gospel According to Mark." *Review and Expositor*, 75 (1978), 619-622.

_____. "The Passion and Resurrection in Mark." *Review and Expositor.* 75 (1978), 583-600.

Danker, Frederick W. "Postscript to the Markan Secrecy Motif." *Concordia Theological Monthly.* 38 (1967), 24-27.

Dewey, Joanna. "The Literary Structure of the Controversy Stories in Mark 2:1-3:6." *Journal of Biblical Literature*, 92 (1973), 394-401.

Donahue, John R. "Jesus as the Parable of God in the Gospel of Mark." *Interpretation*, 32 (1978), 369-386.

Dunn, James D. G. "The Text of Mark 16 in the English Bible." *Expository Times*, 83 (1971), 313.

_____. "The Text of Mark 16 in the English Bible." *Expository Times*, 83 (1971), 311-312.

Elliott, James Keith. "The Text and Language of the Endings to Mark's Gospel." *Theologische Zeitschrift*, 27 (1971), 255-262.

Evans, C. F. "I Will Go Before You Into Galilee." *Journal of Theological Studies*, 5 (1964), 3-18.

Fee, Gordon D. "Review of William R. Farmer, *The Last Twelve Verses of Mark*." *Journal of Biblical Literature*, 94 (1975), 462.

Fleddermann, Harry. "The Flight of a Naked Young Man." *Catholic Biblical Quarterly*, 41 (1979), 412-419.

Fowler, Robert M. "Who is "the Reader" of Mark's Gospel?." *Society of Biblical Literature Seminar Papers*, 22 (1983), 31-53.

Fuller, Reginald H. "The Resurrection of Jesus Christ." *Biblical Research*, 4 (1960), 8-13.

Goulder, Michael. "The Empty Tomb." *Theology*, 79 (1976), 206-214.

_____. "Mark XVI. 1-8 and Parallels." *New Testament Studies*, 24 (1977), 235-240.

Gourgues, Michael. "A Propos du symbolisme christologique et baptismal de Marc 16:5." *New Testament Studies*, 27 (1981), 672-678.

Haefner, Alfred E. "The Bridge Between Mark and Acts." *Journal of Biblical Literature*, 77 (1958), 67-71.

Hamilton, N. Q. "Resurrection Tradition and the Composition of Mark." *Journal of Biblical Literature*, 84 (1965), 415-421.

Harnack, A. "Neues zum unechten Marcusschluss." *Zeitschrift für Theologie und Kirche*, 33 (1908), 168-170.

Hebert, Gabriel. "The Resurrection-Narrative in St. Mark's Gospel." *Scottish Journal of Theology*, 15 (1962), 66-73.

Henaut, Barry W. "Empty Tomb or Empty Argument: a Failure of Nerve in Recent Studies of Mark 16." *Studies in Religion/Sciences religieuses*, 15 (2, 1986), 177-190.

Hodges, Zane C. "The Women and the Empty Tomb." *Bibliotheca Sacra*, 123 (1966), 301-309.

_____. "Review of William R. Farmer, *The Last Twelve Verses of Mark.*"
    Bibliotheca Sacra, 133 (April, 1976), 178.

Horvath, Tibor. "The Early Markan Tradition on the Resurrection." *Revue de
    l'Universite d'Ottawa*, 43 (3, 1973), 445-448.

Karnetzki, Manfred. "Die galiläische Redaktion im Markusevangelium."
    Zeitschrift für die neutestamentliche Wissenschaft, 52 (1961), 238-272.

Kee, Howard Clark. "Mark's Gospel in Recent Research." *Interpretation*, 32
    (1978), 353-368.

Kelber, Werner H. "Mark and Oral Tradition." *Semenia*, 16 (1980), 7-55.

Kingsbury, Jack Dean. "The Gospel of Mark in Current Research." *Religious
    Studies Review*, 5 (1979), 101-107.

Koch, H. "Der erweite Markussluss und die kleinasiatischen Presbyter." *Biblische
    Zeitschrift*, 6 (1908), 266-278.

Knigge, Heinz-Dieter. "The Meaning of Mark: The Exegesis of the Second
    Gospel." *Interpretation*, 22 (1968), 53-70.

Knox, W. L. "The Ending of St. Mark's Gospel." *Harvard Theological Review*,
    35 (1942), 13-23.

Kraeling, Carl H. "A Philological Note on Mark 16:8." *Journal of Biblical
    Literature*, 44 (1925), 357-364.

Katz, Peter. "The Early Christians Use of Codices Instead of Rolls." *Journal of
    Theological Studies*, 44 (1945), 63-69.

Lane, William. "From Historian to Theologian: Milestones in Markan
    Scholarship." *Review and Expositor*, 75 (1978), 601-617.

_____. "Gospel of Mark in Current Study." *Southwestern Journal of Theology*,
    21 (1978), 7-21.

Lincoln, Andrew T. "The Promise and the Failure: Mark 16:7,8." *Journal of
    Biblical Literature*, 108 (2, 1989), 283-300.

Lindemann, Andreas. "Die Osterbotschaft des Markus: zur Theologischen Interpretation von Mark 16:1-8." *New Testament Studies*, 26 (1980), 298-317.

Linnemann, Eta. "Der Wiedergefundene Markusschluss." *Zeitschrift für Theologie und Kirche*, 66 (3, 1969), 255-287.

Lührmann, Dieter. "The Gospel of Mark and the Sayings Collection Q." *Journal of Biblical Literature* 108 (1 1989), 51-71.

McIndoe, J. H. "The Young Man at The Tomb." *The Expository Times*, 80 (1968), 125.

Mangatt, G. "At the Tomb of Jesus." *Biblebhashyam*, 3 (2, 1977), 91-96.

Masson, Charles. "Le Tombeau Vide." *Revue de Theologie et de Philosophie*, 32 (1944), 161-174.

Meye, Robert P. "Mark's Special Easter Emphasis." *Christianity Today*, 15 (March 26, 1971), 4-6.

_____. "Mark 16:8--The Ending of Mark's Gospel." *Biblical Research*, 14 (1969), 33-43.

Morgan, R. "Review of C. H. Talbert, *What is a Gospel?*" *Journal of Theological Studies*, 30 (October, 1979), 531.

Moule, Charles Francis Digby. "St. Mark XVI. 8 Once More." *New Testament Studies*, 2 (1956), 58-59.

Neirynck, Frans. "Mark 16:1-8: tradition et rédaction, pt. 1." *Ephemerides Theologicae Lovanienses*, 56 (1980), 56-88.

_____. "The New Nestle-Aland: The Text of Mark in N^{26}." *Ephemrides Theologicae Lovanienses*, 55 (1979), 331-356.

O'Collins, Gerald. "The Fearful Silence of Three Women [Mark 16:8c], a Conference at the Centro Pro Union." *Centro Pro Union Bulletin*, 33 (Spring, 1988), 3-8.

Ottley, R. R. "ἐφοβοῦντο γάρ, Mark XVI 8." *Journal of Theological Studies*, 27 (1926), 407-409.

Palmer, D. W. "The Origen, Form, and Purpose of Mark XVI. 4 in Codex Bobbiensis." *Journal of Theological Studies*, 27 (1976), 113-122.

Paulsen, Henning. "Mark 16:1-8." *Novum Testamentum*, 22 (1980), 138-175.

Perrin, Norman. "The Christology of Mark: A Study in Methodology." *Journal of Religion*, 51 (1971), 173-187.

_____. "The Interpretation of the Gospel of Mark." *Interpretation*, 30 (1976), 115-124.

Petersen, Norman R. "When is the End Not the End?" Literary Reflections on the Ending of Mark's Narrative." *Interpretation*, 34 (April, 1980), 151-166.

Reedy, Charles J. "Mk. 8:31-11:10 and the Gospel Ending: A Redaction Study." *Catholic Biblical Quarterly*, 34 (1972), 188-197.

Richardson, L. J. D. "St. Mark XVI. 8." *Journal of Theological Studies*, 49 (1948), 144-146.

Roloff, Jürgen. "Das Markusevangelium als Geschichtsdarstellung." *Evangelische Theologie*, 29 (1969), 73-93.

Sanders, Henry A. "The Beginnings of the Modern Book." *Michigan Alumnus Review*, 54 (1938), 95-111.

Schmithals, Walter. "Der Markusschluss, die Verlärungsgeschichte und die Aussendung der Zwölf." *Zeitschrift für Theologie und Kirche*, 69 (1972), 379-411.

Schweizer, Eduard. "The portrayal of the Life of Faith in the Gospel of Mark." *Interpretation*, 32 (1978), 387-399.

Scroggs, Robin and K. I. Groff. "Baptism in Mark: Dying and Rising with Christ." *Journal of Biblical Literature*, 92 (1973), 531-548.

Smith, Robert H. "Darkness at Noon: Mark's Passion Narrative." *Concordia Theological Monthly*, 44 (1973), 325-338.

_____. "New and Old in Mark 16:1-8." *Concordia Theological Monthly*, 43 (1972), 518-527.

Stein, Robert H. "A Short Note on Mark XIV. 28 and XVI. 7." *New Testament Studies*, 20 (1974), 445-452.

Stock, Klemens. "Methodenvielfalt Studien zu Markus." *Biblica*, 62 (1981), 562-582.

Stone, Jerry H. "The Gospel of Mark and Oedipus the King: Two Tragic Visions." *Soundings*, 66 (1984), 55-69.

Tannehill, Robert C. "The Disciples in Mark: The Function of a Narrative Role." *Journal of Religion*, 57 (1977), 386-405.

Thomas, John Christopher. "A Reconstruction of the Ending of Mark." *Journal of Evangelical Theological Society*, 26 (1983), 407-419.

Trocmé Etienne. "The Beginnings of Christian Historiography and the History of Early Christianity." *Australian Biblical Review*, 31 (1983), 1-13.

Trompf. Garry W. "The First Resurrection and the Ending of Mark's Gospel." *New Testament Studies*, 18 (1972), 308-330.

_____. "The Markusschluss in Recent Research." *Australian Biblical Review*, 21 (October, 1971), 15-26.

van der Horst, P. W. "Can a Book End With ΓΑΡ? A Note on Mark xvi.8." *Journal of Theological Studies*, 23 (1972), 121-124.

van Kasteren, P. "Het slot van het Marcusevangelie." 86 (1916), 283-296.

_____. "Nog een woord over het Marcusslot." *Studien*, 87 (1917), 484-490.

Waetjen, H. "The Ending of Mark and the Gospel's Shift in Eschatology." *Annual of the Swedish Theological Institute*, 4 (1965), 112-121.

Ward, Wayne. "Gospel Sources: A Reconsideration From the Perspective of Redactional Theology." *The Yearbook Annales* (1974-1975), 75-97.

Weeden, Theodore J. "The Heresy That Necessitated Mark'S Gospel." *Zeitschrift für die neutestamentliche Wissenschaft*, 59 (1968), 145-158.

Wichelhaus, Manfred. "Am ersten Tage der Woche." *Novum Testamentum*, 11 (1969), 45-66.

Williams, Clarence R. "The Appendice to the Gospel According to Mark: A Study in Textual Transmission." *Connecticut Academy of Arts and Sciences, Transactions*, 18 (1915), 353-447.

V. NONPUBLISHED WORKS

Blevins, James L. "The Messianic Secret in Markan Research, 1901-1964." Ph. D. dissertation, The Southern Baptist Theological Seminary, 1964.

Farmer, William R. "A Note on J. N. Birdsall's review of *The Last Twelve Verses of Mark* in *JTS* April, 1975."

Francis, Dan R. "A Critical Survey of Contemporary Literature Concerning the Empty Tomb in Mark." Unpublished Th. M. thesis, The Southern Baptist Theological Seminary, Louisville, Kentucky, 1980.

Helzle, E. "The Ending of the Gospel of Mark (Mark 16:9-20) and the Freer Logion (Mark 16:14W), Its Tendencies and Its Mutual Relationship, a Word-Exegetical Investigation." PhD Dissertation, Tübingen, 1959.

Odom, Stephen. "Paradox in the Kingdom Sayings of Jesus: An Exegetical Study of Selected Logia." Unpublished Th. M. thesis, The Southern Baptist Theological Seminary, Louisville, Kentucky, 1980.

Pack, Frank. "The Methodology of Origen As A Textual Critic in Arriving at the Text of the New Testament." Ph. D. Dissertation, University of Southern California, 1948.

Ruef, John S. "The *Sitz im Leben* of the Gospel Accounts of the Appearances of Jesus after the Crucifixion and the Ending of the Marcan Gospel." Paper presented at the meeting of the Society of Biblical Literature, 1965.

Stacy, Wayne. "Fear in the Gospel of Mark." Unpublished Ph. D. dissertation, The Southern Baptist Theological Seminary, Louisville, Kentucky, 1980.

Wright, G. Al Jr. "Markan Intercalations: A Study in the Plot of the Gospel." Ph.D. Dissertation, The Southern Baptist Theological Seminary, 1985.

VI. OTHER SOURCES

Hughes, John J. *Bits, Bytes, & Biblical Studies* Grand Rapids, Mich.: Zondervan Publishing House, 1987.

Miller, Paul A. *Project Gramcord.* Trinity Evangelical Divinity School, 2065 Half Day Road, Deerfield, Il., 60015.

Packer, David W. *Ibycus Scholarly Computer.* Ibycus Systems, P. O. Box 1330, Los Altos, California, 94022.

Index of Authors

Index of Manuscripts

Index of Scripture

Index of Subjects